Narratives of Love & Loss

Narratives of Love & Loss

Studies in Modern Children's Fiction

MARGARET RUSTIN
AND
MICHAEL RUSTIN

VERSO

London · New York

First published by Verso 1987
© Margaret Rustin, Michael Rustin

Verso
UK: 6 Meard Street, London W1V 3HR
USA: 29 West 35th Street, New York, NY 10001 2291

Verso is the imprint of New Left Books

British Library Cataloguing in Publication Data

Rustin, Michael
Narratives of love and loss: Studies in modern children's fiction.
1. Children's literature — — History and criticism
I. Title   II. Rustin, Margaret
823'.912'09   PN1009

US Library of Congress Cataloging in Publication Data

Narratives of love and loss.

1. Children's stories, English--History and criticism. 2. Children's stories,
American--History and criticism. 3. Love in literature. 4. Loss (Psychology)
in literature. 5. English fiction--20th century--History and criticism.
6. American fiction--20th century--History and criticism.
I. Rustin, Michael. II. Rustin, Margaret.
PR888.C5N37   1987   823'.914'099282   87–21040

ISBN 0-86091-187-X
ISBN 0-86091-899-8 (pbk.)

Typeset by Pentacor Ltd, High Wycombe, Bucks
Printed in Great Britain by Biddles Ltd, Guildford, Surrey

For Susanna and Emily

Contents

Acknowledgements

We would like to thank the Institute for Advanced Study, Princeton, for their hospitality and support during the academic year 1984–85 when most of the writing of this book was undertaken.

We were given invaluable encouragement with our project by friends who were kind enough to read various chapters as we completed them. Among these were Myra Barrs, Sarah Hirschman, Norma Klein, Jeffrey Praeger, Deborah Silverman, and Michael and Judy Walzer.

The public library of Princeton, New Jersey, is to be thanked for the availability of its admirable stock of children's literature. While we were working on children's books, three schools were successfully teaching and encouraging our children to read them – Malorees Infant and Junior Schools, in the London Borough of Brent, and Community Park School, Princeton. For Margaret Rustin, work on these stories had to fill the place of her work with child patients during her year's leave of absence from the Tavistock Clinic in London.

At the Institute we received secretarial support of a wonderfully enthusiastic and generous kind from Peggy Clarke, Lucille Allsen, and Lynda Emery. And with earlier drafts we were admirably helped by the secretaries in the Sociology Department at North East London Polytechnic, especially Jane Ward. We thanks Mrs G. M. Barrett for her kind help with the proofs.

Our publishers and editors at Verso, Neil Belton, Robin

Blackburn, and Charlotte Greig, have made the production of this book as efficient and pleasant a process as it could be.

Finally, we would like to say that the main inspiration for this book has come from the works of fiction that are its subject.

Introduction: Deep Structures in Modern Children's Fiction

The post-wàr period in Britain has seen a remarkable flowering of literature written for children. In quality, this body of writing is comparable to the work of the two earlier periods[1] in which the first major classics of the genre were produced – the middle decades of the nineteenth century in which the works of Lewis Carroll, Edward Lear, Charles Kingsley, and Robert Louis Stevenson appeared, and the late Victorian and Edwardian years which saw the writings of, among others, A.A. Milne, J.M. Barrie, Kenneth Grahame, Beatrix Potter, and Rudyard Kipling.

In this book we seek to explore the distinctive themes and concerns of some of the best writing of these post-war years, and to examine the social and cultural conditions which made this development possible. Our method is to provide a number of detailed readings of stories, not an encyclopaedic review or general history. This is because we think the qualities of this work can best be demonstrated by attention to particular texts, which in any case have rarely been given the careful critical analysis they deserve. Most of these stories are in the genre usually called fantasy, because of our primary interest in the imaginative and emotional aspects of children's experience.

We have chosen to write about works all of which we value highly. One of our primary aims in writing this book was to understand and, we hope, explain the astonishing emotional depth and moving power of works which might at first sight appear deceptively simple to adult readers, written as they are to be read by children. One of the criteria which led us to write about an author was therefore the perception of latent depths of meaning (usually related to states of feeling) which distinguishes some of the best writing for children. In no sense is this selection intended to be a nomination of the best writing of the period. We are not attempting to construct a 'great tradition' of children's fiction, in part because we think rigid canons of this kind are more of an obstruction than a help to first-hand response to books, and because in any case we do not have the professional expertise to assess this now extremely extensive field of writing as a whole. We want to make strong positive claims for the works we do discuss, but we already know that there are other works of comparable quality which we have not had time or space to consider.

Most if not all of the works we discuss are already deservedly famous, and have also been bestsellers since they were first published. We want to make claims about the ways in which these works depict states of mind and feeling, and also sometimes experiences of the social world, which have a representative and truth-bearing quality in relation to their intended readerships. We argue for the 'poetic realism' of these works. The fact that the stories are in fact very widely read and celebrated therefore provides some indirect corroborative support for our thesis.

All the writers we discuss are concerned, in one way or another, with issues of emotional development in children. Each writer has found ways of representing some themes of emotional experience and crises in childhood in imaginative and often poetic terms. It is because of our specific interest in these issues that we have chosen to discuss works in this genre. The stories selected have been writen mainly for children of primary school age – between five and eleven years – with some variation between them. The children who figure as characters in the stories are also of this age. This is a time in which family relationships, whatever their quality, usually remain central to a child's preoccupations, while at the same time some independent exploration of the social world – through school, brief periods spent away from parents, and increasing time with friends, – is beginning to take place. This period also begins the more obvious development of an inner identity independent of and sometimes hidden from parents; the in-between space between family and social world which children begin to negotiate in these years is vitally connected with their developing sense of personal self. It will be seen that the recurrent experience of separation and reunion provides a central topic for most of the works we discuss.

These stories can be approached in three somewhat different ways, all of which we make use of in our detailed discussions. We seek to explore their emotional resonance from a psychoanalytical point of view. That is to say, we seek to understand the emotional depth of reference of a story through thinking about the states of mind that it depicts in its child characters, and their development through the narrative. In few cases is this an explicit or conscious issue within the story – such self-consciousness, especially theoretical self-consciousness, would defeat the purposes of writing for young children. These stories are about the representation of feeling, and about the resolution of conflicts of feeling, not about their explanation or interpretation, though interpretation is something that we are interested in. The authors we discuss have found symbolic equivalents or containers for states of feeling, often we would say not just unnoticed but truly unconscious states, referred to in psychoanalytic theory as 'phantasy' and it is these which connect the stories, at the deepest level, with the inner lives of their readers. This is a kind of poetic communication, analogous to the symbolizations of children's imaginative play. Indeed, in some instances, such as Rumer Godden's doll stories, or Lynne Reid Banks's *The Indian in the Cupboard*, dramatic descriptions of children's play is a central element of the story. What we try to bring to this from a psychoanalytical point of view are some conceptions of the states of mind of children, of a more or less typical or universal kind, by which we can, we hope, illuminate the particular realizations of each story. We hope to show what it is in the common experience of children that these stories reflect, usually in indirect and metaphorical ways.

At this point we would like to clarify our own use of terms. 'Phantasy' with 'ph' is a term used in psychoanalytic writing to describe the content of the inner or unconscious mental life of a person, and we use it here in this sense. 'Fantasy' with an 'f' we use to describe the literary form; it is also the more everyday term for various forms of imaginative mental life.

Our second point of departure is a sociological one. We seek to explore how far these stories represent and explore

3

the social world, within the cognitive limits of what young child readers can be expected to understand. We suggest that in some instances the stories offer a powerful if miniaturized image of a society in which child readers can locate themselves, and about which they can learn. This representation is usually charged with a particular moral and emotional standpoint. Sometimes, as in the cases for example of Philippa Pearce's *Tom's Midnight Garden* and E.B. White's *Charlotte's Web*, this represents deeply held values in a national culture. More generally, the emergence of a major genre of 'children's fiction' itself calls for sociological explanation as a social fact in its own right.

Finally, we will consider these stories in specifically literary terms, as artifacts constrained by the capacities of their readership (exceptionally sensitive and vivid in some respects, unavoidably restricted in others) to develop with distinctive formal properties. We argue broadly that this is a genre of distinctively metaphoric writing. It creates metaphoric ways of representing the experiences and development of its own characters. Its stories also function as metaphors or poetic containers for the typical life experiences of its readers. Sometimes the role of play, symbolic representation, or story-telling as the bearer of emotional meaning is a theme within the story itself. Children display intense feelings about fictional characters – they are loved/hated and often identified with in a total way, whereas the sophisticated adult reader holds him or her-self at much greater distance. Where writers are in touch with this quality in their readers, they can involve them very deeply in their imaginative creations. This fantasy genre of stories aims for and achieves depth over a necessarily limited canvas of topics and referents. It finds highly charged symbols from within the common culture of childhood experiences. Its readers are relatively fresh to both language and feelings. Children are also able to re-evoke in adults their own capacity for intensity of feeling. For these reasons, and because its primary subject matter is a life-stage so important to both children and the adults in touch with them, fiction for children has been able to achieve a particular distinction and, at moments, perfection.

The issue which links these three perspectives is the emergence of childhood as a distinctive and internally-differentiated life-stage in the latter half of the nineteenth century for a small privileged minority of the population, and increasingly, in this century, for nearly all. The preconditions of this development seem to have been the decline in infant mortality, making it probable that most children in each family would survive into adult life, and the lessening of privation and economic pressure, providing more social and emotional space for children's development, and also making feasible a general growth and literacy. The reduction in average family size which has taken place in the last hundred and fifty years also made it possible for adults to give more personal attention to children, especially in the domain of feeling.

Lawrence Stone[2] and Philippe Aries[3] have each described the evolution of families in which more equal and intimate conjugal relations, and a greater emotional attention to the needs of children became normative, initially in the middle class, from the eighteenth century. One might also see the increased concern with feelings and personal relationships visible in the literary culture from this period, with the rise of the novel,[4] as part of some increased 'feminization' of English culture. The pattern was also of a greater splitting between 'masculine' attributes, oriented towards the combative and competitive external worlds, and 'feminine' ones, confines within the family and oriented towards the home and family life. Women provided the largest readership of the novel from the eighteenth century onwards, and the novel was one of the major vehicles for a developing culture of individual sensibility. These social structures enforced a bifurcation of the bisexual elements in human nature imposing a rigid normative division of gender identities. However, in recent decades, post Freud, there has developed at least in parts of the culture a greater acknowledgement and tolerance of the complexities of sexuality and the different possible distribution of 'masculine' and 'feminine' traits within individuals.

Writing for children, as it emerged, soon began to reflect this split between male and female worlds, between activity and sensibility. The sentimental quality of the classics of the Edwardian period (Milne, Barrie, Hodgson Burnett and so on[5]), reflects the mawkish quality of family life lived within these confines, though some writers, such as Beatrix Potter writing from the somewhat marginal position of a grown-up daughter still living at home with her parents, remained able to write with a distinctive irony about domestic life.[6] The clubby male alternative to this setting was represented in Grahame's *The Wind in the Willows*, and for older readers by Jerome K. Jerome. On the other side of the late Victorian gender divide, new genres of boys' adventure and school stories burgeoned[7], in comic and book form (G.A. Henty, Rider Haggard, Frank Richards, et al), featuring a world of men and boys in which hardly any women appeared at all. The obverse of this gender division amongst readers was the emergence of girls' school stories by Angela Brazil and others. While gender divisions in fiction have lessened in the post-war period, it seems clear that the genre of writing which we mainly discuss does represent a transformation of the English novel of sensibility to this new terrain of writing about and for children. The majority of writers in this genre, and seven of our ten authors, are women.

In the twentieth century, concern for the development of children became characteristically professionalized, with the extension of popular education, and of various occupations allied to it which were concerned to devise a theory and practice of child development. The dominant conceptions of education broadened and shifted away from initially restrictive and overtly stratifying concerns with basic skills and didactic religious instruction for the lower orders (where they were educated at all) and away from the acculturation of the upper classes into the values and skills imparted through classics and physical sports. While the next stage, the emergence of the curriculum of modern subjects with English and Maths at their centre was used to stratify and select by different and more middle-class criteria, the emergence of English as a key educational vehicle was at least a step towards a genuine universalism. One influential vanguard of this broadened educational vision was provided by the new discipline of English literature, whose most vigorous ideologists in Britain were the group around F.R. Leavis and his quarterly journal *Scrutiny* (published between 1932 and 1953).[8] This group was concerned both to construct an appropriate literary canon and professional-critical method, and to extend these into a common educational practice. They were also more concerned with capacities for feeling and moral judgement than with evaluations based on social style and taste. From their particular standpoint of an intense commitment to conjugal sexual relationship seen as a lifelong intimacy they also furthered some partial reduction in the

acute oppositions of gender identity and associated repression of sexuality in English cultural life. (The fact that at
the centre of this group was an intellectually creative couple,
F.R. and Q.D. Leavis, seems to have been crucial to this
project, though the situation was greatly complicated by the
lack of academic recognition accorded to Mrs Leavis throughout most of her career.)[9]

The positive valuation of English literature as the deepest
exploration of personal and social experience in the national
culture has had a profound and lasting influence, for example
on the post-war development of the English theatre as well as
on educational practice. It made the teaching of English in
ways centred on the pupil rather than on the grammarian's
formalism, the centre of the primary school curriculum. In
the primary, if not the grammar school, this emphasis on self-
expression in one's native language was a genuine step
towards the creation of a democratic culture, more recently
extended in multi-cultural directions. This also prepared the
way for the development of a growing body of serious
writing for children, which could relate itself to the main-
stream literary tradition, as well as to its own forerunners.[10]
One can see some indirect influence of the *Scrutiny* school on
English children's writing in the widespread commitment to
a poetic method and to organicist and familial values, as well
as perhaps in a limiting concern with middle-class experience. Certainly there can be little doubt about the importance
of this line of influence among those committed as active
advocates of writing for and by children – David Holbrook for
example.[11] The field of children's fiction has developed not
only from the example of particular writers, but also by the
agency of sponsoring institutions, often highly conscious of a
mission of cultural improvement directed towards children,
as well as concerned to entertain and amuse them. Certain
publishers, for example Penguin's Puffin imprint and its chief
editor Kaye Webb, movements among teachers such as the
National Association of Teachers of English, BBC Children's
and Schools' Broadcasting, children's theatres such as the
Unicorn in London, and children's librarians, were thus
concerned to improve and enlarge what was available to
children and to make available and popular both old and new
classics in this field. (One instance of this consensus has been
the hostility of all these groups to the enormously popular
writings of Enid Blyton.) It is interesting to note that one of

7

the finest post-war writers for children, Philippa Pearce, herself worked for many years for BBC Schools' Broadcasting and for seven years as children's books editor for the publisher André Deutsch.

Parallel with the advocacy of English as *the* humane discipline, and also influential in educational thinking, was the emergence of child psychologies of various kinds, which provided new theories of personal development around which the curriculum of infant and primary education came to be built. Basil Bernstein has discussed this change of educational codes, from 'positional' to 'personal' modes of socialization, and the importance of various kinds of developmental theories to them.[12] Among the psychologies which were influential in educational thinking, especially in regard to young children, were the psychoanalytic ideas of Melanie Klein and Donald Winnicott. Susan Isaacs, one of Klein's collaborators in the 1940s, had a major influence on the field of teaching, through her books, through the experimental school she opened, and later through her post at the London University Institute of Education.[13] One of us has suggested elsewhere[14] that there are some similarities between the values of the movement which gave primacy to the teaching of English literature and Kleinian psychoanalysis, for example in their shared emphasis on moral and emotional development, and on the importance of imagination and understanding to personal growth. The theoretical absence which critics have noted at the core of the *Scrutiny* view of literature might have been more effectively filled by a psychoanalysis which shared its preoccupation with issues of morality and feeling.

Inner Worlds

It may clarify our methods of analysis of particular works in later chapters if we indicate the main theses of our psychoanalytical, literary, and sociological arguments. Our psychoanalytic starting-point is the idea that there is an internal dimension of children's experience. In the inner world of unconscious phantasy to which we have access in dreaming and through the part of our personalities which responds to symbolic or cultural experiences, the primary focus is on our intimate emotional experiences. The inner meanings we give to our relationship to parents, siblings and our own selves are thus contained in our mind, in an ever-evolving flux. The centrality of family relations for young children is ubiquitous, for example. How to deal with the loss of the near-exclusive attention of mother, initiated in the process of weaning but extending beyond this in terms of emotional intimacy, is a universal developmental task. E.B. White's *Charlotte's Web* provides a particularly subtle rendering of this state of mind, representing it both through Fern's interest in the baby pig, and in Wilbur's relationship with the maternal Charlotte. Lynne Reid Banks's *The Indian in the Cupboard* explores the same situation from another point of view, counterpointing a boy drifting away from intimate contact with his mother, but simultaneously taking the responsibility for looking after the little Indian, who amazes him by making many of the demands on him of a lively infant.

In the period of latency, children ordinarily become much more involved with each other, and move to a greater distance from parents. This exposes them to additional anxieties about rejection and abandonment (feelings by which all children feel threatened at times). It is particularly characteristic of the personality of children in these middle years to split experience in over-simplified ways. Boys and girls tend to separate into single-sex friendship groups; moral issues are seen in very black and white terms; there is a strong urge to define 'us' (however delimited) against 'them' – race, class, sex, neighbourhood can all serve as the basis for such collective identifications. Children are then tempted to deal with painful feelings by pushing them into others. The unconscious purpose of this is to make others feel bad or worthless in order not to have to feel so themselves. The strong concern with issues of right and wrong often shown by latency-age children can serve as a means of regulating conflicts over good and bad feelings, which may seem to need to be ordered strictly in accordance with principles if they are not to get out of control. There is a major genre which describes children coping with the situation of living without the support of parents, struggling between gang-like projections of feeling and consequent feelings of persecution and more integrative and co-operative ways of living to-gether. William Golding's fable *Lord of the Flies* is one famous exploration of this theme for 'adult' moral purposes. Incidentally, many of Enid Blyton's stories represent poor outcomes of this situation in terms of character, in a thoroughly complacent and uncomfortably cheerful way. We discuss two fine stories which explore these dilemmas. One of them, *The Lion, the Witch, and the Wardrobe* by C.S. Lewis, (part of his six-volume *Narnia* series), sensitively traces the defensive manoevres by which the children deal with their phantasied abandonment, which include splitting and projection within the group and competition for adult favour. It also shows the ultimate integration of their feelings of love and hate, as Edmund recognizes the White Witch for what she is, and the other children become less moralistic and more understanding about their brother. This story skilfully connects child readers' innate preconceptions of morality with an allegorical version of the Christian story, ending in the Aslan-Christ's death and resurrection. The interweaving of the drama of emotional splitting and reintegration with the doctrinal pattern of the story is, however, so subtle as to give the series a deep appeal which extends well beyond those who share its religious assumptions.

We examine a story by one other author who pioneered this theme, Edith Nesbit's *Five Children and It*. This story, published in 1903, was written in a different period from the others we discuss, but its description of the moods and feelings of the children during the time in which they are on holiday away from their parents anticipates the explorations of emotions by later writers in this new sub-genre, and seems well worth presenting in these terms. These themes are also important to Philippa Pearce's work, and to a large body of pre- and post-Second World War writing for children, including for example that of Arthur Ransome, the emergence of holidays reflecting no doubt the new prosperity of middle-class life. Where being abandoned, kidnapped, or orphaned was the initiating trauma for much nineteenth-century writing for and about children (Dickens, Stevenson, Hodgson Burnett, for example), in the twentieth century this frequently becomes scaled down to adventures on holiday where absence of parents and the containing structures of ordinary life is only temporary or symbolic, and where this is in any case welcomed by children in the stories for its possibilities for excitement.

Paula Fox in *The Slave Dancer*, by contrast, returns to the potentially more tragic event of a kidnapping, locating her story in the brutal circumstances of the slave trade in the nineteenth century. This more extreme situation enables her to explore a boy's identifications in his isolation with alternative parent-figures, with his remembered parents, and with slave-victims much worse off than himself. Though much of the drama of this story is in its description of the sea voyage, with echoes of *Treasure Island* made much more sombre and realistic by the kidnappers' pursuit of slaves from Africa instead of pieces of eight, its strength is that it also describes an interior drama in the developing mind of the boy. The other Paula Fox stories we discuss deal with related themes, in a more humorous and less tragic way. *A Likely Place* describes a boy merely left in the care of a babysitter for a few days, who makes friends with an old man in the park who is as lonely as he, while *How Many Miles to Babylon?* describes a kidnapping of a fatherless boy whose mother is also temporarily absent. The kidnapping is a short-lived affair, and enables the author to explore in subtle ways the relationships of some homeless boys living in the streets with her main character who does after all have a real home. In each case, Fox is as interested in the state of mind of her child characters, and the ways that they manage to keep alive a sense of a good parental object, as she is with the external events of her stories. Fox incidentally is an American writer who lives in Brooklyn, New York. She explores areas of risk and social conflict, not least those arising from race, in terms that are those of an urban social realist, in contrast to the more common devotion to fable, fantasy, and the countryside of most English writers for children.

One way in which these writers explore children's inner experience – we might say their relation to the figures of their internal world or to the internal objects of psychoanalytical theory – is by describing the meaning for the child of feeling contained and understood in symbolic terms. The capacity to think, to maintain an internal resilience to temporarily bad experiences through the memory of the good, is crucial to development, and depends in part on powers of language, play, and imagination. Many of these stories explore the role of such symbolic containers as themes within their narrative, as well as themselves constituting symbolic containers or emotional metaphors for the inner experiences of their readers. Rumer Godden's characters' relation to their dolls, and in the case of the Kitchen Madonna to the icon which Gregory has made for Marta, Omri's relationship to his toy

Indian in Banks's story, the relationship of the various children to the animals in Pearce's *The Battle of Bubble and Squeak* and *A Dog So Small*, are examples of benign projections of feelings which bring about creative development and increased integration. Play, like art, to which as Winnicott has shown it is closely related,[15] creates a setting in which conflicts can be expressed and change can therefore occur. In many other stories, in fact, the children's encounters with events, people, and creatures outside their immediate relationships allow the discovery and development of new aspects of the self, and sometimes unlock more hopeless, blocked or depressed states of feeling.

The creative functions of language and fiction are themselves the explicit theme of some of the works we discuss. This is the case, for example, with *Charlotte's Web* where the act of writing by Charlotte is hailed as a magical and life-saving achievement, and with *Tom's Midnight Garden*, where Tom sends postcards to his brother about his adventures, and where in the end the old lady Mrs Bartholomew herself tells him about her history. Arrietty reads to her friend Tom in Norton's *The Borrowers*, and in a different version of this theme of creativity, (White's *The Trumpet of the Swan*) Louis, like his great jazz trumpeter namesake, is able to make his way in the world through his music. Just as there are film-makers such as Truffaut and Fellini whose films about the experience of film-making have had a particular lyricism and intensity, so some writers of children's fiction seem to have written some of their best work when reflecting on the power of fiction itself.

Language is also vivid and important in the form of dialogue in several of these stories, exemplifying and celebrating the child's capacity to find fresh words to deal with unexpected experiences and so maintain hopefulness in adversity. The toy Red Indian has this capacity in a most independent and spirited way, in Banks's story, and thus inspires his friend. So do many of the characters in *Charlotte's Web* and in Hoban's *The Mouse and His Child*. Both these authors demonstrate, through the words of their nastier characters, Templeton and Manny (both incidentally rats, a conventional symbolism hard for writers to resist) that a devastating power of speech is not a monopoly of the good (as John Milton's Satan had demonstrated for all time), even though the capacity usually itself has something good about

12

it. The main virtuosity of another of E.B. White's heroes, Stuart Little the mouse-child, lies more in his physical dexterity and pluck than in his verbal capacities. We can learn from Buster Keaton that the mastery of the everyday perils of the physical world is a large issue in the minds and thus memories of the small child. In another work beloved of children and adults, Sergeant Pepper's Lonely Hearts Club Band (The Beatles, 1967), there is a song in which the celebrated Mr Kite is going to jump, with others, through a hogshead of real fire.

The symbolic meanings of these stories are contained in characters with whom child readers can identify, in the development of narratives which explore different kinds of personal development, and through the associations of images which reverberate throughout a story. The miniature size of the Borrowers, and the additional vulnerability of small-animal characters (Stuart Little, for example) are an obvious point of identification for young readers. Beatrix Potter in her stories creates a whole gallery of social types and personalities in the guise of animals. Many of these stories work through images and their transformation, as well as through plot. This additional level of metaphoric resonance and depth is indeed one of the main qualities which distinguishes the best works in this genre, as in other kinds of fiction. The meaning of the river and its freezing over and thawing in *Tom's Midnight Garden* is an instance of an image of development; the twin mountain peaks covered in snow is an instance of a representation of a deadly maternal object for Edmund in *The Lion, the Witch, and the Wardrobe*.

All of the writers whom we discuss show particular sensitivity to children's feelings. Nina Bawden, for example, shows in *Carrie's War* how the two children cope so differently with their evacuation from home. Carrie, the painfully vulnerable heroine, has an intense desire to reconcile Mr Evans, in whose house she is living, with his estranged sister. The author lets us see how this is stimulated by her own anxiety about what has happened to her absent parents, and by a phantasy of parental conflict. Nick, her brother, on the other hand, is able to cope with separation from parents by depending on his elder sister, who thus carries a double weight of anxiety. This also frees Nick to accept the affection of Louisa, in whose house he is living, in a less ambivalent way than Carrie. The idea of a conflict which requires a magical resolution, whether for good or ill, is related in this story to the wider fears of wartime, in which many people are exposed to death, as these are internalized by a sensitive child. Carrie can identify with the legendary slave-boy whose skull must be kept in the house in order for it not to be destroyed. She also feels herself to have been brought to the village against her will, and she finds it difficult to believe that places retain an existence when she is not present in them. This is also true of people important to her – the children push their mother, in her absence, from their mind, and hurt her by showing her this when she visits. Carrie only fully overcomes these anxieties in middle age, when she is helped by her own children to find that this childhood home and those who cared for her there did after all survive her leaving it so abruptly.

In discussing these stories, we frequently write about characters as if they possessed all the complex and inter-related feelings of actual people, though of course we know that they can have no qualities other than those described in the pages of the story. We may seem to be making inferences which are appropriate to analytic psychotherapy, from a particular sequence of thoughts or actions to a whole set of implied relationships or states of mind, in a fictional context in which such speculations can have no actual referent. Our view is, however, that authors have imagined situations and persons *as if* they were real. They have made connections between the different events of their story and the feelings of their characters with an intuitive grasp of the way people thus imagined are or would be. What we are wishing to do is to demonstrate how the grasp by these authors of children's feelings and behaviour has some parallels with the more generalized understanding obtained from child psycho-analysis.

Many modern literary critics have become hypercritical of the supposed realist fallacy of imagining fictional characters as real, and attributing motives and histories to them beyond what is actually stated.[16] The concern of such critics has shifted from these 'realist' preoccupations (what lies behind the representation) to an interest in the procedures of representation themselves. We think however that our procedure is only an extension of ordinary readers' response to works of fiction. If they cannot be responded to as plausible representations of some reality, whether internal or external, whether of the writer's or some other people's experience, they will seem to have little point or connection with the reader's world. In any case, the 'real world' which is held up as a solid contrast to the fictional, rarely presents itself to us in so unmistakably distinct a way. In the real world too, we have to rely on momentary impressions, third-party reports, interpretations of expressions and remarks, letters, faces in the crowd, inferences based on knowledge of our own feelings, to understand others. We may in fact know more and not less about a fictional character than about most real people of our acquaintance. This is why fiction, including children's fiction, is so irreplaceable a form of human knowledge.

Both the processes of fictional creation, and the psychoanalytic understanding of children's states of mind which we are linking to it, are necessarily selective and typifying. Each explores only certain aspects of experience, and excludes others. This is why the selectiveness inherent in children's fiction in particular is nevertheless compatible with commitment to realism of certain kinds.[17] Certain typical forms or deep structures of experience (notably those which correspond to psychoanalytical understanding) are disclosed more effectively by the deliberate partiality and concentration of metaphorical writing, than in a social naturalism of surfaces. In other words, such stories share some of the virtues of poetic writing.

The fluidity of the boundary between the imaginary and the real in the lives of children, and the uncertainties and openness surrounding both, make children especially capable of being moved by stories which give form to the experience of their inner worlds. An analogy may be drawn between the importance of dream, phantasy and play in analytic work with children, as the major medium of self-understanding, and the play-like qualities of much writing for children. Such writing, like the most successful moments of analytic therapy, links inner and outer experience, finds external form in language or shared symbolism for unconscious states of feeling. Children's potential openness to their own inner states allows them to be especially 'good readers' for writing of this special kind.

The method which we adopt in thinking about these stories may be similar to that which actors and producers seem to adopt in thinking about the text of a play. In order to imagine what it is like to act a part, it seems to be necessary to imagine what that person would be like, to fill in, so to speak, the spaces which the author has left, through the unconscious swiftness of perception which enables coherence to be achieved from presented fragments, or by deliberate simplification. We are attempting to do no more than fill in such spaces, in order to clarify how these representations correspond to more general truths of childhood experience.

We don't of course, wish to suggest that the authors we discuss necessarily at all share or are sympathetic to our modes of thinking in this respect. The methods of imaginative writing, of discovery through creative fiction, are of their own kind, and owe nothing to more deductive or scientific procedures. They generate equally truthful and usually much more compelling descriptions of the world, in their imaginary mode. Some writers cordially hate these more explicit and analytic procedures, especially perhaps those derived from psychoanalysis, as potential threats to their own creativity. We wish to celebrate this quality of creativity, however, and the capacity to realize intuitively the nature of a person, a situation, or an imaginary possibility related metaphorically to these. But we contend that there are different ways of understanding childhood, and we hope that it will be illuminating to have juxtaposed these together.

Fictional Worlds

'To tell a story', says Umberto Eco, 'you must first of all construct a world, furnished as much as possible, down to the slightest details.'[18] Writers for children in England during this century have made many such worlds, spaces for imaginative exploration which have been one positive result of and contribution to the cultural construction of childhood as an enlarged and deepened life-stage in modern societies.

Literary theorists have pointed to a crisis in the modern novel arising in part from the differentiation and segmentation of the life experiences of readers in modern complex societies.[19] Literary realism especially becomes problematic when readers share little common experience of social worlds, except that mediated to them by mass communications. The radical simplifications of 'artificial worlds' such as those created in the genres of science fiction, detective stories, or spy novels like those of Le Carré, come to seem more lifelike and believeable than 'realism' on a broader canvas. Within the constraints of these more 'specialized fictions' it becomes possible to create a complexity which is nevertheless felt to be intelligible, and more satisfying in this respect than readers' experience of their real-life worlds. Or writers can remove themselves from these social issues altogether, limiting themselves as documentarists to a particular area of life, or looking inwards to the exploration of subjective mental states. One of the sources of these problems of realist writing is the vast increase in the numbers of people who have access to reading and writing, and who expect their experiences or views of life to be represented in literary forms. The break-up of a common literary culture and the proliferation of subcultural differences is in part an unavoidable consequence of cultural democratization.

Writers for children may enjoy a paradoxical advantage in this cultural situation. This is the benefit of certain kinds of constraints which are imposed on the writer for children by the nature of his or her readership, and which become embodied in established literary conventions and expectations, familiar to child readers from their earliest age of reading or being read to. As Eco says, 'It is necessary to create constraints, in order to be able to create freely.' Child readers can be assumed to experience their world mainly from the vantage point of a family (of one sort or another); their other experiences will usually be filtered, in one way or another, by this normal social location of childhood. Child readers are not yet equipped with the excess of information imposed by modern societies on adults as a condition of their survival. Like the audiences for epics in oral cultures (fiction for children is often listened to rather than read), child readers like stories that provide familiar plots, landmarks, and motifs. Children can be assumed to share some threads of common experience of emotional life within a family, however various the patterns of family life may be. The memories of childhood now normally extend over a long period of dependence, which will have been gratifying and painful in different degrees. Children also share exploration of and gradual detachment from their family base, in the normal course of the life cycle. The writer for children thus finds herself or himself with readers who can be assumed to know and care about central life experiences which they share, and which are the source of universally powerful feelings.

Child readerships share common attributes which are helpful to their authors. They can be expected to be curious and exploratory about the world, and interested in the business of making sense of it, while being an audience little burdened or divided by overmuch factual knowledge about it. They will thus very often be interested to explore imaginary worlds as acceptable representations of the real thing. It thus becomes as important to achieve authenticity at the level of deep as at surface structures, deep so far as children are concerned referring above all to the unconscious feelings aroused in the context of dependent relationships. Children are also likely to be responsive to the surprise and amusement inherent in the use of language, since they are experiencing it with the freshness of first-time learners. For children, the boundary between internal and external reality is more fragile and permeable than it is for most adults. This creates a propensity for make-believe, and for the investing of imaginary creations with strong feelings and self-identifications. The child reader is thus, potentially at least, unusually open to the pleasures and imaginative power of fiction.[20]

These various considerations require that good writing for children be highly condensed in the way it communicates significant experience. Adult writers for children have to find symbolic vehicles for *their* understanding of the world (or those aspects of it that they think interesting, relevant or appropriate for children) which are going to be accessible to *children's* understanding. These requirements press children's writers in the direction of writing through metaphor and allegory – symbolic forms which can carry depths of reference and meaning within deliberately simplified systems of natural objects, persons, and actions. The pleasures of learning and problem-solving (important to the child as he or she goes about the world) can be represented more effectively to the 'common child reader' by setting imaginary agents (miniature people, mouse-children and other animals, or whatever) to solve problems posed by their relation to the child's constructed environment, than in a more literal or realist mode. As is often the case in good writing, the construction of an appropriate formal container for a life experience (the realist novel was itself such a form) is a necessary condition for making the experience available for exploration by writers and audiences. In the case of writing for children, the physical experience of being a child in a large, strange, unpredictable, and potentially threatening world has been represented in a whole genre of 'miniaturized' stories in which, for example, Peter Rabbit strays into Mr McGregor's garden, Stuart Little descends on a string to rescue a ring which has fallen down the plughole, and Pod the Borrower climbs up curtains like a mountaineer (using hatpins as belays). Swift's *Gulliver's Travels* is the first and most important exemplar of the method of making the world newly real by having it encountered out of scale. Unexpected changes of size are also one of the many bewildering aspects of Alice's experience in Wonderland. The fictional worlds thus created are intricate in their details and the possibilities they create for action, and they are also models or metaphors for the child reader's own exploratory relation to his physical environment, which he or she can identify with and enjoy. The delight of such an imaginary universe lies in its consistency with its premises, in the order created from an initial disturbance of everyday assumptions.

There are some similarities between the account we present here of works in the genre of fantasy for children written in the twentieth century, and Bruno Bettelheim's important study of classic fairy tales from a psychoanalytic viewpoint, *The Uses of Enchantment*.[21] His argument that many fairy tales can be read as condensed metaphors of unconscious conflict (who, in phantasy, do we think Little Red Riding Hood is getting into bed with?) is a convincing one, and our own analyses have some parallels with his. The universe of the classic fairy tale is however usually much more catastrophic than the fictional worlds of most modern children's classics. Hansel's and Gretel's family are threatened with starvation; the cruel punishment meted out by the witch in *Rapunzel*, and also by Rumpelstiltskin, requires a mother to give up a baby; Snow White is poisoned by her jealous stepmother. By contrast, it is as if in twentieth century children's fiction, the direct and overwhelming fear of famine and death fades, and the magic by which these perils can be escaped thus becomes less seductive. This change of mood between the world of the fairy tale and modern middle-class children's experience is noted ironically by some early twentieth-century writers for children. Potter's *The Tale of Jemima Puddleduck* is comic in a way that Little Red Riding Hood is not.[22] The Psammead, a quasi-fairy, in Nesbit's *Five Children and It* drily teaches the children not to hope too much from wishes, which so easily cause trouble, and are so painful to perform. Jack Zipes, in *Breaking the Magic Spell*,[23] pointed out that the classic fairy tales reflect a world of pressing scarcity and bitter social conflict – their violent narratives have a social as well as an unconscious referent. Certainly the absence in many modern classics of direct physical cruelty seems to reflect a change in the common experience of their readers. Even though adults live in a world of unparalleled violence and threats of violence, children in Britain and America (at least in those social groups most likely to be reading these books) are now likely to be insulated from the direct effects of this.

The effect of this change of conditions has been in some cases to shift the themes of writing for children from directly-experienced threats of death, to less severe experiences of loss or separation. Several of the stories we discuss deal with the phantasies evoked by experiences which are far from catastrophic in their literal meaning. *Tom's Midnight Garden* as we shall see, is one example. Another response has been to explore the effects of turmoil or crisis in the wider society as these bear indirectly on the smaller world of the child. Examples of this are *Carrie's War*, whose child characters are subjected to wartime evacuation, or, perhaps, *The Borrowers*, which seem, in a number of respects to reflect the changes brought about in wartime Britain. In some instances, a world of social violence and conflict has been successfully transformed into an allegorical form. We suggest for example that Russell Hoban's *The Mouse and His Child* can be read as a story of the experience of European immigrants in America. The uncompromising battle to overcome the forces of evil in Tolkien's *The Hobbit* and C.S. Lewis's *Narnia* stories contain many echoes of the war against Nazism, and the ideological struggle against totalitarianism more generally. Madeleine l'Engle and several other widely-read authors also deal with struggles against the forces of evil. Another way of dealing with the harsher events of the world is to place them in the past, like Hatty's loss of her parents in *Tom's Midnight Garden*, or Jessie's voyage in *The Slave Dancer*. Or, finally, the experience of loss and death can be explored through the life cycle of creatures metaphorically a little distanced from the child reader's experience, like Charlotte the spider in *Charlotte's Web*. While Charlotte's death provides one of the most poignant moments of children's fiction, it is also contained within a form which makes it deeply moving and integrative rather than overwhelming and destructive for its readers.

Bettelheim castigates modern writing for children for its evasion of the central issues of sexuality, aggression, and death which he finds symbolically explored in the classic fairy tales. We think his view neglects the fact that these tales were determined by stark social factors in their world of origin, as well as reflecting universals of unconscious experience in infancy. It also neglects the lack of differentiation between child and adult readers in the original contexts of these stories. As childhood comes to be seen as a more specific, extended, and protected stage of development, at least in more privileged parts of the world population, it seems intelligible that its cultures correspondingly evolve into a more differentiated and hopeful form. It is not only magic which can lead to happy or relatively happy endings for children, for children in more favoured conditions may have both internal resources and external support. What we find is a diversity of modes of exploration of central life experiences, reflecting the complexity of society as it is experienced by child readers. Since real life-and-death tragedies are a less common experience of childhood than they once were, it seems understandable that they should figure less directly as the subject-matter of writing for modern children, and can leave more space for the exploration of the child's inner world whose joys and terrors may correspond less directly to externally-perceived reality.

Perhaps the most important quality we identify in these works, by contrast to their fairy tale predecessors, is to be found in their moral assumptions. They are integrative and forgiving in their morality, rather than splitting and punitive. Where lasting loss occurs, as in *Charlotte's Web*, the dead remain alive in memory. There is a symbolic reconciliation between the boy member of the ship's crew and one slave-boy at the end of *The Slave Dancer*. Even Manny Rat is rehabilitated as Uncle Manny, in *The Mouse and His Child*. It is because these books are written for children, and with children as their central figures, that their authors are so reluctant to leave their readers without hope that life might at any rate be different in the future. For similar reasons, child psychoanalysis is often seen as a more hopeful enterprise than psychoanalysis in general.

This is not to say that the range of subject-matter of

children's fiction is not often too narrow, and too confined in particular within the relatively privileged locations of middle-class life. Some writers like Roald Dahl have been able to achieve a huge appeal by writing against this polite grain, allowing space for the unsocial and tabooed impulses of childhood, saying out loud what children might say out of the presence of adults. Other writers, such as Leila Berg, have made conscious efforts to write for working class children, and there is a corresponding movement to connect with the experience of children from different ethnic backgrounds. We recognize, incidentally, that the genre of stories about which we are writing, substantially concerned as it is with relationships and feelings, has more appeal for girl readers than for boys, even in these times of less sharp gender divisions. Some writers, such as Paula Fox, are particularly to be admired for their achievement in broadening the social and moral scope of writing for children, enabling readers to explore the more cruel and oppressive aspects of their society, while remaining committed to the importance of self-knowledge and authentic relatedness to others as a precondition of development. It is important that work that seeks to engage with experiences of social conflict and brutality should not itself be made shallow and brutalized by its subject-material.

Social Worlds

We have already indicated the extent to which modern children's fiction can be read through sociological eyes, as offering representations of particular social worlds from a child's eye view. We view the development of the whole field of literature for children in these terms, as one element of an emergent culture of childhood in Western society. We have pointed out some affinity between the development of fictional writing specially attentive to young children's feelings, and the parallel rise of discourse in psychology, educational theory, and psychoanalysis, which were during the same period evolving a theory and practice of child development. Each of these cultural movements seems to be part of a broader process of the elaboration of childhood as a field of social practice (schooling, publishing, family policy and advice, therapy) and as a differentiated sphere of culture.

One can explain this development in various ways – for example, as means towards the expanded production and reproduction of human capital, servicing new forms of production which depend on heightened symbolic and relational capacities; or, alternatively, as beneficial enlargements of cultured life-space, effected in opposition to the utilitarian values of business, but made possible by greater material wealth and by an ethos of common citizenship and the entitlements it has brought.

Different stories represent different social worlds. E. Nesbit's *Five Children and It*, from a much earlier period, has its child characters looked after by a housekeeper – it is actually a fairly modest middle-class domestic setting for its time – and locates them socially in between Lady Chittenden, remote and very rich, and an encampment of gipsies whom they fear as child-stealers, but whom they come to discover are human beings after all. This story conveys the idea that if middle-class children behave considerately they will survive their encounters with rough bakers' boys and fairground men. So long as they learn to be appropriately modest, these social divisions can be lived with. It is a suitably modern morality for a progressive middle-class author, teaching her readers the obligations of democratic life, and the uselessness of extravagant wishes and ideas about oneself.

The Borrowers (five books which were published between 1952 and 1982), on the other hand, represents a version of the English social landscape a generation or two later, under pressure from below to democratize and liberalize itself. Arrietty's wish to escape from the Clock family's cramped life under the floorboards, and into a wider world, and her parents' anxious support for this, seems to us to have resonance with changes in the English class system of these times. It reflects, in its oblique way, the widespread experience of the children of working-class families finding opportunities, with the support of their parents, to open up their lives to a new freedom and opportunity. Especially important was the post-war extension of education, which is indirectly evoked in the importance to Arrietty of having learned to read. The imprisonment of the Borrowers in a household managed by a repressive servant class (while the upper-class owner lies amiably drunk in bed upstairs) can be read as a parable of pre-war Britain, just as the experience of the Clocks having their home destroyed and having to become refugees seems to echo both the physical and social changes brought about in Britain, and to a more destructive degree elsewhere, by the Second World War.

From the beginning, and with increasing emphasis throughout her series, Mary Norton is sensitive to the meanings of material possessions. The positive and negative impact of material acquisition is in fact a central theme of these books. Pod and Homily work to create a real home with whatever humble materials they can find, but Homily is overwhelmed with greed when Tom showers luxury objects upon them (from his aunt's old doll's house), and this brings about the discovery and near-destruction of the Borrowers' home. The reaction of Mrs Crampfurl to the Borrowers' appropriations echoes the resentment in the middle classes in this period of the rising aspirations of working people. *The Borrowers* conveys an atmosphere of fear and hostility which represents real qualities of class feeling in England. The moral ambiguity in the idea of 'borrowing' (the little people live by taking things that the human beings don't need and wouldn't normally miss, implying that there should really be enough for everyone given a lack of greed on all sides) delicately explores the problematic category of 'property' both for adults (in this period) and for children in their relation to adults (in all periods, perhaps).

The later volumes update these issues into the period of 'affluence' of the later 1950s and 1960s. A thoroughly synthetic and empty version of consumer civilization is embodied in the character of Mr Platter and his wife, humans who put the Borrowers on commercial exhibition. This grasping and ruthless version of modern affluence is contrasted with the attitudes of people rooted in village life, including a retired railwayman, Mr Potts. These representatives of an older social world work together to preserve the memory of the past, and are capable of acknowledging a place for the Borrowers as something new and unexpected in their world, deserving care rather than exploitation.

This version of British life is clearly as much a moral and ideological reading as a factual description, however transposed and miniaturized in the Borrowers' adventures. An 'organic', conservationist view of the good society and a romantic view of the importance of imagination, are widely-shared elements in English literary culture. These values were fashioned by the Leavisites into what they hoped would be a radical challenge to materialist forms of the thinking both of the right and of the left. Raymond Williams, in his *Culture and Society*,[24] subsequently sought to reappropriate this tradition as the root of a distinctively English socialism, rooted in cultural critique.

A world view very influential in English literary culture[25] became formed from these elements derived directly from the romantic critique of urban industrial society. It positively valued nature, imagination, relation to the past, and capacity for emotion, against merely mechanical and rootless ways of living. Its social attitudes, in their most radical phase during and after the Second World War, were integrative, expressed in an organic but sometimes democratic idea of one classless nation. Culturally, and especially in the context of progressive educational movements, this approach urged the importance of the imagination, and the value of understanding and sympathy in regulating the relations of members of different social classes, and of adult and child generations. These organicist values are evident in the work of several others of the English authors we discuss – Nina Bawden and Philippa Pearce, for example, and of many leading writers we do not, such as Alan Garner. The importance of the genre of 'fantasy' itself indicates a strong commitment in this culture to the creative role of the imagination.

We also suggest 'social' readings of the American works we discuss – the stories by Paula Fox, E.B. White, and Russell Hoban's *The Mouse and His Child*. These books are each very different in their implied social vision, though all are in their own ways more exposed to extremes of experience than the works we discuss which were written in Britain. A parallel might be found in the contrast drawn by A. Alvarez between British and American poetry in the post-war period.[26]

We think that it is far from fanciful to see real societies refracted in the imaginary worlds of children's books. It seems that child readers must learn from these writings, to some degree, the implicit tones of voice, unconscious social assumptions, and definitions of right and wrong embedded in their social structures. While these are inflected in very individual ways by different writers, these particular world views can nevertheless be seen to be structured within and by particular national and class cultures. Edmund Leach has memorably pointed out, in relation to another national context, how unmistakably *Babar the Elephant* proclaims the rights and claims of French culture.[27] The texts we discuss are no less specific in their implicit social vision.

*

The main part of this book is devoted to a more detailed discussion of particular works. We hope through these chapters to demonstrate the value of our method of interpretation by reference to the deep structures of meaning which we think can be found underlying the best writing for children, and which we think helps to explain its moving and memorable qualities.

We have arranged these chapters in a loosely thematic way. The first group of stories considered, *Tom's Midnight Garden*, *The Lion, the Witch, and the Wardrobe*, and *Five Children and It* (the latter story is the anomaly in terms of its time of writing), are framed by an experience of separation of children from their parents. They describe adventures which take place away from parents; we are concerned here with the theme of separation and its effects.

The four chapters of the next group are devoted respectively to four stories for young children by Rumer Godden, Lynn Reid-Banks's *The Indian in the Cupboard*, two other stories by Philippa Pearce, *A Dog So Small* and *The Battle of Bubble and Squeak*, and *Charlotte's Web* by E.B. White. These stories are concerned fairly directly with themes of emotional development, and are literally or metaphorically about younger children. In particular we are interested in the way these stories explore the role of play and symbolic containment more generally as a means of growth.

In the final group of chapters, on *The Borrowers*, *The Mouse and His Child*, *Carrie's War* and three stories by Paula Fox, we are specially concerned with social issues and the representation of children (or, in one case, an animal-child) learning about a world outside their immediate families. But these stories all succeed also in linking these external aspects of learning with the emotional dimensions and preconditions of development. We hope that our analyses will demonstrate that the different levels of meaning of each of these stories have been successfully integrated by their authors. We believe that the multivalent depth of meaning of these stories goes a long way to account for their outstanding quality.

1

Loneliness, Dreaming and Discovery: *Tom's Midnight Garden*

Philippa Pearce's *Tom's Midnight Garden* is one of the finest stories for children to be published in Britain since the war. It was a Carnegie Medal-winner in 1958, it has been many times reprinted, and it is now widely regarded as a modern classic. It exemplifies in a particularly clear way each of the three themes we have outlined in the introductory chapter above. We try to account for the moving quality and beauty of this work in terms of the emotional and imaginative states of mind that it makes real, and we interpret these mental states through the modes of thinking of (broadly) Kleinian psychoanalysis. The story also describes the way in which a child of modern times comes to enter imaginatively into the lives of a period two generations ago. The story explores in quite complex ways the balance of gain and loss involved in this process of change. Thirdly, the story achieves its effect in part through its intense power of metaphor. The story involves its readers in understanding that loving communication between children and adults often takes place through the medium of language and story-telling itself. In these ways this story is a perfect exemplar of the view of children's fiction we want to develop through this whole book.

At the beginning of the story, a boy called Tom whose age is not given but who seems to be about ten, has to leave his family at the start of a holiday which he'd greatly looked forward to, because his brother Peter has measles. He is to go and stay with his uncle and aunt, in a town called Castleford in the Fens. He finds his uncle didactic and uncomfortable with children and his aunt affectionate but too anxious for him to feel readily at home. They live in a flat which has been converted from a larger house. There is no garden, and he feels he is going to be cooped up, especially as he is in quarantine and mustn't be in contact with other people. There is a grandfather clock in the hall of the house, which belongs, he is told, to old Mrs Bartholomew, the house's owner. She is regarded as crabby and reclusive – 'old Ma Bartholomew'. The clock has eccentric habits, and sometimes strikes thirteen. Tom is intrigued by this clock, and goes downstairs when it strikes thirteen at midnight during his first night in the house. He opens the back door, and finds a large moonlit garden, where there are hyacinths – spring flowers – even though he knows it is actually June.

He returns every night to this garden, and meets there a little girl called Hatty, and also her cousins, their friend Barty, her Aunt Melbourne, the gardener Abel and the maid, Susan. It's a spacious garden with interesting trees to climb, hiding places and tunnels in the hedges, a pond, and a gateway leading out to meadows and a river. He gradually realizes that the time he is entering when he goes into the garden is long ago, and also that he visits it at different seasons and at different moments of Hatty's childhood, sometimes earlier and sometimes later. Once he meets Hatty dressed in black just after she has come to her aunt's house, her mother and father having died. She has been taken in, as a 'charity child', and is bereaved and unhappy. While one of her cousins, and Abel the gardener, are kind to her, her aunt and the other cousin are not. In her play, she imagines herself as a princess, and her dead mother and father as a king and queen; we realize that her elaborate games in the garden help to make an imaginative, compensatory space to protect her against her loneliness and rejection. Tom becomes deeply involved in his night-time adventures in the garden, which, however, because of the strange properties of time in the thirteenth hour, seem to take up no real time at all.

To his uncle and aunt's surprise, he doesn't want to go home; he manages to catch a cold and is thus able to stay for a few days longer. The daytimes are boring, and he does little that interests him, but the nights see him deeply absorbed in his friendship with Hatty. She, however, is growing up (though Tom does not recognize this) and her playmate Tom appears to her in the garden less and less often, and grows thinner and more ephemeral in her eyes when he does. There have been various hints in the story that connect Hatty with Mrs Bartholomew, and we begin to realize that Hatty is Mrs Bartholomew when she was child, and that these childhood experiences are being brought alive in Mrs Bartholomew's dreams. Towards the end of the story there is a great frost, and Hatty, now a young woman, skates with Tom all the way to Ely. They go up the cathedral tower together, Hatty and the ghostly Tom, and there meet an equally spectral Peter, who has been missing Tom and dreaming of the picture postcard of Ely Cathedral which Tom has sent him. Hatty is given a ride home from Ely by young Barty in his gig, and this is the beginning of their courtship and subsequent marriage.

After this, Tom has a terrible dream that he is going to lose the garden and Hatty, just before his return to his own home. He wakes up and cries out Hatty's name, and old Mrs Bartholomew is woken up and disturbed. The following morning she demands that he go and apologize personally. She explains to him that *she* is Hatty, and talks to him about her childhood. On the doorstep, Tom says goodbye to Mrs Bartholomew 'with still politeness'. But then he rushes back upstairs to her:

> Afterwards, Aunt Gwen tried to describe to her husband that second parting between them. 'He ran up to her, and they hugged each other as if they had known each other for years and years, instead of only having met for the first time this morning. There was something else, too, Alan, although I know you'll say it sounds even more absurd . . . Of course, Mrs Bartholomew's such a shrunken little old woman, she's hardly bigger than Tom anyway, but, you know, he put his arms right round her and he hugged her goodbye as if she were a little girl.'

In this story, the imaginations of the two children, Hatty and Tom, are deepened and extended by their experiences of separations. Hatty suffers a dramatic and deep loss, through the death of her parents; Tom's is a more minor separation through illness and holiday. But Tom also feels rejected (even though he knows, when he compares himself with Hatty, that he has not really been abandoned), and bitterly misses his brother (who seems almost like a twin) with whom he had so wanted to play during the holiday. It's through experience of Hatty's loss, and exploration with her in play of what for both of them is a somewhat unfriendly and persecuting place, that Tom is able to make something of his separation and of the opportunities for new experiences which it brings about.

The question of what is alive in feeling, and what is dead, is a recurrent theme in the story. We learn through the story of the many catastrophes in Mrs Bartholomew's life – the death of her parents, then of her two sons in the Great War (this explains to us her interest not only in Tom, but also in his brother Peter), and finally, some years before, of her husband Barty – Mr Bartholomew. She is perceived by her neighbours as a 'shrunken old woman' – a dead sort of person. We see Tom as merely resentful and lifeless when he is with his uncle and aunt – though nothing really terrible has happened to him. He experiences their house as lacking in anything alive for a boy (except for his aunt's good food) when he arrives there. The midnight garden is first seen by moonlight, with its life-in-death associations, and the idea of a gravelike place is also conveyed by its yew trees. Trees are important to all the children – Hatty, Tom, and his brother Peter. While Peter is listlessly carrying on with the tree-house at home which he was to have spent the holiday with Tom in building, Hatty hurts herself falling out of a tree-house she has built with Tom. But this leads to development for her, as her cousin James shows concern for her injury and decides to help her, in face of his mother's indifference. Illness or the threat of illness are (as sometimes in life) catalysts of growth for the children, evoking especially intense devotion in others, and bringing recognition of bonds that otherwise are taken for granted. Tom is desperately anxious that he hasn't hurt Hatty through his dangerous tree-games. Hatty is in turn protective and sisterly towards Tom, as she grows older and no longer so involved in their play together. At a moment of crisis in the story, on the eve of Hatty's wedding when she is having to say goodbye to her childhood and its imaginings, the tree in the centre of the garden is struck by lightning, and she is heard by Tom to cry out. But this, like other moments of loss in the story, also makes possible its new beginnings. For 'then I knew, Tom, that the garden was changing all the time, because nothing stands still, except in our memory'.

One of the most beautiful images in the story is of the great frost in the Fens, around the turn of the century, and of Hatty as a young woman, with her childhood companion Tom, skating all the way to Ely. This is her last great experience of the freedom of childhood, an extension of the earlier wanderings of the two children into the meadows beyond the garden. (These have led her into trouble, as the geese follow the children back on to the lawn.) But because it is frozen, it is somehow safe, even for a young woman on her own, and the adventurousness and independence which she has learned through her solitude are a strength for her. When she returns from Ely, the ice is thawing and she is told it may be dangerous – the figures she now sees on the river banks appear more frightening as it grows dark. It is then that she meets Barty, and the unfrozen world of sexual love begins, as Tom and her childhood fade from her mind. So the great freeze becomes a metaphor for latency, suggesting an infinite expansiveness and pre-pubertal space – also the space of childhood memory – while for the time being other aspects of the self are hidden and safe. As the ice melts, Tom is displaced in Hatty's mind by Barty, whom she is later to marry.

The theory of art developed by psychoanalysts in the object-relations tradition is helpful in understanding the beauty of this story. Symbol formation, in the work of both the Kleinians[1] and Winnicott,[2] is linked with the capacity to retain an internal memory of loved objects in their absence. Imagination and play provide a space in which primary preoccupations with images of parents and feelings towards them are held in mind and explored. Tom is able to explore the experience of loneliness through identification with Hatty's loss of her parents, and his hostility to his uncle and aunt through Hatty's experiences of her adoptive family. Hatty's much greater deprivation enables Tom to come to terms with his lesser experience of loneliness and separation. The heightened feelings Tom has about the mignight garden, and about his aunt and uncle's home when he has to leave it, recall the strong attachments which children can develop for a holiday home, which are so intense in part because of the initial anxiety and strain of coming to a strange place. Even Uncle Alan's didactic lectures on time and its scientific properties are a provocation to him, to think about it for himself, from his own experience. His recognition of Mrs Bartholomew at the end, as the Hatty he knew as a child, seems to be a coming to life of a dead person, the old lady, as someone with feelings, and with love for him. In his separation from his home, Tom has had difficulties keeping alive a real awareness of his mother and father, and in accepting his uncle and aunt as substitutes for them. At the end of the story, his aunt witnesses and thus in part shares in Tom's unfrozen capacity for affection, the rediscovery of his capacity for love, in this transformed and unusual way.

For Hatty too, play is a way of coping with loss. We may think of her ghostlike playmate, Tom, as an echo of her own preoccupation with her dead parents. Abel's fear of Tom, and the danger he seems to be to Hatty (his knife, his climbing on the garden wall and the tree) suggest Hatty's preoccupations with death, as well as Tom's potential destructiveness. For old Mrs Bartholomew, the reliving of her childhood experience of bereavement and recovery enables her to renew her capacity for love and feeling in the present. Tom's arrival in her house seems to bring her back in contact with her childhood. Tom reminds her also of her own sons, for 'whom she had done all her crying . . . so long ago'. Mrs Bartholomew is sustained by her memories of relationships with loved ones as child, as wife, and as mother. While the identifications established in infancy may be primary for psychoanalysis, this picture of an old lady shows that 'object relations' are re-made throughout the life cycle.[3]

Tom's Midnight Garden in fact depicts several characters' experiences in keeping alive good feelings in a state of loneliness and loss, and the relationships between them through which these are brought alive. Being left is shown to stir up quite negative and resentful feelings, as well as a sense of emptiness and deadness, most clearly in Tom, but also in Mrs Bartholomew. We should probably see Tom's uncle's and aunt's limitations as in part the product of his own grudging attitude to his holiday with them – they are made by him to be worse than they are. Tom's over-eating substitutes physical for emotional hunger. His emotional needs break out at night, though his dreaming is prosaically ascribed to his rich meals. Tom's games with Hatty are perceived by Abel to be dangerous, and this seems to be more than the difference between his boy's and her girl's pastimes. The bow and arrow which Tom teaches Hatty to shape with a knife breaks a pane of glass, and his tree-house causes her to hurt herself – Tom's destructiveness is real, and he has to face its potential consequences. He is on the edge of puberty, and his relationship with a girl is a new and positive development for him. She arouses feelings of compassion, for example when he learns of her bereavement, and when she is hurt in her fall. Through Hatty he gets back into contact with his softer and more dependent feelings. For Hatty, there is an opposite development – her adventures with Tom support her in the independence that she will need, and help her to break out of the restrictive and submissive role in which her aunt, and the conventions of the time, have cast her. The unruly geese – introduced into the garden by the 'pauper child', and contaminating the rigid household order in the way that *she* does in her aunt's view – represent the more robust and ordinary life of a family, managing as Abel and Susan later do to raise their children when Hatty's more privileged cousins get into difficulties. The geese are like an irruption of a more ordinary and democratic social order into the world of inherited property and status. (They also evoke the story of the ugly duckling, in Hatty's complicity with them.) There is a suggestion that Tom is troubled by his aunt and uncle being together as a couple, in his irritation at their preparations for bed, as they are listening out for him (as he is listening out for them), and in his wandering around the house at night. His presence in the house does in fact seem to divide them, quite frequently, and his perception of their relationship is denigrating: 'Uncle Alan . . . would be reading aloud from his favourite, clever weekly newspaper; Aunt Gwen would be devotedly listening, or asleep'. One might suggest that the author has intuited in Tom a deeply buried envy and jealousy in relation to his brother Peter, who is still at home with their parents.

While less is said about Mrs Bartholomew's state of mind, she too seems to be lost in hostility to the world. She is felt by the tenants of her house to be spoiling and sour; this is the only evidence of her daytime state of mind that we have. Her feelings for life are in dreams; the contrast between her memories and her actual existence is conveyed in the description of her at night: she was 'lying tranquilly in bed: her false teeth, in a glass of water by the bedside, grinned unpleasantly in the moonlight, but her indrawn mouth was curved in a smile of sweet, easy-dreaming sleep. She was dreaming of the scenes of her childhood.' She, like Tom, emerges from this deadness to the discovery of love buried or frozen within her. Being able to call out to someone with intense feeling – Tom crying out Hatty's name, and Mrs Bartholomew asking to see Tom – is what both can do at the end of the story, but not at the beginning. Tome and his brother bring alive her two lost sons, and she the internal mother he has lost and found.

The similarities in the situations of Tom and Hatty – each feeling lonely and abandoned in their different ways – allows the writer to contrasts the time and place in which they live, and thus to provide an imaginative entry into the past for her readers. Comparison between the lives of the two children leaves little doubt that Tom's life is the easier one, for where he has to put up only with a temporary absence from home through his brother's measles, and a few weeks with an uncle and aunt who are not accustomed to children, (we sense from her eagerness to look after Tom that having no children has been his aunt's grief and disappointment), Hatty's parents have died, and her aunt is harsh and unkind to her.

Nevertheless, the story projects into the past a more spacious and humanly connected environment which Tom can explore through his contact with Hatty. A contrast is defined between a unified, hierarchical, safe world, cultivated inside its garden boundary but close to nature and the river outside it, and a blank and uninteresting suburb of the present day. The river has become polluted, between the time of Hatty's childhood, and the present. A sense of greater community in past time is conveyed by the scenes on the ice, in which the banter among strangers seems gentle and friendly. Whereas the old household was, for all its inequality, a set of relationships, the present-day inhabitants of the flats into which the house had been converted seem scarcely to be acquainted with one another, and live in silent animosity towards their owner. The beauty and mystery of the garden, with its flowers, trees, secret places and long history in which tracings and carvings can be left, is contrasted with the mean little dustbin yard which is all that remains. Tom's lifeless journey in his uncle's car contrasts with the expedition on the ice, and the eventful return journey in Barty's gig.

Mrs Bartholomew's childhood is underpinned by the presence of religious beliefs, which are especially important to the God-fearing Abel and lead him to protect and care for Hatty when his employer is harsh to her. The garden has associations to a pre-pubertal (and for Tom pre-oedipal) Garden of Eden, except that to Abel it is Tom that appears as a spirit of evil, tempting Hatty into danger. There is a suggestion of Blake in the description of the Angel painted on the clock face, announcing the day of judgement. Altogether, religious associations pervade the old house, providing an expressive if a somewhat fearsome language for feelings. In contgrast to this religious outlook is the dry mechanistic rationalism of Uncle Alan, who seems out of contact with feeling altogether. The grandfather clock, a male counterpart to Mrs Bartholomew, screwed immovably to the wall and still tended carefully by her, metaphorically unlocks these associations as it provokes arguments between Tom and Uncle Alan about scientific, regular time, and the imaginary 'time no longer' which Tom experiences in the midnight garden, and which he defends, with some intuitive sympathy from his aunt, against his uncle's cutting scepticism.

Greater hardship and harsh social attitudes are located in the past – Hatty is despised as a 'pauper child' whom her aunt wants to exclude from the family property; Hatty has no money for the train when she wishes to return from Ely. She has, after all, lost both her parents from bereavement, a rare occurrence in Tom's world. The author balances a feeling for the greater spaciousness and connectedness of the Edwardian social world with knowledge that it was also frequently more cruel and pain-filled for children than the present.

Love of place is a powerful theme in several of Philippa Pearce's books. We are told that the house of this story was based on the millhouse where she grew up, and where her father was born. (While the landscape of the fens is lovingly described in this story, the more complicated associations of Cambridge are filtered by its renaming as Castleford.) One can regard the feeling of this book for nature, for the past, and for the spirit of place, as conservative themes, though they have recently been revived in a 'green' radical politics which perhaps draws a particular strength from people living close to the countryside. It is a characteristic feature of English culture that positive feelings are so much more easily symbolized in a kind of historic, rural pastoral setting, than in representations of the modern world. Even so, it is the contemporary Tom who has the experience, and children like Tom for whom the book is written. The principal commitment of the author is not to the past as a preferred world, but to the need to remain connected to it, in memory and relationship.[4]

The modern quality of this work can be particularly pointed

up by comparison with an earlier children's classic, Frances Hodgson Burnett's *The Secret Garden* which was in fact written and set in roughly the period of Hatty's childhood in *Tom's Midnight Garden*. Philippa Pearce's story must surely contain and respond to this earlier book as one of its formative influences. In *The Secret Garden* another bereaved little girl finds a locked garden in which her new guardian's wife, the mother of a child she discovers in the house, has died in an accident. She and this ill and unhappy boy try to restore this garden, and through this persuade the father to return and care for his son. There is also a gardener, as in *Tom's Midnight Garden*, who befriends the girl, and supports her project.

While Hodgson Burnett's fine book achieved a representation of children's feelings, and their ways of coping with loss and loneliness, *The Secret Garden* works in a much more literal and moralizing mode than *Tom's Midnight Garden*. The girl, Mary Craven, *really* has to reform the spoilt boy whom the servants cannot manage, through the unlikely beneficial confrontation of two deprived and selfish natures. The garden has to be actually restored, and be the physical means of recreating the father's sense of relatedness to his dead wife, and his capacity to care for their child. By contrast, the author of *Tom's Midnight Garden* understands that what happens in imagination and play has a reality too, and can lead to growth and change without dramatic external deliverances. *Tom's Midnight Garden* doesn't need to be told in the realist mode of *The Secret Garden*, nor do the children have to effect miracles to survive. Reparation and restitution take place in the mind, as well as in outward action. Yet *The Secret Garden* does make the crucial discovery that imaginative experience in childhood is related to absence and separation, and it is from this important achievement that more subtle realizations of children's states of mind subsequently develop.

A number of evocative metaphors enable the narrative of *Tom's Midnight Garden* to communicate states of mind which could not be described for children in more literal ways. The midnight garden itself is a metaphor of imaginative, dreamlike space, related to the space in between internal and external reality which is described by Donald Winnicott.[5] The story insists on the real existence of this world for Tom, through his passionate belief in it, and later in the confirmation that it exists in Mrs Bartholomew's mind too. Also metaphorical is the description of the great freeze and of Tom and Hatty's expedition on the ice. As Hatty, she jokes with the men on the bank about her imaginary companion, with whom she will be safe. The frozen river suggests the spaciousness and safety of pre-pubertal childhood, but also enables the writer to evoke the change about to occur in Hatty as the ice melts, and as Tom is displaced in her mind by Barty.

The visit to Ely Cathedral also has a metaphoric; symbolic meaning. The tower gives Tom and Hatty, now at their different points of development, a vast new perspective on the landscape and the world. They meet by the font to go up the tower, and spend the afternoon visiting the Lady Chapel. The tower makes up, with the body of the cathedral, the bringing together of male and female at the onset of Hatty's adult life.[6] This story is given a poetic as well as narrative coherence by recurring themes. The trees in the garden, the clock, Mrs Bartholomew, the river in its different states, the nature of time, Ely Cathedral, are referred to throughout the story, which is unified for the reader by these recurring images and topics.

Such metaphors of stages of emotional development play a crucial part in the best fiction for children, especially in the genre of so-called fantasy with which this book is mostly concerned. The greater tolerance of young readers for departures from realism, and for interpretations of 'realist' and 'non-realist' modes of expression, have allowed writers to incorporate some of the metaphoric virtues of 'modernist' literary methods, while remaining within the framework of conventional narrative. The restriction of descriptive scope made necessary by the limited worldly experience and indeed vocabulary of their readers also imposes on children's writers the imperative that they must communicate with them about serious matters of life metaphorically and poetically, or not at all. Such writers have also been able to count on the existence of a common readership which shares many essential life experiences, where adults rather feel cut off from one another by the fragmentation and the scale of urban society. In the period after the Second World War, they could also share in a culture which for the time being felt hopeful about and strongly committed to the possibilities of childhood. This combination of factors may be what has made possible this flowering of metaphoric fiction for children.

It must be evident to child readers as well as adults that the events of the narrative could not really occur, yet the story in a number of ways refuses to trivialize them as 'mere' dreams, and insists on their deeper truth. There is, for example, a beautiful moment in the story when Tom finds the skates that Hatty has left for him, both moments after she has left them, in the midnight garden time, and in Tom's real present, fifty or sixty years later. There is a note left with the skates: 'To whomever may find this. These skates are the property of Harriet Melbourne, but she leaves them in this place in fulfilment of a promise once made to a little boy'. The skates themselves are one of the few signs of Tom's encounters with Hatty which remain as visible traces in the daytime world.

The other crucial conjunction of the two worlds is Tom's recognition that old Mrs Bartholomew is Hatty, grown old, and their childlike embrace which so startles the onlookers, (though Aunt Gwen, always emotionally attentive to Tom, does notice the strange quality of their contact). Is this just magic for children, the wish-fulfilment of being 'really' able to enter the past, or is something more truthful being said?

We believe that the ambiguities of this story regarding what is and what is not to be taken as real, are expressions of the nature of fiction itself. Tom's adventures in this story can be taken as themselves a metaphor for the experience of reading and story-telling. The passionate commitment, almost at times the addiction, of the children to their play with one another depicts the compelling power of the imagination. This state of mind in Hatty worries Abel, who fears that it will lead her into danger, and both flatters and dumbfounds Gwen and Alan who don't understand why Tom is so desperate to prolong his stay. This reference within the story to the power of fiction is made explicit. Tom has been writing letters about his adventures to his brother Peter, and when he forgets to write one day Peter is filled with such pangs of loneliness that he comes to find Tom and Hatty on the cathedral tower. (Incidentally, it is at this point that we see through Peter's shocked eyes that Hatty is now a young woman, and are prepared for Tom and Hatty's separation.)

The last chapter of the book, where Mrs Bartholomew meets and talks with Tom after the night-time crisis when he cries out and wakes everyone in the house, is called 'A Tale for Tom Long'. This hint enables us, if we wish, to re-interpret the whole story as Mrs Bartholomew's tale for Tom.

It is open to us to imagine it as made up from her childhood memories, and from her multiple identifications with Tom (as her childhood self, and as a reminder of her dead sons), but not necessarily as the whole truth. Tom's absorption with Hatty can be imagined as an equivalent to, or a metaphor for, his involvement in a story about Hatty, who lived in the garden of the house long ago. It is certainly only through listening to stories told by people with memories ('What was it like when you were little?', children ask their grandparents) that children can enter the past through their imaginations. Mrs Bartholomew and Tom are strangers to one another, but they are emotionally the grandchild (Mrs Bartholomew's sons were killed in war) and the grandmother that they each at that moment need.

From this point of view, pursuing this level of interpretation of the story as itself a metaphor for a story told to a child, the trace left by the skates also has another quality of meaning. For Mrs Bartholomew, the house reminds her continually of her past life. But for Tom, it is the fen-runner skates, unmistakably from the past, but sent through the years with a note for him, (or at least, to a 'little boy' who might be him) which brings this connection with Hatty so vividly alive. Within the story of *Tom's Midnight Garden*, this is the key that makes it come so alive. But we can also imagine this as the imaginative point of departure from which 'A Tale for Tom Long' could be successfully told to a real child like Tom. One explanation of the outstanding qualities of *Tom's Midnight Garden* lies in the way that its author has brought her understanding of the nature and transformative process of fiction within the narrative of her story. It is this which makes this work of fantasy into such a moving description of emotional possibility.

2

Narnia: An Imaginary Land as Container of Moral and Emotional Adventure

C.S. Lewis's *Chronicles of Narnia* are among the most successful of a long line of books for children which use the device of transporting children into a world outside our everyday world of experience.[1] In such worlds, we can encounter different kinds of tiny creatures, different historical moments and landscapes, and child heroes can have adult-scale adventures. The child reader can bear the terrors of moral choices in which the death of goodness is at stake, in the knowledge that the children facing these also have a secure place back home in the ordinary world of family life and school, where adults are of human dimensions, and children's responsibilities are limited. Lewis described the books as 'fairy tales', and drew attention to the implicit appeal to both adults and children of this genre and his writing, and the series is one which can be read at multiple levels of sophistication. The popularity of the Narnia books is in part based on the satisfaction available to adult and child in a shared reading, and the possibility for a child to re-read old favourites at changing levels of understanding.

The argument of this chapter concerns the meaning of the children's entry into Narnia, its relation to their situation at that moment, and the kind of experiences they have in Narnia, which we shall show to be explorations of emotional dilemmas children feel faced by in their everyday lives. There are many other facets of these stories which a different form of analysis would highlight, and some of them will be touched on as they relate to our thesis, particularly the idea that the central Christian allegorical structure can be seen as a religious framing of unavoidable human problems which the children are enabled to struggle with in their lives in Narnia.

The story begins, as so many children's adventure stories do – from the classics of E. Nesbit and Arthur Ransome to the superficial but immensely popular tales of Enid Blyton and their numerous modern television cartoon equivalents of super-heroes – with a family of children separated from their parents. In this case it is a wartime evacuation, to protect the children from the danger of air raids in London. They are sent to a remôte house in the country inhabited by a benevolent but eccentric professor and his housekeeper. The children are impressed and a little frightened by the hugeness of the house and quickly try to turn their backs on feelings of strangeness and potential homesickness by defining the house as a new world of freedom. The four children in the family introduce themselves to us distinctively at once: Peter, the eldest, leading the plan to master their environment by exploration; Susan, busy as the big sister shepherding the younger ones; Edmund, angrily aware that Susan may ape mother but that mother is not there; and Lucy, the youngest, timid and anxious:

'We've fallen on our feet and no mistake,' said Peter. . . . 'That old chap will let us do anything we like.'

'I think he's an old dear,' said Susan.

'Oh come off it!' said Edmund, who was tired and pretending not to be tired, which always made him bad-tempered. 'Don't go on talking like that.'

'Like what?' said Susan; 'and anyway, it's time you were in bed.'

'Trying to talk like Mother,' said Edmund. 'And who are you to say when I'm to go to bed? Go to bed yourself.'

'Hadn't we all better go to bed?' said Lucy. 'There's sure to be a row if we're heard talking here.'

'No there won't,' said Peter. 'I tell you this is the sort of house where no one's going to mind what we do. Anyway they won't hear us. It's about ten minutes' walk from here down to that dining room, and any amount of stairs and passages in between.'

'What's that noise?' said Lucy suddenly. It was a far larger house than she had ever been in before and the thought of all those empty passages and rows of doors leading into empty rooms was beginning to make her feel a little creepy.

'It's only a bird, silly,' said Edmund.

'It's an owl,' said Peter. 'This is going to be a wonderful place for birds. I shall go to bed now. I say, let's go and explore tomorrow.'

The next day it rains, so they explore the house and Lucy investigates a huge wardrobe. It contains long fur coats and she steps into its warm darkness, for 'there was nothing Lucy liked so much as the smell and feel of fur'. Perhaps on this first day away from mother and home, the fur coats comfortingly recall mother's softness and warmth. The wardrobe leads her into the frozen land of Narnia where 'she felt a little frightened, but very inquisitive and excited as well'. Lucy's exploration of the feelings aroused by the absence of and distance from her mother have begun: she goes beyond the fur coats into the unfamiliar interior, an inner world of fantasy where human-scale adults are absent and she will encounter a witch-queen, a god-like lion, talking animals and many mythic creatures – nymphs, satyrs, fauns, giants and so on. This first exploration of Narnia is Lucy's, and in *The Lion, the Witch and the Wardrobe*, (volume I of the *Chronicles*), she has a special place as heroine. As the smallest of the children, most sensitive to the impact of leaving home, she is the one who can lead them all into a world where they can discover what this experience means to them, how it changes them.

She meets a Faun, Mr Tumnus, a tragicomic character carrying an umbrella and parcels, like anyone in a London street, and talking in a polite, educated English fashion, thus familiar and yet profoundly strange to Lucy. He introduces her to Narnia, the land of eternal winter. The extreme cold is contrasted with the cheerful interior of his home and the perfect English high tea he produces for Lucy, followed up with stories of 'life in the forest'. The mixture of comfortable domesticity and magic entrances Lucy; Mr Tumnus plays a strange flute 'and the tune he played made Lucy want to cry and laugh and dance and go to sleep all at the same time'. These mixed and contradictory feelings are the point from which the Narnian experience begins, and Lucy's capacity for being internally alive to her own complexity and ambivalence is the source of her position as heroine.

When she prepares to leave, Mr Tumnus weeps and confesses that his kindness has been hypocritical – he has 'taken service under the White Witch' who makes eternal winter, who has 'all Narnia under her thumb'; his tears reveal that while pretending to be friendly, he has in fact been seducing ('kidnapping') her with the aid of a nice tea, exploiting her trust in order to hand her over asleep to his White Witch mistress. The Faun confronts his terror of the witch, including her possible vengeance, and promises to help Lucy return home safely. 'If I don't . . . she's sure to find out. And she'll have my tail cut off, and my horns sawn off, and my beard plucked out, and she'll wave her wand over my beautiful cloven hoofs and turn them into horrid solid hoofs like a wretched horse's. And if she's extra and specially angry she'll turn me into stone . . .'

'Of course I can't give you up to the Witch; not now that I know you.' Mr Tumnus's battle with his cowardly self ('I'm a bad faun') is relevant to the reader's understanding of Lucy's own emotional state at this moment: in dealing with the loss of her mother and the whole cluster of loved people, places and things, one option would be to make an inner alliance with a cold-hearted maternal object, like the Faun's White Witch. Can Lucy hold on to a good image of mother, or may this be displaced by her anger and hurt which could persuade her that their being sent away from home is evidence not of parental concern but of chilly neglect and abandonment? Her loyalty to good memories is being tested. The infantile aspect of her personality might associate the temporarily absent mother of this moment with the mother who weaned Lucy in babyhood,[2] exposing her to the pain of loss, the need to develop and protect internal resources, the ambivalence evoked by the experience of desiring what is not part of the self. Mr Tumnus asks if he can keep Lucy's handkerchief, which symbolizes the tender concern for him that his tears evoked in her and which enabled him to escape the tyranny of submission to the cowardly part of himself in alliance with the White Witch. Warm feelings, interest in and affection for Lucy, break through the structures rooted in terror, and revive his 'good' self.[3]

When Lucy returns home through the wardrobe and tells her story, the other children think she is crazy. Their ways of dealing with the transition from the family home have rendered them out of touch with their deeper feelings and imaginative capabilities, and Lucy experiences a very lonely and miserable few days. For she knows that what she has described is truly what happened to her, but her siblings' defensive clinging to the more easily managed 'facts' of external reality leave her isolated in her awareness of the inner world of psychic truth. This is made more painful for her because of Edmund's spitefulness – he is not so far from feeling the small child's sense of loss, as his sharp objections to Susan's taking on mother's role have testified. His nearness to feeling distressed intensifies his wish to dissociate himself from such unwanted humiliating dependent longings, and he 'sneered and jeered at Lucy and kept on asking her if she'd found any other new countries in other cupboards all over the house'. So for a while Lucy is the despised 'baby' while the other three bask in complacent superiority.

As befits the situation, the next entry into Narnia is made by Lucy and Edmund in the course of a game of hide-and-seek. Lucy is wondering whether Narnia and the Faun were all a dream, and goes to the wardrobe with this question in mind, and Edmund is eager to plague her with teasing. Edmund, after closing the door and thus metaphorically closing his retreat to the 'real' world, finds himself alone in Narnia. He is afraid to be alone, shouts for Lucy, and angrily blames her when he cannot find her.

> 'She's angry about all the things I've been saying lately,' thought Edmund. And though he did not much like to admit that he had been wrong, he also did not much like being alone in this strange, cold, quiet place; so he shouted again . . . Still there was no answer. 'Just like a girl,' said Edmund to himself, 'sulking somewhere, and won't accept an apology.'

He feels his lonely anxiety at this moment is being purposely inflicted on him in revenge by Lucy; what he had forced into her now feels to him as if it is hurled back at him in order to hurt and punish. An experience of persecution replaces the guilt he cannot tolerate.

Just at this moment the White Queen appears in her sleigh, all magnificence,

> a great lady, taller than any woman that Edmund had ever seen. She also was covered in white fur up to her throat and held a long straight golden wand in her right hand and wore a golden crown on her head. Her face was white – not merely pale, but white like snow or paper or icing sugar, except for her very red mouth.

We are encountering a Queen like the bad stepmothers of

fairy tales, or the Snow Queen of Hans Andersen. Her furs are a reference to the reversal of good into bad mother – a good mother's fur coat might be cuddled by a child, the Queen's furs are a narcissistic glorification of her cold beauty. She inspires terror but also awe, and she proceeds to seduce Edmund in age-old fashion with delicious food. When she raises her wand, Edmund is very frightened of her; he 'seemed unable to move' (paralysed by terror); however, her harsh tones melt into an irresistible invitation to join her in the sleigh and be taken care of. Magic food is created, 'Turkish Delight'. Edmund is momentarily alert to a nasty quality in the Queen and her dwarf-driver, but this intuition is quickly dulled by her exploitation of his greed; his sensuous pleasure in the sweet food fills his mind and an addictive dependence on the Queen develops.

> While he was eating, the Queen kept asking him questions. At first Edmund tried to remember that it is rude to speak with one's mouth full, but soon he forgot about this and thought only of trying to shove down as much Turkish Delight as he could, and the more he ate the more he wanted to eat, and he never asked himself why the Queen should be so inquisitive.

So she pumps him for all the information she wants about him and his brother and sisters, and implants the idea of bringing them all to visit her. Edmund is bewitched: 'When he had first got on to the sledge he had been afraid that she might drive away with him to some unknown place from which he would not be able to get back, but he had forgotten about that now.' The Queen taps his resentful younger-brother ambition, to pursue her aims: 'I very much want to know your charming relations. You are to be the Prince and – later on – the King; that is understood. But you must have courtiers and nobles. I will make your brother a Duke and your sisters Duchesses.'

The alliance made between Edmund and the Queen rests on her astute recognition of his weak spot – the part of himself that is feeling hungry for mother's love and care can be drawn into a relationship with her based on his longing both for comfort at an infantile level, which the food represents (this is reminiscent of so much of the consumption of sweet stuff by children) and a simultaneous freeing of himself from uncomfortable knowledge. As he eats, his mind gets emptier and emptier. The image of the serpent's offering of the apple to Eve in the Garden of Eden is reworked in this story in a particular way; Adam and Eve, in eating of the tree of knowledge, became conscious of sin and sexuality, and open to a possible loss of contact with God and goodness. Edmund is already feeling poisoned by his own emotions and seeks relief from persecution and terror through moral oblivion achieved by abandonment to infantile sensuality. The geography of Narnia underlines this; Edmund is invited to walk from the lamp-post, the point of entry into Narnia which also metaphorically represents order, light and insight, to the Witch's house which stands 'between two hills', the place of regressive temptation, where the infantile part of Edmund is promised perpetual gratification from the Witch's sweet food, as a baby might nestle between two breasts.

Because of his guilty pact with the Witch which he must keep secret, Edmund betrays Lucy, and denies the existence of Narnia to Peter and Susan. The older children consult the Professor about Lucy, who they feel is out of her mind. Lucy, however, holds to her own sense of reality, and seems to feel that there might be support for her somewhere: 'I don't care what you think, and I don't care what you say. You can tell the Professor or you can write to Mother . . . I know I've met a Faun in there . . .' To their surprise, the Professor does not seem as convinced as they that 'if things are real, they're there all the time,' and he draws their attention to the discrepancy between their current worry about Lucy's 'lies' and their experience of her as ordinarily truthful. This prepares the way for Peter and Susan to enter Narnia, for their comfortable omniscience is shaken, their pseudo-grownupness revealed to them. All four children one day hide in the wardrobe to escape from a party of trippers being conducted on a tour of the house by the housekeeper, Mrs Macready, 'who was not fond of children, and did not like to be interrupted when she was telling all the things she knew'. This is a moment of multiple meaning, for the trippers come from beyond the immediate world of the house, reminding the children of the world they have left, their parents, London, the war, and also of their present temporary status as visitors and their unimportance to Mrs Macready. From all of this they flee into the wardrobe, where they can blot out anxieties roused by links to a frightening reality and merge into the permanent structure of the house.

They enter Narnia, where Edmund gives himself away by unguarded recognition of the landscape. His brother's moralistic denunciation only intensifies Edmund's isolation, in which he sustains himself by dreams of revenge: 'I'll pay you all out for this, you pack of stuck-up, self-satisfied prigs.' They discover that Narnia is in the chilly grip of the White Queen, whose hatred freezes everything. It is always winter and Christmas never comes – there is never any hope of change, neither the change towards the longer-light days of the spring nor the symbolic hopefulness of Christmas celebrations. Mr Tumnus, Lucy's friend, has been arrested by the Secret Police, and his house is in ruins. The methods of a police state are in evidence: 'The door had been wrenched off its hinges and broken to bits . . . The crockery lay smashed on the floor and the picture of the Faun's father had been slashed into shreds with a knife.' There is an official notice on the door announcing the police action. Domestic peace and family relations have been trampled underfoot, for the relation to the state is pre-eminent, and a trial for treason is underway. The children feel afraid to be without food, being now literally hungry, but also in sore need of emotional sustenance as they experience the impact of the icy state of Narnia. But Susan is touched by the devastation of Mr Tumnus's home, unconsciously aware of the echoes within herself whereby terror would lead to silent acquiescence in an emotional disaster, and she joins Lucy in arguing for an attempt to rescue the Faun.

As in many a fairy tale, a bird appears to help them, a robin, who leads the way. Edmund's fears of being led into a trap are countered by Peter's argument: 'Still – a robin, you know. They're good birds in all the stories I've ever read. I'm sure a robin wouldn't be on the wrong side.' Robin Redbreast is the childish name, and the difference of opinion reflects two sides of the children's position – Edmund gives voice to the paranoid fear that there is no good maternal image (the redbreast) which they can rely on, Peter to the hope of re-establishing a link with a living creature which can help them deal with the cold nightmare of Narnian existence. Their hopes are strengthened when they meet up with Mr and Mrs Beaver, a practical couple who make excellent arrangements to feed the hungry children. Peter helps Mr Beaver catch fish, the girls help Mrs Beaver with her other preparations (the sexual division of labour is entirely conventional as is apportionment of sensitivity and intuition to the girls and courage and decisiveness to the boys); but Edmund cannot really enjoy the 'good ordinary food' because he is tormented by the desire evoked by 'the memory of bad magic food. He thought about Turkish Delight and about being a king . . . and horrible ideas came into his head.' Perhaps also his dream of being the favourite of the White Queen is more attractive to him than the appreciation of the good care provided by the domestic Beaver couple – the pre-oedipal delights of a special position with mother draw him away from making a relationship with a couple who might awaken a painful echo of his parents. Learning how to fish from Mr Beaver involves an acceptance of his expertise and local knowledge which is beyond Edmund, in his state of aroused ambition and delusions of grandeur. The children's painful separation from their parents would tend to foster an unconscious hostility towards the relation between the parents who continue to enjoy each other's presence. The Beavers' generosity reopens a current of affection, in contrast to the children's experience of Mrs Macready.

The Beaver speaks to them of Aslan, the Lion, of whom they know nothing. The mention of his name has a particular effect (clearly, in Lewis's frame of reference, parallel to the religious impact of the name of Jesus). Each child responds individually, for Aslan represents the inner hopes and goodness (good aspects of the self and attachments to valued persons and identifications) which are personally specific; in psychoanalytic terms, the internal good object.

> Each one of the children felt something jump in his inside. Edmund felt a sensation of mysterious horror. Peter felt suddenly brave and adventurous. Susan felt as if some delicious smell or some delightful strain of music had just floated by her. And Lucy got the feeling you have when you wake up in the morning and realize that it is the beginning of the holidays or the beginning of summer.

The children learn what has happened to Mr Tumnus. The Witch's vengeance is to turn her enemies to stone, squashing their life and independence which arouses her tyrannical hatred. Aslan, on the other hand, is described in 'an old rhyme':

Wrong will be right, when Aslan comes in sight,
At the sound of his roar, sorrows will be no more,
When he bares his teeth, winter meets its death
And when he shakes his mane, we shall have spring again.

This Old Testament characterization of the power of goodness personified arouses both anxiety and excitement in the
children. Mr Beaver goes on to differentiate between the
human (potentially good) and the not-fully-human:

'No, there isn't a drop of real Human blood in the Witch.'
'That's why she's bad all through, Mr Beaver,' said Mrs Beaver.
'True enough, Mrs Beaver . . . there may be two views about
Humans . . . but there's no two views about things that look like
Humans and aren't.'

Edmund slips away, declaring his alliance with the Witch
by his departure, but as he nears her house apprehension
breaks through his grandiose and revenge-dominated fantasies of life as King of Narnia; the pointed spires, the huge
stone lion, the giant-turned-to-stone and the wolf doorkeeper
all frighten him. His only recourse is to relieve his own
feelings of panic by mocking the creatures turned to stone,
but their impervious statuesque quality makes them unsuitable recipients for his unwanted emotions, which bounce
back at him disconcertingly. Edmund begins to experience
his solitary state as less than ideal, and when he sees a stone
faun wonders if it is Lucy's Mr Tumnus, for Lucy had been a
much more responsive recipient of his projections and he is
missing her, though he does not yet know it.

The problem of maintaining loyalty to an absent loved
person is the psychological core of the story. C.S. Lewis
explores this by a division of labour between the four
children. Edmund's pursuit of power, to which he is impelled
by greed and by envious resentment, is one manner of
dealing with a painful sense of deprivation, and the other
three children are in touch with this potential response in
themselves through their attachment to Edmund; but they
protect themselves through idealization and deposit the
nasty side of themselves self-righteously in Edmund. Such
gross splitting between good and bad is characteristic of
much of the cruder writing for children, but here the focus is
on the problem of integration. This is discernible on two
levels, in the character of Aslan, and in the changes within

the children themselves. These two are implicitly intertwined – the appearance of Aslan, the Christ-like saviour, heralded by the arrival of Father Christmas with gifts for the children, is simultaneous with the 'breaking of the spell', and the structure suggests a religious interpretation along the lines of the working of the Holy Spirit in the children's hearts. The description of the children's feelings allows us to consider what such an idea might mean psychologically. Edmund's disillusion with the Witch begins with his realization of his terror of her and is confirmed when the food she offers turns out not to be mind-dulling Turkish Delight but dry bread and water, prison fare, enabling him to see how he has become her prisoner. This separation of her perspective from his own prepares the way for his response to an encounter with a group of animals celebrating Christmas with a wonderful dinner; the Witch is enraged, as this is evidence of her waning power, and turns them to stone despite Edmund's pleas. He, however, feels pity for them, because the longing of the little child part of himself for the family circle has been awakened by this vision of a family party. His heart is melting, and the revived sympathy for his own vulnerability is echoed in the thaw in the countryside, of which he becomes aware with relief. Forgotten experience is recovered and he recognizes the spring, and his own capacity for love, which had been lost. Just as Edmund's inner condition, frozen by hatred, is coming alive, so the spring flowers begin to grow and birds to be heard.

The other three with Mr Beaver are tackling the issue of healing the split between good and bad parts of the self from another angle. They move from an idealization of a magical kind, 'a delicious dream', to a meeting with Aslan, who seems to them both 'good and terrible'. The biblical resonance is profound, but the children's difficulty in looking Aslan in the face, a fear expressed in their trembling limbs, is also representative of their inadequate grasp of their own natures. Aslan can combine within himself love of good-ness and truth with a capacity to face and integrate hatred and violence, and his strength derives from this inner contact between opposing elements. Peter is hauled out of his moralistic superiority through a perception of the possibility of taking responsibility for his unwanted emotions and admits that Edmund's betrayal of them is in part his fault – his self-righteous anger had left Edmund too alone and exposed. He has, also, in order to save Susan who is attacked by a wolf, to kill the wolf, and in doing so face his own terror and harness his capacity for aggression.[4] Fairy-tale heroics and psychological growth are working together in the story (as so often in fairy tales, which do deal with serious moral conflicts). Aslan demands this step of Peter: 'Let the Prince win his spurs' – and very often has the role of drawing the children's attention to what they are capable of and preventing them from a passive reliance on his god-like powers.

The psychological truth of the story and its religious allegorical purposes part company in an interesting way as the struggle proceeds. Edmund is rescued from being murdered by the Witch-Queen and the dwarf, and the reunification of the children is achieved without any working through of what has happened to them all. Aslan talks to Edmund and then says to the others, 'Here is your brother, and – there is no need to talk to him about what is past'. Forgiveness is asked and given in a moment, and then all are concerned to avoid feeling 'awkward', to band together as a friendly company who have no difficulties with themselves or each other. The problems of painful guilt, remorse, depression are swept aside in Christian forgiveness. Not surprisingly this turns out to be based on a fresh split, for the dwarf appears as messenger and it is clear that all the evil is now firmly located in the Witch and her allies. She is demanding that the traitor must be sacrificed – there is an ancient law which enshrines this. A primitive morality erupts to dominate when guilt cannot be adequately experienced. There is a regression from an ethic of personal responsibility and inner integration and the human relations made possible by this to an externally imposed morality of talion; the Emperor of the story is like a vengeful Jehovah who does not forgive, but exacts vengeance. Lewis's Christian faith demands that sinful man be saved by a Jesus-like sacrifice of Aslan, who puts himself in the place of Edmund. This shift is perhaps reflected in an important change in the tone of the writing – medieval, heraldic and crusading images appear, prefiguring the children's translation to royal status, a language of gothic old-worldliness which unites elements of folklore, patriotism and myth.[5] The children leave behind their ordinary selves, so vividly made known to us, and become idealized representations of the good, with characters stereotypically fixed: King Peter the Magnificent, Queen Susan the Gentle,

King Edmund the Just, Queen Lucy the Valiant. We shall return to discussion of the relative importance of human and religious themes in discussion of the final volume of the series.

There are, however, shifting emphases in the story's structure which keep the emotional intensity alive. One of the interesting developments is the differing mode of involvement of the boys and the girls in Aslan's crisis. Aslan discusses with Peter the planning of the battle which will soon take place; as the active disciple, Peter was entrusted with much by Christ, so Peter in Narnia is handed the task of marshalling the forces of the good, in partial realization that Aslan himself may not be with them in the battle. The two girls, however, are intuitively aware of Aslan's intended separation from them, and cannot sleep. They go in search of him and are allowed to follow him and witness the cruel humiliation and sacrifice on the stone table at the hands of the Witch. The biblical echoes are again much in evidence; the Witch says to Aslan bound by chords, 'Understand that you have given me Narnia forever, you have lost your own life and you have not saved his [Edmund's]. In that knowledge, despair and die.' When the girls tend Aslan's lifeless body they call to mind the women caring for Jesus's body in the Garden of Gethsemane. The despair of Aslan's death is not total, because it is observed by Susan and Lucy who are able to contain their fear of the Witch and her frightful horde of spectres, minotaurs, vultures and the like because of their profound pity and sadness. Aslan has shared his sadness with them, and their mourning keeps alive a memory of his vitality, beauty and strength. They are helped in their efforts to restore some dignity to the corpse by a party of field-mice who gnaw through his bonds (like the mouse or rat of Aesop's fable, freeing the lion who has spared him and whom he thus repays).

The two girls support each other through this ordeal. Their task involves bearing the awareness of the possibility of loss of contact with their good object and the triumph of the forces of evil. This refers both to the death of Aslan at the hands of the Witch and to the anxieties the children outside their Narnian lives feel about the survival of their parents and their country presently under attack by a Nazi enemy. In the inner world, there is the problem of whether the internal parents, the memories of loved and loving parents, can be adequately protected from attacks launched by bad parts of the self, fuelled by emotions like terror, greed, intolerable deprivation, envy. Susan's and Lucy's capacity to stay with Aslan signals their refusal to retreat from the agonising encounter with their own limitations. Lewis attributes this capacity for suffering to the girls, and an active fighting role to the boys. There is a conventional line drawn here between attributes of the sexes, but at a deeper level the different experiences of the girls and boys represent an unintegrated psychic state, in which masculine and feminine aspects of the personality cannot be adequately brought together, and this seems to arise because of the overwhelming fear aroused by the Witch as an image of femininity. There is a good Father (Aslan) and a bad Mother (the Witch) and no representation of a couple; the link with the Beaver couple has been replaced by more primitive preoccupations. The seductive sexuality of the Witch, which ensnared Edmund, makes it evident that women whose sexual natures are acknowledged are profoundly to be feared. The oedipally preoccupied child and a Christian ascetic distrust of sexuality are here combined. This theme crops up again in later volumes even more strikingly; when Susan grows up and becomes a sexually aware young woman, interested in clothes, make-up and parties, she is no longer able to enter Narnia, which is only open to children (like the Kingdom of Heaven). The latency child's hatred of sexuality is thus enshrined in the rules of access to Narnia.

The girls' endurance breaks the stranglehold of the eye-for-an-eye morality; 'deeper magic' has been released, and the stone table, the place of heartless assault on the good object, snaps in two. Though this is described in a somewhat mumbo-jumboish magical way, referring to an age of 'stillness and darkness before Time dawned' (evoking images of pre-birth experience), the idea of 'Death . . . working backwards', while overtly presented as a god-like resurrection, can be understood in the story's own terms as the natural result of the mourning process, since Aslan is alive in the children's minds. His rebirth is for them like the re-finding of the primary parent, one who can 'carry' the child, both physically and psychically and is available for exactly this purpose, the perfectly trustworthy ideal mother of the infant.

'You must ride on me.' . . . That ride was perhaps the most wonderful thing that happened to them in Narnia. Have you ever had a gallop on a horse? [The child reader is invited to lose himself in the flow of words that follow.] . . . Take away the heavy noise of the hoofs and jangle of the harness and imagine instead the almost noiseless padding of the paws. Then imagine instead of the black or grey or chestnut back of the horse the soft roughness of golden fur, and the mane flying back in the wind. And then imagine you are going about twice as fast as the fastest racehorse. But this is a mount that doesn't need to be guided and never grows tired.

The blissful unity between the Lion and his riders seems most deeply to recall the experience for infant and mother of coming close together again after birth, when death may have been a vivid fear for each, relived in subsequent separations. The overwhelming sexual quality of the experience is alive in C.S. Lewis's prose, which carries the reader through the whole physical world of Narnia in waves of excitement which perhaps also bring alive, in the context of infant/parent interaction, the potential sexuality of the children. The creative power of Aslan's rebirth is dramatized as he breathes life into the stone statues surrounding the Witch's palace.

> Instead of all that deadly white [cold and virginal] the courtyard was now a blaze of colour; glossy chestnut sides of centaurs, indigo horns of unicorns, dazzling plumage of birds. . . . And instead of all the deadly silence the whole place rang with the sound of happy roarings, brayings, yelpings, barkings, squealings, cooings, neighings . . . songs and laughter.

Death is conquered, as the Christian story would put it, and the liveliness and beauty of the inner world of creative imagination is restored. Aslan leads the search for all the prisoners who need to be released; the windows are all opened, letting in light and air to clean out 'the dark and evil place'; the Queen's domains have anal connotations, where all that was alien is reduced as in infantile unconscious phantasy to manipulate lifeless stuff, imprisoned and thus dominated.

In the battle which follows, Edmund plays a crucial role, for it is he, who knows from experience the seductive powers of her magic wand, who can perceive that the smashing of the wand, of her capacity to petrify metaphorically and literally, is the essential priority. Lucy observes him, once healed of his wounds by her magic cordial, 'looking better than she had seen him look, oh, for ages; in fact ever since his first term at that horrid school which was when he had begun to go wrong. He had become his real old self again and could look you in the face.' The theme comes full circle, for the problem the story begins with, of the children's response to the war-imposed evacuation, is now connected by Lucy (always the most emotionally astute of them) with an earlier separation from home which had catastrophic consequences for Edmund. We might understand this along these lines – for Edmund, the departure to boarding school was too stressful. (There is an implicit doubt about the desirability of school as a place of education and socialization for children, as a couple of pages later, when the Narnian way of life under the reign of the new Kings and Queens is described, one feature is a 'good law' which 'liberated young dwarfs and young satyrs from being sent to school'.) The pain of separation from parents and siblings, the loneliness and uncertainty were too much for Edmund to bear. This situation was made worse by the culture of the school – 'horrid' (Lucy's word) conjures up images of insensitive teachers, brutality, bullying. Maybe the Witch-Queen's castle is an image with elements of a remote prison, like a Gothic boarding school where the children are controlled by the wand/cane. There is a rich literature by twentieth-century writers about their excruciating experiences of harshly unimaginative brutalizing school environments,[6] particularly painful to the child who misses home and maternal care. Edmund's turning away from people (not being able to look them in the eye) implies a growing despair about being able to re-establish relations based on love, an inner cynicism in which he decides that the only bearable position is to ally himself with the persecutors and thus rid himself of his misery by inducing it in fresh victims. Such was the interaction with Lucy at the beginning of the story, and it is a well-known escape from terror in contexts of tyranny. The particular quality of Edmund's new personality (he had lost) contact with his 'old self') involves excitement as well as submission; he is afraid of the Witch, but also sensuously enchanted by her, and his sadistic fantasies of revenge are thoroughly satisfying to him. The helplessness of the victim is replaced by an excited state of mind suffused with unconscious masturbatory phantasies of omnipotence, powered by hate, not love.

In contrast, when the children find themselves home again via the wardrobe and tell the Professor about their adventures, he says to them, 'Yes, of course you'll get back to Narnia again some day. . . . But don't go trying to use the same route twice. Indeed, don't *try* to get there at all. It'll happen when you're not looking for it.' The life of the imagination, this implies, cannot be brought about by effort; it is more to do with being attuned to possibility. 'Keep your eyes open,' the Professor says. Adventures will come to those who are ready to have them. The eyes kept open are part of a mode of responsive experiencing of inner and outer worlds. This is unlike Edmund's turned-away gaze, which became ossified because there was too much distress to digest, and he could not find sources of help. Lewis has a grasp of and fascination for such states of mind, which not surprisingly crop up in other characters in the later volumes. For example, in *Prince Caspian*, Nikabrik is described as having 'gone sour inside from long suffering and hating,' while Caspian, though exposed to the loss of his parents as a young child and subsequent care by his usurping and affectionless uncle and aunt, is sustained in hopefulness by his relationship with his nurse and tutor, who are capable of genuine parental concern for him.

The varied adventures of *The Chronicles* culminate in *The Last Battle*, and in this story the overarching Christian allegory is pursued very fully. This necessitates a division into 'sheep and goats' and an impermeable division between the inhabitants of heaven and hell, which belies the subtlety with which Lewis has earlier on been able to investigate the children's differing capacities over time, the moments at which their worst selves have dominated, a complex ongoing fluctuation of inner forces within the personality. For example, whereas Edmund is the bad apple in volume 1, Susan is the faint-hearted doubter of volume 3; she is getting on badly with Lucy, possibly because Lucy is about to join her at boarding school, which may be a change she fears. (The adventure starts on the station platform as they await the train to school.) The realism of this shifting perspective is replaced in the Last Judgement reworking of the final story by a finite moment of judgement which casts out evil, the bad choices which might always be made, and preserves in perfect unambiguous bliss the elect. However, it is in death that such a simplification is placed, the end of the vital flow of life (which has earlier on been celebrated in these stories), and the element of tragedy in death, particularly the death of children in an accident, is ignored. For in Christian theology, death is an entry to eternal life and the loss of life in the world is not important, and mourning can thus be translated into joy.

For the adult or older child reader who does not share Lewis's Christian beliefs, the biblical references become intrusive; the imagery has to be made parallel in so many detailed ways that the writer's own imaginative flair seems deadened by the intellectual effort involved in a complete blending of the Narnian world and the religious conception of Man's relation to God. The attractiveness of the oblique reference, which does not force itself into one's awareness, is lost. Thus the donkey dressed up in a lion skin and presented as Aslan recalls the 'false gods' of the Old Testament; the donkey's stable is transformed into a stable where 'the inside is larger than the outside' and we are reminded that 'a stable once had something inside it that was bigger than our whole world.' Entry into heaven is by belief, and the dwarves' scepticism blinds them to the Heaven they could enter; they 'chose cunning instead of belief'. Peter becomes doorkeeper, as St Peter was entrusted with the keys of heaven. There is also an implicit political frame of reference, with racist and probably anti-communist overtones: the enemies are described as 'dark men . . . in a thick crowd, smelling of garlic and onions, their white eyes flashing dreadfully in their black faces' (this goes a lot further than the 'Turkish Delight' reference to the suspect sensibility of the East). The ape, overwhelmed by greed and hubris, who leads the anti-Aslan conspiracy, explains, 'You think freedom means doing what you like. . . . That isn't true freedom. True freedom means doing what I tell you.' So the creatures of Narnia are to be enslaved via trickery (the false lion) and distortions of truth, and forced into slave labour for the benefit of their master. The echoes of a militantly anti-communist Christian cold-war stance are unmistakable, and the gullibility of the population from Puzzle, the donkey, onwards (unable to puzzle his way out of the monkey's web of confusing lies) suggests no great confidence in the people's capacity to think. There have been hints of this earlier, in the condescending rather than truly democratic way in which the lesser characters (in social status or intelligence) are spoken

57

of. Their countrified, quaint talk in contrast to the courtly converse of the Royals suggests a conservative hierarchical social framework in which each is rightly placed.

Perhaps this is the background for *The Last Battle*, for such pessimism does make an ongoing life of moral experience hard to bear. In this respect, Lewis's religious views may be in accord with the simplifying moral preferences of the latency child; it is so much easier to live with clearly distinct versions of good and evil, and the falsity of this absolutism may be ignored for the comfort it brings. However, the special popularity of *The Lion, the Witch and the Wardrobe* may also be a testament to its greater richness and emotional veracity.

3

Magic Wishes and the Self-Explorations of Children: *Five Children and It*

E. Nesbit's *Five Children and It* and its two later sequels (*The Pheonix and the Carpet* and *The Story of the Amulet*) are early and influential examples of a whole genre of fiction for children. This is the genre of stories about holidays, which take a family of children out of their everyday environment, away from the daily experiences and constraints of school, and often away from their parents too. With the wider experience of annual summer holidays among the middle classes and, later on, among most of the population, child readers are prepared by the initial setting of such stories to read about *adventures*: a world of strange places and people, and days or even weeks in which to play freely as stray events and the imagination suggest. These stories often evoke the distinct emotional rhythm of a holiday – the first excitement, the explorations of new places, deep immersion in a self-contained world of play, and a final sadness and reflective-ness as the holiday comes to an end. This distinctive framing, with its clearly-marked beginning and ending, and its location out of normal time and space, allows these stories to be shaped by the imaginative or internal experience of the children they create, since the routines of the everyday world can be ignored or taken up just as the writer wishes. The intense emotions often aroused by holidays also become important themes in the best of this writing, and have to be dealt with somehow even in the worst. The experience of a holiday can be elaborated into a metaphor of 'internal experience' or of space for emotional development, speaking to and moving the child (and adult) reader through this latent depth of meaning.

Characteristically, such stories are often set in what we think of as holiday places – houses in the country, as in *Five Children and It*, the Norfolk Broads and Lake District scenes of some of Arthur Ransome's stories, and the Cornish seaside of coves and lighthouses in some of Enid Blyton's fiction. The genre is perhaps itself a cultural by-product of the social institution of the annual holiday as it emerged in the late nineteenth century (helped by the railways and rising standards of living). Its converse – the world it deliberately leaves behind – is the school story. In the holiday stories, school is often pictured as the mundane daily life from which the children have been liberated as the story begins, and to which they will have to return at its end.

In *Five Children and It*, the beginning of the holiday is a moment of high expectations: ' "Aren't we nearly there?" "Oh is this it?," ' the children start to ask, three miles before they have arrived. (Today, on long car journeys from London to Wales, such questions may begin at Hammersmith Broadway!) The expectations are, among other things, for the complete availability of the parents for their children. *Five Children and It*, like many such stories, dashes these hopes at the outset by sending the parents away. After four pages,

> Father had to go away suddenly on business, and mother had gone to stay with Granny, who was not very well. They both went in a great hurry, and when they were gone the house seemed dreadfully quiet and empty, and the children wandered from one room to another and looked at the bits of paper and string on the floors left over from the packing, and not yet cleared up, and wished they had something to do.

The parents' absence creates the space which then has to be filled somehow, by the children in their relationships with each other, through other adults, and in *Five Children and It* by the children's encounters with the magical, wish-granting Psammead ('pronounced Sammyadd') or Sand-fairy. Often in stories of this kind, the absence or virtual absence of the parents is important not only in the literal freedom it gives children to explore as they want, but in the push to psychic work which is given by the pain of (temporary) loss. We discuss this theme also in chapter 2, on *Tom's Midnight Garden*.

60

Even a writer as apparently uninterested in emotional pain as Enid Blyton has a way of acknowledging that *something* happens inside when parents go away suddenly. At the beginning of one of her many versions of the children on holiday theme, *The Famous Five*, the children hear about a change in their parents' plans:

'Mother, have you heard about our summer holidays yet?' said Julian, at the breakfast-table. 'Can we go to Polseath as usual?'
'I'm afraid not,' said his mother. 'They are quite full up this year.'
The three children at the breakfast table looked at one another in great disappointment. They did so love the house at Polseath. The beach was so lovely there, too, and the bathing was fine.
'Cheer up,' said Daddy. 'I dare say we'll find somewhere else just as good for you. And anyway, Mother and I won't be able to go with you this year. Has Mother told you?'
'No!' said Anne. 'Oh Mother, is it true? Can't you really come with us on our holidays. You always do.'

These hammer-blows are, however, registered by Blyton's children with the most enthusiastic of manic defences:

The children began to feel rather excited. It would be fun to go to a place they had never been before, and stay with an unknown cousin . . . 'Oh Daddy, do telephone to Aunt Fanny and ask her if we can go there!' cried Dick. 'I just feel as if it's the right place somehow. It sounds sort of adventurous.'

Nesbit's children on the other hand find that after their parents have left the house seems dreadfully quiet and empty. It evokes desolation, and they find more consolation in the garden and the country beyond. They have their father's words still in mind when they decide what to do:

It was Cyril who said, 'I say, let's take our Margate spades and go and dig in the gravel pits. We can pretend it's the seaside.'
'Father said it was once,' Anthea said; 'he says there are shells there thousands of years old.' So they went.

Once at the gravel pit, where the 'little front doors of little sand-martins' little houses' are another reminder of home, they decide to dig to Australia to find the upside-down children there (perhaps because Australia and their parents both seem so far away). They remember what father told them about the sea having been there in prehistoric times, but it is hard to play sandcastles without the sea (they are remembering their last Margate holiday at least two years ago) and they can't find any seashells. Then they find what they *do* need, someone to talk to them – the sand-fairy, buried in the sand.

> The children stood round the hole in a ring, looking at the creature they had found. It was worth the looking at. Its eyes were on long horns like a snail's eyes, and it could move them in and out like telescopes; it had ears like a bat's ears, and its tubby body was shaped like a spider's and covered with thick soft fur; its legs and arms were furry too, and it had hands and feet like a monkey's.

The sand-fairy had indeed been there for thousands of years, since the time when it was seashore as Father had said. It tells them of the time when 'people used to send their little boys down to the seashore early in the morning before breakfast to get the day's wishes, and very often the eldest boy in the family would be told to wish for a Megatherium, ready jointed for cooking.' The Psammead asks them about their breakfast, and who gives it to them ('Mother gives it us' they reply). The providing of food is important throughout this story, and it is a continuous reminder of the children's external and internal dependence on adults. They ask the sand-fairy if it can still give wishes, which it can. It says it came out of the sand because they wished it. They visit it every morning, before or after breakfast, and the story describes the adventures that follow the wishes the sand-fairy grants.

The Psammead is an invention with perhaps *too* many different physical qualities – like spider, snail, bat, monkey, and later, in respect of its whiskers, even rat. Its strangeness and its shoreline history (and its eyes on stalks) suggest animal associations that the author doesn't mention, to sea creatures like crabs. But it is perhaps more important that the Psammead should be warm-blooded, and its queerness is adequately conveyed in these other ways. More significant than its physical attributes are its qualities of mind and speech, and these are distinctive and memorable. The Psammead is very old, and behaves to the children somewhat like a very old and quirky person. It is outspoken:

'What on earth is it?' Jane said. 'Shall we take it home?'

The thing turned its long eyes to look at her, and said: 'Does she always talk nonsense, or is it only the rubbish on her head that makes her silly?'

It remembers the old days when children simply chose between healthy breakfasts. It is a lover of dryness and warm sand. In the old days, it said, the children used to let the 'nasty wet bubbling sea' into the sandcastles they built, and 'of course as soon as a sand-fairy got wet it caught cold and generally died'. Now the Psammead is upset and endangered even by the wetness of the children's tears. It has hidden away for thousands of years, but now it has come out it seems interested in the children, and likes them, especially when they are kind to it. It is its nature to grant wishes, but to do so it has to swell up and stretch its skin, and this is exhausting. At the end of the story it tells us how painful this exertion has been.

Perhaps there is an association between the Psammead and the granny that we have heard is ill and whom Mother has had to leave them to look after. We discuss an even stranger mental link of this kind in chapter 4 on Rumer Godden's *The Fairy Doll*. This old, vulnerable, somewhat frighteningly direct Psammead, who does however have this wonderful knowledge and even understanding of children, and who can meet their wishes in the absence of their parents, is a representation of a composite internal object, drawn from memories of parents and grandparents, and, in its furriness (Anthea later manages to cuddle it), of children's own 'transitional objects' like cherished soft toys. It has 'bad' (spider, bat, snail) and 'good' (furry) qualities combined in it, and this duality is important for its role in psychic integration for the children. They are able to use the Psammead as a way of helping them through their deprivation. Its aversion to wetness (and thus tears) helps the children not to give way to feelings of missing their parents – it has after all been able to to survive for a long time by itself. It also functions as a 'better self' or remembered parental voice, in its making them take responsibility for the consequences of their desires. Anyway, when Mother finally returns and Granny has recovered from being ill, the Psammead (now 'almost worn out') is allowed by the now more considerate children to stop exhausting itself by giving them wishes (it has really tried all it can to help them), and to go back to sleep in the sand. The children will not have to make such huge internal demands of themselves for a while.

In our account of *Five Children and It*, consistent with the main approach of this book, we are chiefly concerned with the theme of some important children's feelings – that is to say those experiences of loss, internal conflict, and pressure towards emotional development which are best examined through our perspective of psychoanalysis. Nesbit's work preceded the reception of psychoanalysis into English culture, and her work explores these themes in implicit and probably unselfconscious ways, though, as we hope to show, with great sensitivity. But her stories are moral and social comedy, as well as representing serious feelings, and this may explain the fact that they lack the more powerful evocation of loss, and the natural tragedies inseparable from life found in some more recent children's fiction – the death of Charlotte the spider in *Charlotte's Web* (discussed in chapter 7), or the passage of time in *Tom's Midnight Garden*, for example. Nesbit is a writer who believed in both moral and social improvement, and her writings have a consistently optimistic note not always found in her successors, however gifted. Before going on to a more detailed discussion of the narrative of *Five Children and It*, some consideration should be given to the moral and social dimensions of the story.

Nesbit was not a directly didactic writer, and has a joke with her readers (both adult and child) which conveys that she is on her child readers' side early on in this story:

> Now that I have begun to tell you about the place, I feel that I could go on and make this into a most interesting story about all the ordinary things that the children did – just the kind of things you do yourself, you know – and you would believe every word of it; and when I told about the children's being tiresome, as you are sometimes, your aunts would perhaps write in the margin of the story with a pencil, 'How true!' or 'How like life!' and you would see it and very likely be annoyed. So I will only tell you the really astonishing things that happened, and you may leave the book about quite safely, for no aunts and uncles either are likely to write 'How true!' on the edge of the story.

But in fact, though *Five Children and It* has a sand-fairy in an important role, it is nevertheless to a large extent the story of an ordinary holiday. The children's adventures don't take them very far from conventional country holiday surroundings or from what they might imagine in normal play. (The two later sequels to this book move further afield in both time and space.) Furthermore, Nesbit *is* concerned about the moral dimensions of the children's experiences. They are given some licence by the author to break the rules – for example taking fruit from an orchard, demanding buns from a shop, helping themselves to some supper from someone's window, pouring water inadvertently over the nursemaid, taking a mild revenge on a too-violent boy. But these misdemeanours are kept within narrow confines, and the children are shown to worry a lot about doing the right thing, paying for the things they take, and so on. What the children think about during and after their adventures are often questions of ethics: What feelings should they have for their baby brother? Can they steal if they are really hungry? How can money be fairly earned? How should they co-operate with each other? The main problem the Psammead poses for them is how to think of wishes that won't get them into trouble every time. Many works of children's fiction (Beatrix Potter's tales, for example), explore the boundaries between nature and culture[1] – the antithesis between children's deviant desires and the rules of the grown-up world. This is one implicit pattern of *Five Children and It*.

Nesbit explores these dilemmas of childhood chiefly in the mode of comedy. She allows different wishes to be measured by their minor triumphs and disasters. The reactions of the children to each other, and of the Psammead and Martha, the baby's nurse, for example, to what they do, provide an exploration of moral meanings *within* the story. But though Nesbit avoids overt didactics, worries about moral duties are not usually far from her characters' minds. Sometimes she even offers a direct narrator's judgement on an escapade. For example, she excuses the children's taking food from the clergyman's window in the chapter devoted to their adventure on wings:

> I cannot pretend that stealing is right. I can only say that on this occasion it did not look like stealing to the hungry four, but appeared in the light of a fair and reasonable business transaction. They had never happened to learn that a tongue – hardly cut into – a chicken and a half, a loaf of bread, and a syphon of soda water cannot be bought in shops for half a crown. These were the

necessities of life which Cyril handed out of the larder window . . .

The author takes a sympathetic and understanding view of the children's enforced purchases, but this is because she notes that they themselves have worried about them: 'He felt,' she reports in her narrative voice, that 'to refrain from jam, apple turnovers, cake and mixed candied peel was a really heroic act – and I agree with him.' Nesbit was one of the first children's writers to be able to enter a child's world in its own terms (the contrived absence of parents is a narrative device which helps to effect this), but she was born in 1858, and also shared the customary moral seriousness of her time.

Five Children and It shows the middle-class children exploring a social as well as a moral and emotional world.[2] Their wishes bring them into contact with different kinds of people. There are the servants who are looking after them, especially Martha, who is in charge of the house. There are shopkeepers, farmers, a baker's boy who is bigger than they are, gypsies, a horse-and-carriage dealer at the Saracen's Head, showmen at the fair, a policeman, and their snooty neighbour, Lady Chittenden. More centrally, it is an adult world and they have to learn what it means for children to find out about it on their own. Much of the comedy is about the juxtaposition of children and adults.

Nesbit was a Fabian socialist, and in one passage towards the end of the book she makes fun of her own views. She has the Psammead make a last wish that grown-ups should never be told about it:

> 'Why, can't you see, if you told grown-ups I should have no peace of my life. They'd get hold of me, and they wouldn't wish silly things like you do, but real earnest things; and the scientific people would hit on some way of making things last after sunset, as likely as not; and they'd ask for a graduated income-tax, and old-age pensions and manhood suffrage, and free secondary education, and dull things like that; and get them, and keep them, and the whole world would be turned topsy turvy.' [This was in 1903.]

She describes the Kent countryside and its old and distinctive features: 'And when the big chimneys were smoking, and the sun was setting, the valley looked as if it was filled with golden mist, and the limekilns and oasthouses glimmered and glittered till they were like an enchanted city out of the *Arabian Nights.'* It is an ancient settled countryside in fact; even the gravel pit and chalk quarry which mark the edges of the wood near the White House are old man-made workings. But she contrasts it favourably with the city: 'And nearly everything in London is the wrong sort of shape – all straight lines and flat streets, instead of being all sorts of odd shapes, like things in the country.' Like many reformers of the town planning movement, she accounts for social problems by the contrast of town and country:

> Trees are all different, as you know, and I am sure some tiresome person must have told you that there are no two blades of grass exactly alike. But in streets where the blades of grass don't grow, everything is like everything else. That is why so many children who live in towns are so extremely naughty. They do not know what is the matter with them, and no more do their fathers, and mothers, aunts, uncles, cousins, tutors, governesses, and nurses; but I know.

Nesbit thus introduces into her children's fiction an antithesis between the 'organic' world of the imagination and the countryside and the mechanical world of the modern city, which has been so important in the romantic critique of capitalism in Britain.

She shows a social world divided by status, and the children (from a middle-class family of relatively modest means) inclined to fear the lower orders (the baker's boy, the gypsies), to resent the upper classes (Lady Chittenden) and to lord it over 'the servants'. But the children's pretensions and anxieties are played off against the mostly decent reality of the people they meet. Martha and the other local people are given a vital turn of phrase, and her commitment to the care of her charges marks her out above all as a parental figure on whom the children can depend, even when they like to patronize her in their minds as a servant. The world of the village and the country town are represented as basically safe for children, and the rebuffs they receive on their adventures are mostly ironic, and are no more than they invite. When Robert attempts to buy a horse and carriage with the golden guineas they have wished for, the dealer responds thus:

'We should like to buy some, please,' said Robert politely.

'I daresay you would.'

'Will you show us a few, please? To choose from.'

'Who are you a-kidden of?' inquired Mr Billy Peasmarsh. 'Was you sent here of a message?'

'I tell you,' said Robert, 'we want to buy some horses and carriages, and a man told us you were straight and civil spoken, but I shouldn't wonder if he were mistaken.'

'Upon my sacred!' said Mr Peasmarsh. 'Shall I trot the whole stable out for Your Honour's worship to see? Or shall I send round to the Bishop's to see if he's a nag or two to dispose of?'

Nesbit recognizes the hierarchical nature of society in this story, but suggests that in the country anyway children can safely learn to explore the world, and to develop a healthy respect for people of different kinds. (In one of the sequels, *The Story of the Amulet*, she has a passage which offers a more utopian vision, similar to that of William Morris's *News from Nowhere*.)

*

The first wishes of the children in this story show how difficult it is to make any sensible use of wishes. She tells her readers:

I daresay you have often thought what you would do if you had three wishes given you, and have despised the old man and his wife in the black pudding story, and felt certain that if you had the chance you could think of three really useful wishes without a moment's hesitation. These children had often talked this matter over, but, now the chance had suddenly come to them, they could not make up their minds.

By this remark she reminds the child reader of fairy tales, and of wishing games that they mostly will have played. But she is also in touch with her fictional children's immediate situation. The Psammead is cross with them, having already given them a wish unwittingly (to come out). '"Oh, please, mayn't we have another?"' the children ask. '"Yes, but be quick about it. I'm tired of you,"' says the Psammead. The children can't think of anything, and the hurried wish which Anthea manages to remember – 'a private wish of her own and Jane's which they had never told the boys' – is a response springing from unconscious preoccupations. Anthea wishes 'we were all as beautiful as the day,' and this is because her mother's departure, and the Psammead's crossness, have made her feel that the children must be anything but beautiful, or they wouldn't be abandoned like this.

The wish is not a great success. 'Then the children looked at each other, and each child suddenly found itself alone with three perfect strangers, all radiantly beautiful.' They barely recognize each other, and this enables the author to have some fun at the expense of idealized images of beauty, much as we might now of glamour. '"You girls are like Christmas cards, then – that's all – silly Christmas cards," said Robert angrily. "And Jane's hair is simply carrots." It was indeed of that Venetian tint so much admired by artists.' Worse, the baby doesn't recognize them, and they have to make friends with him. 'It took over an hour, and the task was not rendered any easier by the fact that the Lamb [all the children have pet-names] was by this time as hungry as a lion and as thirsty as a desert.' Then far from its being the case that 'the servants will admire us most awfully, you'll see', Martha indignantly slams the door on them, and when they persist pours cold water over them out of a window. They just have to wait till sunset till the wish wears off and they become themselves again.

Their wish may also be understood as their holding on to a memory of themselves as loved children, even while they actually feel deserted. They are very concerned for the Psammead when it wishes for them. They also manage to bear the baby's rejection of their new selves, 'radiantly beautiful' and different-looking after their wish. Their own capacity to care for others is thus brought very much alive. They are relieved to discover that they don't turn to stone at sunset (they don't depend completely on magic wishes for their existence) and they realize how much they like each other as they normally are:

'Wake up,' she said, almost in tears for joy; 'it's all right, we're not stone. And oh, Cyril, how nice and ugly you do look, with your old freckles and your brown hair and your little eyes. And so do you all!' she added, so that they might not feel jealous.

This is the most important thing the children learn from their first adventure, that despite their disappointments over the start of the holiday, they do have each other.

The children's second wish doesn't work out too well, either.

> Anthea woke in the morning from a very real sort of dream, in which she was walking in the Zoological Gardens on a pouring wet day without an umbrella. The animals seemed desperately unhappy because of the rain, and were all growling gloomily.

Though this dream is induced by her brother squeezing water on her, it seems also to be an association to the Psammead's dislike of water. An extreme way of putting it would be to say it is a dream response to Anthea's anxieties about whether the Psammead can stand the children's misery (in dream metaphor, tears equated with rain) and the burdens they will place on it. The children are somewhat quarrelsome on this morning, and are very patronizing towards Martha:

> 'Servants do like taking babies to see their relations,' Cyril said; 'I've noticed it before – especially in their best things.'
> 'I expect they pretend they're their own babies, and that they're not servants at all, but married to noble dukes of high degree, and they say the babies are little dukes and duchesses,' Jane suggested dreamily, taking more marmalade. 'I expect that's what Martha'll say to her cousin. She'll enjoy herself most frightfully.'

The fact is that Martha does, for quite ordinary reasons of affection, want to take the baby to see her cousins, and is leaving the children behind. While the children claim to be glad to get rid of them, there is also perhaps some jealousy of the dressed-up baby and Martha in these denigrating comments. The Psammead overhears them arguing when they are digging to find it. '"Humph!"' he says, '"Do you know, until I heard you being disagreeable to each other just over my head, and so loud too, I really thought I had dreamed you all. I do have very odd dreams sometimes."'

But the children are too intent on their wish to want to listen to the sand-fairy this morning. Their wish expresses a very literal form of greed:

> 'We want,' said Robert slowly, 'to be rich beyond the dreams of something or other.'
> 'Avarice,' said Jane.

'So it is,' said the Fairy unexpectedly. 'But it won't do you much good, that's one comfort,' it muttered to itself.

The children choose to have the whole gravel pit filled with gold, but of course it is not much use when they have got it. The old-fashioned coins are very heavy to carry, and it is very difficult to persuade grown-ups to take them. They finish up being taken to the police station on suspicion of theft – they certainly have been very greedy in their minds – and it is Martha's unshakeable belief in their innocence and the disappearance of the gold at sunset, that brings about their release. They have earlier asked the Psammead that the servants should not know about their wishes, but this also has the effect of keeping Martha as someone who will go on caring for them whatever they might be thinking. Their omnipotent wish for boundless wealth with which to control adults hasn't helped them very much, though they have learned that adults' ways of seeing them are not so easily changed. There is some amusing social comedy as they learn these lessons. For example, the young lady in the hat shop refuses to take Anthea's money:

> 'It's good money,' said Anthea, 'and it's my own.'
> 'I daresay,' said the Lady, 'but it's not the kind of money that's fashionable now, and we don't care about taking it.'

The children's appreciation of Martha's defence of them is in contrast to their earlier patronage of her. It is perhaps their rescue by Martha that enables the children really to worry about their obligation to the gentleman to whom they had paid a guinea to take them to Rochester. But everything is all right: 'The guinea had not disappeared, and he had bored a hole in it and hung it on his watch-chain.' Anthea even secretly sends money to the pastrycook from whom they had bought twelve buns for a guinea – unnecessarily, the author suggests. At any rate, a better relationship between the children and the adult world is more or less restored by the end of the chapter. Anthea and Robert are cross with the Psammead for being '"a spiteful brute. If it can give us our wishes I suppose it can give itself its own [Robert says], and I feel almost sure it wishes every time that our wishes don't do us any good."' But the other two are more hopeful and Cyril says that perhaps the trouble the previous day was really their own fault, for having such a silly wish. They begin to get on better and to plan more sensible wishes. But the author subtly notes how precarious their state of mind is when she describes them:

> If you had been there you could not possibly have made head or tail of the talk, but these children were used to talking 'by fours', as soldiers march, and each of them could say what it had to say quite comfortably, and listen to the agreeable sound of its own voice, and at the same time have three quarters of two sharp ears to spare for listening to what the others said.

Thus preoccupied with themselves, it is not surprising that they don't want to include the Lamb on their proposed visit to the Psammead. Martha tells them off for this:

> 'Not want him indeed! Why everybody 'ud want him, a duck! with all their hearts they would! and you know you promised your ma to take him out every blessed day,' said Martha.
> 'I know we did,' said Robert in gloom, 'but I wish the Lamb wasn't quite so young and small. It would be much better fun taking him out.'
> 'He'll mend of his youngness with time,' said Martha; 'and as for his smallness, I don't think you'd fancy carrying of him anymore, however big he was . . .'

The Lamb turns out to be the unintended subject of the third day's wish. While they enjoy having him with them at first, they soon find that they can't concentrate on their wishes when he is around and getting into trouble with the sand. It is then that Robert, usually a very patient brother (but earlier the one most angry with the sand-fairy), so far forgets himself as to say:

> 'Anybody would want him, indeed! Only they don't; Martha doesn't, not really, or she'd jolly well keep him with her. He's a little nuisance, that's what he is. It's too bad. I only wish everybody *did* want him with all their hearts; we might get some peace in our lives.'

The children realize that Robert shouldn't have said that, and then in the silence they hear the particular sigh of the Psammead after it's given a wish: 'And everyone saw the sand-fairy sitting quite close to them, with the expression which it used as a smile on its hairy face. "Good morning," it said; "I did that quite easily! Everyone wants him now."'

The rest of the day was spent in stopping the Lamb from being stolen by nearly everyone they meet. People who don't normally like children, such as Lady Chittenden, suddenly have a passion to take the baby from them. It is as if they are surrounded by irresponsible adults who don't care when they should (like Martha) and pretend to care when they don't really. Their baby brother has become the part of themselves that they feel is unwanted, and seems to be seducing every adult in sight. They find the gypsies particularly frightening; the gypsies are, as one of them later says, like an image of the bad parents to whom bad children can be given away, with their apparently enormous numbers of ragged children. But Cyril has the idea that if they stay with the Lamb until sunset, the wish will wear off, and the gypsies won't want him any more. They have to play with the Lamb, to keep him happy, but the gypsies' admiration of the baby helps them do this. They begin to feel that the gypsies are not wholly bad, and accept the supper the gypsies offer. When the wish wears off at sunset, they are able to slip away with the Lamb, and one of the gypsy women, who has lost her own children, comes after them to say that 'Us gypsies don't steal babies, whatever they may tell you when you're naughty.' She gives the baby a gypsy blessing, and the children, especially the two girls, are able to realize that there are people who really care for babies in the world after all. Their experience with the baby has made them understand their own feelings better. '"I certainly thought I didn't want him this morning," said Robert. "Perhaps I was a pig. But everything looked so different when we thought we were going to lose him."'

The next day is filled with rain, and with floods of ink all over their letters to Mother which stop them from writing to tell her about the Psammead. (We could see this as further metaphors for tears.) But the day after this, they are taken out by a real uncle for a completely perfect outing, with presents from a shop for each of them and also to share, a trip on the Medway in a boat, and tea at a beautiful pastrycook's. 'When they reached home it was far too late to have any wishes that day'; but the children don't have any need of them. This experience fills the children for the first time with a feeling of being fully looked after. The next day Anthea wakes herself up at five, and goes to see the Psammead in the beautiful early morning. It is cross to be woken up, but she wraps it gently in her pinafore.

> 'Thank you,' it said, 'that's better. What's the wish this morning?'
> 'I don't know,' said she; 'that's just it. You see we've been really unlucky, so far. I wanted to talk to you about it.'

She says she doesn't want a wish yet, and asks the sand-fairy if it would like to come and sit on her lap, where it would be warmer.

> 'Thank you,' it said, 'you really are rather thoughtful.' It crept on to her lap and snuggled down, and she put her arms round it with a rather frightened gentleness.
> 'Now then!' it said.
> 'Well then,' said Anthea, 'everything we have wished has old you must be wise . . . .. You see,' Anthea went on, 'it's such a wonderful thing – such a splendid, glorious chance. It's so good and kind and dear of you to give us our wishes, and it seems such a pity it should all be wasted just because we are too silly to know what to wish for.'

It's a real development for one of the children to be able to *talk* to the sand-fairy, instead of just wishing for things, and this comes from a greater sense of trust. Anthea, following the perfect day out with her uncle, is able to think about their own part in what has gone wrong, and to think about the Psammead as a source of understanding as well as a means of gratifying wishes. She can think about the sand-fairy's feelings too. She has the good idea of wings, which the Psammead thinks might be all right if they don't try to fly too high.

She is also able to delay actually making the wish until she goes home, and talks to the others over breakfast. She proposes that they take turns in having wishes – an advance in co-operation – and asks for the first turn herself, telling them of her idea. They approve: 'Jane said, "I think it would be perfectly lovely. It's like a bright dream of delirium"', and they find the sand-fairy easily. They have their best adventure so far. Their delinquencies – taking fruit from an orchard in return for a threepenny bit, and supper from a clergyman's window in return for half a crown – are small ones. They seem like angels to the adults who see them, and their visitation causes the farmer to be 'so nice to his wife that day that she felt quite happy, and said to herself, "Law, whatever have a-come to the man!" and smartened herself up and put a blue ribbon bow at the place where her collar fastened on, and looked so pretty that he was kinder than ever.'

They go to sleep on the church tower (two wishes end in sleep, suggesting their dreamlike quality), and are then marooned on the tower after sunset when their wings vanish. When they are rescued they confess their minor crimes to the vicar and he excuses their incomplete explanations by the idea that they are pluckily shielding someone, which in a sense they are. Their direct appeal to the vicar and his wife leads them to be very kind to the children: '"Is this the whole truth you've been telling me?" asked the clergyman. "No," answered Jane suddenly; "it's all true, but it's not the whole truth. We can't tell you that. It's no good asking. Oh, do forgive us and take us home!" She ran to the vicar's wife and threw her arms around her. The vicar's wife put her arms round Jane. . . .' She offers them cake and milk. This happy adventure is more like one (except for the flying) which children might actually have, and leads to benign contacts with the grown-up world. The keeper who brings them home begins to court Martha from that day, so they are able to be a means for also bringing a couple together who are more important to them than the farmer and his wife. This adventure seems to have been made possible by the children themselves feeling better cared for.

The next morning the children are made to stay in the house, as a punishment for the troubles of the day before. The story tells us that Martha naturally thought it was naughtiness and not misfortune which had got the children into trouble, but also shows how considerate she really is of the children:

'I declare,' she said to the cook, 'it seems almost a shame keeping of them indoors this lovely day; but they are that audacious, they'll be walking in with their heads knocked off some of these days, if I don't put my foot down. You make them a cake for tea tomorrow dear. And we'll have Baby along of us as we've got a bit forrard with our work. Then they can have a good romp with him out of the way. Now Eliza, come get on with them beds. Here's ten o'clock nearly and no rabbits caught.' People say that in Kent when they mean 'and no work done'.

But the children feel blamed and mistreated, and the day's adventure shows that they feel up against the adult world. Robert is allowed out for half an hour 'to get something they all wanted . . . the day's wish,' and goes to find the sand-fairy. But he is too agitated by the punishment and the enforced hurry to respond to the Psammead's unusual friendliness. He finds the Psammead easily, 'for the day was already so hot that it had actually, for the first time, come out of its own accord'. (We might say it has also been warmed by Anthea's affection from the day before.)

'Ha!' it said when its left eye saw Robert, 'I've been looking for you. Where are the rest of you? Not smashed themselves up with those wings, I hope?'

'No,' said Robert, 'but the wishes got us into a row, just like all the wishes always do. So the others are kept indoors, and I was only let out for half an hour – to get the wish. So please let me wish as quickly as I can.'

'Wish away,' said the Psammead, twisting itself round in the sand. But Robert couldn't wish away. He forgot all the things he had been thinking about, and nothing would come into his head but little things for himself . . .

He struggles with his feelings, and finally he says '"I can't think what to wish for. I wish you could give one of the others their wish without their having to come here to ask for it."' This wasn't exactly meant as a wish, but the Psammead to his dismay promptly gives it, and then tells Robert to '"Run along home, or they're sure to wish for something silly before you get there."' When he gets home, the house has become a castle, with the children inside, and a besieging force outside. Nesbit has fun with the dialogue and decor of historical romance, but also represents the mental world of the children feeling themselves under attack from the grown-up (antique) world which doesn't seem to understand them. The castle has neither garrison nor food inside. The house's normal food has become invisible, though the Lamb (who is still in favour) is eating it, and Martha can't see that anything is different from usual. The children really do feel besieged and hungry, and somewhat frightened by the violence of their 'game' and how far away they feel from the everyday world. But Anthea has a valuable idea. 'She went to Martha and said, "May we just have biscuits for tea? We're going to play at besieged castles, and we'd like the biscuits to provision the garrison."' She thus allows Martha to know just enough of what they are doing for her to be able to help them, and give them something to eat.

Though Robert's attempt to think of the other children first hasn't quite worked out with the Psammead, his struggles with himself are not for nothing, and the children are able to co-operate. Robert becomes the captain of the besieged force. Though Jane is frightened by the competitive violence of her brothers, Anthea manages to reassure her that it is all a game:

> 'Oh dear,' said Jane, 'What does it matter which of you is the bravest? I think Cyril was a perfect silly to wish for a castle, and I don't want to play.'
>
> 'It isn't' – Robert was beginning sternly, but Anthea interrupted –
>
> 'Oh yes you do,' she said coaxingly, 'it's a very nice game, really, because they can't possibly get in, and if they do the women and children are always spared by civilised armies.'
>
> 'But are you quite, quite sure they are civilised?' asked Jane, panting. 'They seem to be such a long time ago.'
>
> 'Of course they are.' Anthea pointed cheerfully through the narrow window. 'Why look at the little flags on their lances, how bright they are – and how fine the leader is!'

Thus are little girls seduced by soldiers. But the siege adventure shows the frightening feelings that become engaged in play, and how these children cope with them. It only gets a little out of hand. Just at the moment of sunset, when the house is turning back to normal, Robert pours water out of the window, on to the besieging enemy. But it is actually on to Martha,

> and they could tell by her voice that she was very angry indeed. 'I thought you couldn't last through the day without getting up to some doggery! A person can't take a breath of fresh air on the front doorstep but you must be emptying the wash-hand jug on to their head. Off you go to bed, the lot of you and try to get up better children in the morning.'

The children continue the next day to find it difficult to decide on wishes, and Cyril and Robert fight about it. They can't magic into existence what they really want, because they don't know what it is. Cyril proposes that they should 'just play bandits, or forts, or soldiers, or any of the old

77

games. We're dead sure to think of something if we try not to.' These are all somewhat aggressive forms of play, and though bandits is all right for a bit (once Anthea has borrowed Martha's red-spotted handkerchief to tie up Robert's head with), it begins to pall and become quarrelsome. When the game is dragging they meet the baker's boy and the boys are carried away into challenging him: '"Stand and deliver!" cried Cyril. "Your money or your life!" said Cyril.' But the baker's boy, who 'was of an unusually large size . . . did not seem to enter into the spirit of the thing at all.' There is a fight, and Robert is again hurt, and ends up sobbing. The boys both feel humiliated and furious with their sisters for trying to protect them. Robert angrily says, as any boy might, 'I only wish I was bigger than him, that's all,' and finds he has touched something furry with his hands. It is the Psammead, who promptly grants his overheard wish. The Psammead is cross to have been nearly dug out with wet hands (from Robert's tears), and refuses to make them *all* Robert's size. So the children have to live with the huge giant-like Robert as he is.

Robert's strongest feeling towards the baker's boy is about the injustice of being hurt by someone bigger than himself. '"Don't hit a chap littler than yourself, old man," said Cyril' (worried about his great size), but Robert says he's not going to hit the baker's boy but to 'reason with him'. In fact the baker's boy is set down on top of a haystack and scared into 'a sort of trance of terror!' He gets into trouble for being late, and for telling stories about giants, but the narrator says she 'was sorry for him, but after all, it was quite right that he should be taught that English boys mustn't use their feet when they fight, but their fists.'

The children then succeed in making use of Robert's wish, by taking him to the fair and showing him off for fifteen shillings for the day. He gets tea given to him in his tent. 'The crowd was very merry about the giant's meals and their coming so close together.' But the afternoon is boring and hard work for all the children. 'It seemed to them that this was the hardest way of earning money that could have been invented.' By being ingenious and patient, and with the help of the man at the fair who really 'knew his business', they earn some money, and put Robert's desire to be big to practical use.

The children's next two wishes, in the chapters called

Grown Up and *Scalps*, are variations on earlier adventures. In *Grown Up*, they are enjoying the fact that their baby brother is getting bigger and talking in longer sentences. '"Me grow," said the Lamb cheerfully – "me grow big boy, have guns an' mouses an' – an' . . ."' But when he playfully ruins a second watch in one morning, they become fed up, and Cyril unwisely wishes the Lamb was grown up *now*. They then have to cope with a grown-up brother, but also have to look after him so that he doesn't become stranded in a gentleman's club or somewhere after sunset. They enjoy being real pests in bringing this off, puncturing their grown-up brother's bicycle tyre eighteen times, and driving away a young lady he is interested in by telling the awful truth about the baby St Maur (as he is now called). It turns out that they prefer their brother as he is, and by projection themselves as they are, without the divisive complications of growing up and girlfriends and wanting to go off alone.

In *Scalps*, Cyril (who has been reading *The Last of the Mohicans*) wishes for Red Indians without realizing it, and they find the house surrounded by little Indians of their own size. Anthea is frightened for the baby – this perhaps refers back to the earlier violent experience of the besieged castle – but manages to coax Martha into taking the Lamb out for the afternoon and thus saving him from the threat of scalping. Anthea 'cried for about three minutes' after they had gone. The seriousness of her feeling is understandable if one recalls the children's – and especially the boys' – own earlier aggressiveness which has been at times nearly out of control. Nesbit, a woman writer, is also sensitive to the differences between girls' and boys' experience and feelings.

The children's problems with the Indians are perhaps an inversion of their concerns about food and their frequent hunger. (There are at least fifty separate references to meals of various kinds in the story, and there is a pattern by which most adventures begin at breakfast time.) '"Do you really mean to scalp us first and then roast us?"' asks Anthea desperately, when the Indians have captured them, and though this is ostensibly for purposes of tormenting rather than eating their foes, there seem to be fantasies of cannibalism around the idea of roasting. The children's defence this time is under the leadership of Anthea, not Robert, and she employs more pacific strategies. She engages in pow-wow. '"It's our only chance," whispered Anthea. "Much better than to wait for their blood-freezing attack. We must pretend like mad. Like that game of cards where you pretend you've got aces when you haven't. Fluffing they call it."' When this fails, she leads them in flight to the gravel-pit. The Indians can't find wood for the fire, and in scalping them tear off only their black calico ringlets; this adventure is a little less frightening than the siege. Finally, the Sand-fairy grants the Indians' wish that they 'were but in our native forest once more,' and the danger has gone. Martha returns with Anthea's money unspent (she had gone to Rochester to replace a jug that Anthea had deliberately broken to get her to take the baby away), her cousin having given her another. She also announces her impending departure:

> '. . . you'd better make the most of me while you've got me. I shall give your ma notice directly she comes back.'
> 'Oh, Martha, we haven't been so very horrid to you, have we?' asked Anthea, aghast.
> 'Oh, it ain't that, miss.' Martha giggled more than ever. 'I'm a-going to be married. It's Beale the gamekeeper.'

At the beginning of the final chapter the children are finding it much easier than before to think of nice wishes. 'Their brains were now full of the most beautiful and sensible ideas.' But at breakfast they receive two big pieces of news. Firstly, that 'Granny was better, and mother and father hoped to be home that very afternoon'; and secondly, Martha comes in to tell them '"there's been burglars over at Peasmarsh Place – Beale's just told me – and they've took every single one of Lady Chittenden's diamonds and jewels and things, and she's a-goin' out of one fainting fit into another, with hardly time to say "Oh my diamonds!" in between. And Lord Chittenden's away in London."'
The children remember that they don't like Lady Chittenden, and begin to feel jealous of her on their mother's behalf because she has so many jewels when their mother has hardly any. So Jane, after Anthea and Robert have both said how unfair it is, dreamily wishes that her mother might find '"all those lovely things, necklaces and rivers of diamonds and tarrers" ("Ti-aras," said Cyril)' in her room when she came home. The other children realize with horror that the Psammead will give them this wish whether they like it or not. The wish naturally causes great trouble. Their mother

finds the jewels, and is panic-stricken. Father, like Lord Chittenden, is away when he is most wanted. Martha is asked if she has let any stranger into Mother's room, and has to admit that she allowed Beale to help her clean the windows. Beale '"helped me a-cleanin' of the windows – but outside, mum, the whole time, and me in."' So Beale, whom she has just announced she is going to marry, is placed under suspicion as a result of the children's wish, and Martha's good news is spoiled. Mother rushes off to Rochester to the police, and the children are left to keep watch, ruefully admiring her decisiveness.

In constructing this final adventure Nesbit has understood that children are not always filled with loving feelings at the prospect of the return of their absent parents.[3] Memory of deprivation and consequent resentment is stirred by such an event, as well as joy at its impending end. Wanting mother to have as many jewels as Lady Chittenden, who seems to prefer jewelry to children, is an identification of mother *with* Lady Chittenden, and the absence of both husbands when they are most needed reinforces this parallel. Martha has just told the children that she will soon be leaving them, and the suspicion and blame which the appearance of the jewels casts on her and Beale amounts to an attack on her impending marriage. This seems to be no psychological accident.

But there are good feelings around too, and Anthea remembers the Psammead. '"Our one chance," cries Anthea dramatically, "the last lonelorn forlorn hope."' But she realizes that she cannot simply ask for another wish – she has to think of the Psammead too. She insists on talking to it, even holding bravely on to it in face of its threat to bite her. '"Look here," she said, "don't bite me – listen to reason. If you'll only do what we want today, we'll never ask you for another wish as long as we live."' The Psammead then describes how painful it has been for it to grant all their wishes: '"I'd do anything," it said in a tearful voice. "I'd almost burst myself to give you one wish after another as long as I held out, if only you'd never, never ask me to do it after today. If you knew how I hate to blow myself out with other people's wishes, and how frightened I am always that I shall strain a muscle or something. And then to wake up every morning to know you've *got* to do it. You don't know what it is – you don't know what it is, you don't." Its voice cracked with emotion, and the last "don't" was a squeak.' But it does grant a series of wishes to put everything right and have Lady Chittenden find her jewels unstolen after all. It finally asks:

'Is there anything else?'
'No; only thank you kindly for all you've done for us, and I hope you'll have a good long sleep, and I hope we shall see you again some day.'
'Is that a wish?' it said in a weak voice.
'Yes, please,' said the two girls together.

What has happened is that Anthea, with Jane, mostly more in touch with others' pain than the boys, has realized the demands that she has been making of the Psammead, and by transfer from this is in better contact with the burdens on her mother too. The Psammead's description of how painful it is to have to meet someone else's demands all the time – *every* morning – is something like an account of a mother's unceasing obligations, combined with the weakness of a very old person, like the just-recovered Granny. We realize that its swelling up and deep breaths each time it gives a wish are reminiscent of giving birth. The children's consideration for their actual loved object is the precondition for everything ending happily, in a moment of reparation. Once the intimacy of this moment with the Psammead is past, and the exposed 'internal object' buries itself under the sand, normal life can be resumed. '"And oh my dearest dear chicks," Mother said, "I am simply dying for a cup of tea! Do run and see if the kettle boils."' No one remembers what has happened, any more than child readers need to understand consciously the meanings of fantasy stories that describe their unconscious emotional life.

Nesbit's stories are pioneers in the representation of an identifiably modern world of childhood, despite the now-anachronistic presence of servants as primary care-takers. She explores the importance of children's play, their relationships with each other, and their responsiveness to the qualities of contacts with adults which are available to them. She is sensitive to differences in age, and between genders. She recognizes children's innate sense of morality and justice, while being an advocate of affectionate modes of care, especially for babies and very young children. At the moment when Robert is wishing the Lamb out of the way, 'Jane had suddenly remembered that there is only one safe way of taking things out of little children's eyes, and that is with your own soft wet tongue. "It is quite easy if you love the Baby as much as you ought to."'

Nesbit has an intuitive understanding of the feelings of her child characters. While there is little indication that she has any explicit or theoretical understanding of what we might now see as unconscious processes, *Five Children and It* registers in the most subtle way the response in children's imagination, play, and relationships to their experience of adults. She demonstrates through the different adventures the psychic defences of would-be omnipotence, aggressiveness, and denigration. She shows how the children's relationships with each other, and the basic kindness of their environment, enable them to surmount the loneliness and sense of abandonment which is part of this holiday experience. She explores too the children's unconscious hostility to Martha, to their baby brother, and to the mother who has left them – Martha, the gypsies, and finally Mother herself are recipients of this negative feeling – and towards rivals for maternal care such as their baby brother. There is a surprising delicacy and emotional precision in her description of these successive episodes, in a writer whose manifest preoccupations – with more external social observation or sheer enjoyment in make-believe – might seem somewhat different. The subtlety with which she renders the hostility which the children express towards their mother and Martha on Mother's return is perhaps the most remarkable instance of Nesbit's psychological insight.

Our suggestion is that the theme of mental pain and its symbolic realization is as illuminating in its application to this story from the 1900s as it is to any of the later writing we discuss. Nesbit is comparable to contemporary writers in particular in her understanding that painful feelings are evoked by everyday events, like a holiday, as well as by the more literal disasters of the loss of parents or long-term separation which are the points of departure of other writing for children contemporary with Nesbit. She is thus able to make contact with the internal imaginative spaces of normal children, through the devices of fantasy and magic wishing. In these ways Nesbit contributed not only to the development of new fictional genres, but in doing so helped to create the enlarged 'cultural space' of contemporary childhood.

4

The Life of Dolls: Rumer Godden's Understanding of Children's Imaginative Play

In this chapter, we look at four stories for young children by Rumer Godden, three of which are about dolls and children's relationship to them, and the fourth of which is about the image of a madonna and child made by a child for a grown-up woman. The four stories evoke the strength of feeling of small children for dolls and similar fantasy objects. They suggest to us a close correspondence between the themes of these stories and the kinds of play they describe, and the emotional issues with which children are concerned in 'real life'.

The three dolls' stories are *The Dolls' House* (1947), *The Fairy Doll* (1955) and *The Story of Holly and Ivy* (1957). Each of the stories represent dolls as having thoughts and feelings. The dolls can talk to each other, but not to people. In relation to children, who are very important to them, they are passive, and able to do no more than wish. Wishes are powerful, however, and at high points they may be able to make things happen; things fall mysteriously, for example. The stories thus establish a boundary between the humans and the doll people, while nevertheless allowing the dolls to be sufficiently active in their own thoughts and feelings to be figures in a drama. The dolls depend on the children to be made and kept alive. Their conversations with each other are so to speak in the roles which have been made for them in the children's play. 'Dolls are not like us; we are alive as soon as we are born, but dolls are not really alive until they are played with' (*Holly and Ivy*).

The stories thus dramatize in the similarities and differences between their doll and human characters the fact that dolls and playthings are objects of or in the child's imagination. They are available and important to children as representations of aspects of their internal worlds. The passions of the dolls and the children revolve around relationships with home, parents, especially mother and grandmother, and siblings. The subject matter of the stories thus enables them to be intense and moving symbolizations of the emotional preoccupations of children. Dolls are more important play objects for girls than boys, usually, and the main human characters of these three doll stories are small girls.[1] A comparable depth of feeling in relation to maternal symbols by a boy (and a rather cut-off and serious minded boy at that) is achieved in *The Kitchen Madonna* through his involvement in a grown-up's symbolic object, the 'icon' of the madonna.

The Dolls' House

The Dolls' House was Rumer Godden's first book for children. It introduces themes to which she has since returned, the exploration of the parallel and interpenetrating worlds of the children in their family home, and the dolls in the dolls' house. In this story the desire of the dolls for a proper house in which they could then live an ordered life, each with a role and position in the doll family, is the centre. The social and psychological importance of the house is that it safeguards the identities of its inhabitants by providing a boundary within which personal considerations are paramount. The organization of the interior represents an agreed form of life which gives respect to all members. The crisis of the story revolves around the attempt of Marchpane, an elegant and snobbish doll, to take over the house for herself and reduce the other dolls to servant or dependent status. The resistance to Marchpane involves a determined effort to keep a grasp on self-identity, and refuse the diminished identity offered by this new order.

The dolls' house belongs to two sisters, Charlotte and Emily, who are given an old dolls' house which they refurbish with the help of their mother and a family friend. Their passionate involvement in this project is supported by the dolls' intense wishing – the dolls cannot communicate directly with the children, though they talk to each other. But if they wish hard enough, the children will know what they want and need. The doll family consists of Tottie, the undoubted heroine, a tiny 100-year-old wooden Dutch doll; Mr Plantagenet, an anxious father rescued from neglect and abuse by Emily and Charlotte; Birdie, his wife, a celluloid doll from a cracker who is gay but 'not quite right in the head'; Apple, a naughty and lovable little boy-doll; and their dog Darner (made from a darning needle). Later comes March-pane, made of kid and china, whom Tottie knows from an earlier part of her life, and whom the children inherit together with the dolls' house from a great-aunt. The characters of both children and dolls are drawn with great precision and depth so that this world can be the setting for a powerful emotional experience for the reader.

How might one understand what the dolls experience in the story, and what they represent in relation to their child owners? This question is a familiar one in thinking about children's imaginary companions, and the characters that many children create for dolls and other toys which provide the context for fantasy play. *The Dolls' House* offers a particularly vivid opportunity to consider the lives of the doll characters as representations of the emotional development of the relationships between Emily and Charlotte, and also their feelings about the adults who appear, and as deline-ations of different aspects of the character of the children. The battle between Tottie and Marchpane for the house seems parallel to the dispute between the children. Emily, the more forceful child, insists that it must be Marchpane's house, and that everything must be arranged for her gratification. Charlotte is troubled by this because of her loyalty to the old doll inhabitants, and her sense that the integrity of the dolls' personalities is being assaulted by these imposed changes of identity. The reader's identification with this struggle is based in the emotional depths or unconscious awareness of recurrent inner conflicts between different parts of the self. Tottie's loving, solid, good sense and caring involvement with the rest of her doll family are supported by her attachment to her origins; the strong good wood which symbolizes her resilience is felt by her to come from a 'good strong tree'. She is battling with Marchpane's grandiose selfishness, where there is no heart, and no space for anything but self in the mind. Marchpane knows no song to sing to Apple, but wants him to be her little boy as an extension of her own sense of power and to satisfy her greed to possess and her need for admiration. While at the cleaners, Marchpane thinks, 'I am a beautiful little creature, really I am. I must be worth a fabulous amount of money. No wonder they are so careful of me . . . I am so very important.' Her existence is devoted to admiration of herself and a search for any new opportunities for additional glorification.

In the story, both Tottie and Marchpane are shown at a Doll Exhibition. Their contrasting experience of this is an elaboration of their personalities. Marchpane is delighted to be on show, and expects to be the best – that is, the most admired. Tottie, however, is almost heartbroken to be sent there – she is separated from her family and house, and she believes that Emily and Charlotte have sold her and that she will never return to her home. She is suffering both from a sense of loss and despair, but also from shame, not to be precious to her child owners. When the Queen comes to the exhibition and asks to buy Tottie, Tottie's delight is not in her implied importance but in the discovery that she is not for sale, but has only been lent to the exhibition. 'Such happiness flowed through her that she felt as though the sap of her tree had risen in her wood, as it once had every spring.' Tottie's joy is to be loved by children, to be played with, and at the exhibition the dolls are divided into those wanting to be looked at, not touched, and those wanting to be played with, made alive by participation in children's fantasies. The dolls who are open to life in this way are those open to 'good times and bad' as the story shows. They have to be sustained in the bad times by hope and courage, which enable them to 'wish' effectively. The capacity for endurance and hope is Tottie's great gift.

Of course, children themselves have only limited means with which to fulfil their desires, and 'wishing' is a very important mode of being for children. The dolls who can only proceed by wishing convey the essence of this childhood experience. Children's wishes are sometimes communicated directly enough – what is wanted for a birthday present, for example. But the subtler desires may not be even consciously perceived by the child, and yet communicated unconsciously to an adult who might intervene. Most of the communic- ations of babies have this character – a feeling about what is needed has to arise in the mind of the mother, and the study of infants and mothers indicates that this feeling is often the consequence of the emotional impact on the mother of the infant's primitive communications.[2] In our internal psychic life, the inner representations of emotionally significant persons – 'internal objects' as Melanie Klein termed them[3] – are experienced as being in continuous dialogue with us. The dolls of this story who communicate with the children by wishing can be viewed as internal objects reaching into the children's awareness. The children's capacity to play imaginatively is linked with their ability to be in touch with unconscious feelings, as Winnicott has described in *Playing and Reality*. In this connection, there is a fascinating detail in the story. At first, Charlotte and Emily agree to lend Tottie to the exhibition for a fee. They want the money very badly to buy new furniture for the dolls' house. But an uncomfortable realization comes to them in the middle of the following night. Tottie ought not to be 'hired out' because the exhibition is to raise money for a blind children's charity. The children explain to the organizer, Mrs Innisfree, that they want to lend Tottie as a gift – in fact, Mrs Innisfree helps them to re-make the old furniture successfully – and this is because, almost as in a revelation from a dream, they have recognized that in their world Tottie represents love, concern, and unselfishness. She cannot be used as part of a mercenary market relationship, in which self is the only interest taken seriously, without a violation of their relation to her. Much later in the story, when Marchpane is in the ascendancy, it is the observation of her smug carelessness and cruelty, sitting still in her chair while Birdie is burnt up, (when Birdie rushes in to save Apple from the danger of the lamp to which Marchpane has exposed him), that allows the children to relegate her to the museum, and to return the house to its 'true' owners. The museum here is a symbol for the archaic area of the self which houses those primitive elements of emotionality which have been outgrown in the course of development.

The other members of the doll family each contribute to the emotional range of the dolls' house life. Mr Plantagenet combines a longing to be 'master of the house' with a profound insecurity. The story suggests that his fragile hopefulness is a result of his previous maltreatment and abandonment in another household of children. He does grow more confident when he has work as the postmaster, an external sign of his capable adult status, but he often seems to lean on Tottie's greater firmness of purpose. Although he and Birdie are the parents in the dolls' house, it is made quite clear that it is Tottie's resourcefulness on which they really depend. Here is a picture of parents who cannot contain the hopes and fears of their children, but who are in need of someone to hold them together. Possibly this superior capacity of the child is an element in children's play with dolls. The actual parents may sustain the real household (of course sometimes real parents do depend on their children for fundamental support) but in play the children can arrogantly reverse this and show that the children would make better parents themselves. This interpretation is also supported by Apple's character. His naughtiness consists of defiance of his parents and he enjoys denigrating his real parents in favour of an idealized fairytale alternative parent – Marchpane. The young child's vulnerability to seduction into pleasure, excitement and sensuousness is contrasted with Darner's barking when he senses danger. He has a nose for psychological threats, also characteristic of babies and young children. Similar, again, is Birdie's mode of being. She cannot think clearly, and frequently feels confused – although her confusions can also represent the truth, as when she continually 'forgets' that 'her' room is now Marchpane's. But when her feelings are roused she can think; outraged love galvanizes her to take Apple back to the kitchen since he belongs with her, and later enables her to save him from the flames. The intricacies of the events in the doll household following the crisis of Marchpane's arrival and the upsetting of established patterns of life demonstrate both the primitive modes of thought, 'thinking-feeling' we might call it, from which emotional connectedness springs, and Tottie's more developed rationality which is based on careful observation of herself and her world.

The dolls are impotent to effect action except via wishing, and this is true of the relations of the internal objects of our minds to ourselves. These objects can be turned to for alliance and support, for good or bad purposes, but they do not have a capacity to control the actions of the self. Of course we can believe that we are controlled by some alien force within us, as in the madness of 'possession' by spirits, but this is a delusion. Klein's investigation of the process of 'projective identification'[4] whereby a part of the self is projected into an external object and then identified with, enables us to begin to understand how the self can experience itself as obscured or lost in identification with others, in whole or in part. An inner relationship with internalized objects, who are accorded freedom but not weighed down with unfair responsibilities, seems very close to the conception of a relation to God in many religious traditions, or perhaps one should say God and the devil, since both good and bad qualities of being are to be found in our unconscious mental life, as in our everyday life.

In this story the children and the dolls together are able to repair the damaged house and its inhabitants, with the help also of parental figures, and this project represents the inner drama of spoiling and destruction overcome by reparative work. This work is accurately shown to take a lot of time and effort, and to require co-operation and ability to work within one's limits and turn for help when it is needed (in the story, an expert French polisher has to complete the re-upholstering of the dolls' furniture); the work can be done when there is enough hope and imagination to conceive what the restored object might be like. This the dolls embody; they 'know' what a house should be, just as Birdie seems to 'know' that a mother would have to take care of children, not bask in the reflected glory of their charm.

The relationship between the two sisters explores the dynamic interplay of their differing characters. Emily can thrust ahead with ideas and ambitions, and this push can be a good or bad quality. It invests her imagination with power but also leaves her open to being carried away with herself, as when she becomes blind to Marchpane's greedy possessiveness. Charlotte, the younger sister, is more tender-hearted and slow, and cannot stand up to Emily's will on her own. She succumbs, but when Emily gets out of touch with Charlotte's heart, the integrity of the dolls' house life is under threat. Only when the two children are acting in tandem, with Emily's capacity for ideas coming alive in Charlotte (Charlotte thinks of sending Marchpane to a museum) and Charlotte's capacity for empathy in Emily's (when they discuss lending, not hiring Tottie, Emily says 'I want things so hard that I don't think what I am doing') can the life of the children and the dolls proceed without castastrophe. At the close of the story, when the dolls and children have to combine living in and enjoying the restored house and mourning Birdie who is gone, Emily says, 'Shall we let them have a little music?' and winds up the doll musical box, 'Birdie would be happy,' says Tottie to Mr Plantagenet, who is sad. The music is Birdie's, and the 'thinking-remembering', which had alerted Charlotte earlier to Tottie's unhappiness at being hired out, enables dolls and children to bring Birdie alive in the house and their minds while acknowledging the sadness of their loss, and the children are able to bear their responsibility and recover from their guilt.

The Fairy Doll

Each of the three doll stories has its crux in a moment of emotional crisis in the lives of its child characters, which are then echoed and elaborated in metaphorical terms in the lives of the dolls. In *The Fairy Doll*, there is a youngest child who is teased, bullied, and left behind (figuratively, and literally on her tricycle) by her three siblings. A fairy doll from the top of the Christmas tree comes to her aid, but with the help also of visiting Great Grandmother who has observed Elizabeth's predicament. 'H'mm. Something will have to be done,' says Great Grandmother (or the fairy doll?), and just then the fairy doll falls off the tree by her side.

> 'Dear me! How fortunate!,' said Great Grandmother, and now her voice certainly came from her. 'I was just going to say you needed a good fairy.'
> 'Me?' asked Elizabeth.
> 'You,' said Great Grandmother. 'You had better have this one.'
> Elizabeth looked at the fairy doll, and the fairy doll looked at Elizabeth; the wand was still stirring with the rush of the fall. 'What about the others?' asked Elizabeth.
> 'You can leave the others to me,' said Great Grandmother.

Elizabeth discovers that in looking after the fairy doll she finds capacities in herself that she previously did not have. She can make a cave home for the doll, with a bicycle basket, moss, sawdust, and all manner of little objects – berries, burs, toadstools, feathers and hips from outdoors. The fairy doll 'tings' in her mind, and she has ideas, where before she was hopeless at everything. 'A few days afterwards Miss Thrup said in school, "Let's see what Elizabeth can do," which

91

meant, "Let's see what Elizabeth can't do." This time there was a ting in Elizabeth's mind, and she could do the seven times table.'

Great Grandmother combines in Elizabeth's mind with fairy doll to become a strong and caring internal object for her. '. . . To Elizabeth she looked as if she were dressed in white and silver all over; she even had white hair, and in one hand she held a thin stick with a silver top.' The dewdrop on the end of her nose reminds Elizabeth of the twinkling dewdrop on the fairy doll's crown.

Great Grandmother's understanding and hope for Elizabeth gives the child some hope for herself, at a point when her parents are too upset by their daughter's difficulties to be able to help her very much.[5] 'What's the use of giving Elizabeth presents?' she hears her father say, 'She doesn't ride the one she has'; she had failed for a whole year to learn to ride the bicycle she had been given the previous Christmas. Her mother sends naughty children to sit on the chest where the Christmas things are packed away; Elizabeth begins to lavish on fairy doll the care and attention which she herself needs. '"How can I take care of her?" asked Elizabeth. "She is to take care of you," said Mother, "but, as you know if you have read any fairy stories, fairies have a way of doing things the wrong way round."' The fairy doll and Great Grandmother are both real and unreal, and they combine to make a fairy godmother for the child. The fairy doll is able to be the 'container' for many of the child's ideas and feelings and Elizabeth can express herself in play creatively. It wants to be cared for as something very small. It wants to fly in the breeze (on Elizabeth's bicycle). The idea of living in a cave and the doll's food gathered from the woods links the child in her imagination with an earlier humanity, and with a benign nature. (There are echoes of an earlier pagan Christmas in the story, as of more Christian imagery in the others.) The doll is a fairy princess (an ideal girl-baby) but she has a wand (like Grandmother's silver-topped stick) which seems to be able to mete out justice to her enemies. '"Don't be silly,"' says Christabel:

and she said scornfully, 'what a little silly you are!' Thwack. A hard small box of sweets fell off the tree and hit Christabel on the head. The fairy doll looked straight in front of her, but the wand stirred gently, very gently, in her hand.

The fairy doll is a combined father (wand = penis) and mother.

It seems evident towards the end of the story that *The Fairy Doll* is a story of *internal* development. Elizabeth collapses again when the fairy doll gets lost. By now her brother and sisters have become kind to her, in part because of the relief they feel when Elizabeth begins to blossom, and they all look everywhere to help. Great Grandmother comes to tea again, and Elizabeth discovers that she is less dependent on the fairy doll being constantly with her than she thought.[6] She finds she can still think. '"Then were the 'tings' me?" asked Elizabeth, puzzled. "I thought they were Fairy Doll."' She recovers quickly from the loss of the fairy doll, and when it (or a new one) reappears in its box for Christmas, it is able to go back on top of the tree and then be put away afterwards in the cedar chest until next year. '"She has done her work," said Mother.'

In psychoanalytic terms, Elizabeth is a child who has failed to internalize a good object. Her three siblings, and also the schoolchildren, teacher, and her father, persecute her with humiliating criticism. They represent a persecutory gang-like super-ego, a bad-parent part of the self which humiliates the baby-self and leads to loss of hope. We might conjecture that this child of the writer's imagination has been pushed too hard to grow up, and that her parents may have been tired of little children by the time she arrived. Her toys are either cast-offs (the wheezy tricycle) or else too big for her (her feet won't reach the pedals), and she is blamed because she can't be like a big child. She is deeply hurt by the others' mockery of her:

> 'Slowpoke,' said Christabel, whizzing past.
> 'Tortoise,' said Godfrey.
> 'Baby,' said Josie.
> 'Not a slowpoke, tortoise, baby,' said Elizabeth, but they did not hear, they were far away, spinning down the hill. 'Wh-ee-ze, wh-ee-ze, wh-ee-ze,' went the tricycle, and Elizabeth's eyes filled with tears.

Great Grandmother then represents the forgiving understanding super-ego, in contrast to the actual parents who are not available to the child. The very old lady can understand the child's perception more than anyone else, and can imagine how strange she might be to a child. Thus she can come close and help her out of her identification with a dirty, rejected bad-baby, and into the human world of belonging to a family. The fairy doll's 'work' has been to represent the reality in the child's mind of both the understanding-helping parent (mother *and* father) and also the delicate, beautiful and needy baby. Once she has securely internalized these different conceptions of herself and those close to her, Elizabeth can be herself independently of the fairy doll. The story thus dramatizes the role of the imagination in achieving growth. Being a modern story, however, where childhood is understood to have its own life, thus a reality of its own, this Elizabeth-Cinderella is helped not to marry the prince, but just to grow happily in a child's world.

Holly and Ivy

The Story of Holly and Ivy is a more specifically Christmas story, and creates a simple and moving metaphorical representation of the contrasted plenitude and emptiness of what 'Christmas' can mean. It works through a very clear structure of binary oppositions; the story has a poetic and formal resonance as well as giving pleasure through the flow of events of its narrative.

Holly is a doll, with a red dress and green shoes. She is in a toy shop, and is longing for a child to give her a home. 'We shall have a little boy or girl for Christmas,' say the toys, but Holly is not chosen. Ivy is a little girl living with Miss Shepherd and thirty other children in an orphanage. She has a green coat, and red gloves. She is the counterpart and complement of Holly, the doll, and she also wants a home for Christmas. Just as Holly is left in the shop after it closes for Christmas, so Ivy is the only child in the home whom no lady or gentleman has asked for. 'Sometimes in Ivy there was an empty feeling, and the emptiness ached; it ached so much that she had to say something quickly in case she cried, and "I don't care at all," said Ivy.' The toys in the shop are only able to wish for homes and children, but Ivy is able to do more than wish:

> 'I'll go to my grandmother,' said Ivy.
> 'You haven't got a grandmother,' said Miss Shepherd. 'I'm

sorry to send you to the Infants' Home, for there won't be much for you to see there or anyone to talk to, but I don't know what else to do.'[7]

Ivy had wanted a doll for her Christmas present, but in the train with her destination posted on to her coat she finds she has only a pencil-box. 'A doll would have filled up the emptiness – and now it ached so much that Ivy had to press her lips together tightly, and "My grandmother will give me a doll," she said out loud.' She tells the passengers she is going to Aylesbury, and a lady tells her it is two or three stations away. 'Then . . . there is an Aylesbury, thought Ivy'; she gets out of the train and goes to search for her grandmother.

In the children's home one of the boys, Barnabas, knows how she feels and taunts her. 'You haven't got a grandmother,' said Barnabas. 'We don't have them.' Barnabas rubs in Ivy's loneliness, perhaps to keep up his own spirits. In the toy shop there is a cruel toy owl called Abracadabra, who bullies the other toys and mocks their hopes of finding a child. Abracadabra has shining green eyes, and tries to destroy the hopes of the toys with cynical malice; he envies their capacity to hope. He has a mistaken kind of realism, like Barnabas. In the children's home there is the busy Miss Shepherd, looking after the children, without a man. And in the toy shop there is Mr Blossom the shopkeeper, without a woman.

Holly's and Ivy's wishes are very strong. 'We can wish. We *must* wish,' whispered the dolls, and Holly whispered, 'I *am* wishing.' Their wishes correspond also with the wishes of Mrs Jones, a childless lady of between a mother's and a grandmother's age, who is stirred by the sight of Holly in the shop window into a 'feeling that she had not had for a long time, a feeling of Christmas'. She buys a tree and all the decorations for it, and then says to her husband,

'Christmas needs children, Albert.' Albert was Mr Jones's name. 'I wonder,' said Mrs Jones, 'couldn't we find a little girl?'
'What's the matter with you today, my dear?' said Mr Jones. 'How could we find a little girl? You're daft.'

The aching emptiness inside Ivy corresponds to the emptiness of Mrs Jones's womb and her house lacking the child it needs. 'And it was a little sadly that Mrs Jones put holly along the chimney shelf, hung mistletoe in the hall, tied a bunch of holly on the door knocker, and went back to her housework.'

The story continuously moves from Holly to Ivy to Mrs Jones's activities, leaving it to the reader to understand the transitions rather as in changes of scene in a film. Ivy has managed well at first in the crowded streets of the country town, and enjoys the atmosphere of festivity. She finds somewhere warm to sleep in a baker's shed, and in the night she goes to look again at Holly in the toy shop window. There, helped by the wishes of the dolls and overcoming the negative 'Hsst!' and 'T'whoo' of Abracadabra, she finds the key of the toy shop which has been dropped by Peter, Mr Blossom's boy assistant. She dreams of Holly, and Holly dreams of her. The expectations aroused by Christmas preparations are shown to be cruel if one is excluded from the family relationships they celebrate. Ivy wakes up on Christmas morning very cold and hungry. 'Ivy was a sensible little girl: she knew she had to get warm and she did not cry, but "I must m-must h-hop and sk-skip," she said through her chattering teeth, and there in the shed she swung her arms, in-out, out-in and clapped her hands.' This orphan child has learned to be brave in coping on her own. 'Outside she tried to run, but her legs felt heavy and her head seemed to swim. "I m-must f-find m-my g-g-grandmother qu-qu-quickly," said Ivy.'

Ivy finds Mrs Jones's house and looks through the window. She sees the Christmas tree, the fire, and the table set for breakfast. '"My b-breakfast," whispered Ivy, and, oh, she was hungry! She saw Mrs Jones sitting by the fire, in her clean apron, waiting.' (In fact she was waiting for her policeman husband to return from his night duty.) 'Ivy stood quite still. Then: "My g-g-grandmother," whispered Ivy.'

There is one more step in the resolution of the story. Ivy is pricked by a prickle from the holly on the door-knocker. (The pricks of holly and pins recurrently make things happen in this story, like the 'tings' in Elizabeth's head in *The Fairy Doll*. They are the physical expression of unexpected thoughts.) 'The prickle was so sharp that she took her hand down, and, "F-first I must g-get my d-doll," said Ivy.' When she returns to the shop she finds a crying Peter looking for the lost key. She thinks of Barnabas, whom she has never seen cry, and gives Peter the key. Then Mr Jones notices her. '"I think you are lost," said Mr Jones. His voice was so kind that the empty feeling ached in Ivy; it felt so empty that her mouth began to tremble. She could not shut her lips, but, "I'm n-not l-lost," said Ivy. "I'm g-g-going to my m-my g-g-grandmother." "Where does your grandmother live?" asked Mr Jones, and Ivy then takes him to his own house. "This is m-my g-g-grandmother's," said Ivy. Mr Jones realizes the complete correspondence of the little girl's wishes and his wife's. "Sh-shall we kn-knock?" asked Ivy.' But '"You needn't knock," said Mr Jones. "You can come in."'

The corresponding union of Holly and Ivy comes when Peter, who has been told to take a toy for Christmas by Mr Blossom, decides to take Holly for Ivy, whom he believes to be Mr Jones's daughter. So Ivy finds Holly miraculously by the tree. Through her return of the key, and Peter's present to her, Ivy is now able to forgive Barnabas, and she asks Miss Shepherd to tell him all that has happened. The envious Abracadabra on the other hand (being only a bad imaginary object) is taken away with the rubbish. Mrs Jones and Ivy have found each other through the common feeling stirred by Holly.

The story calls to mind W.R. Bion's idea of the innate emotional preconceptions which exist in the mind, and which are there to be filled out in experience.[8] Russell Hoban's story *The Mouse and His Child* has the similar theme of a mouse-child longing to complete his family, and whose extraordinary hopefulness makes this possible. The hopefulness of the child has the capacity to bring out kindness in adults, in what we might see as an evolutionary adaptation of human beings for the survival of their children. Ivy has the preconception of a lost grandmother. (She has presumably learned that her mother is lost beyond return.) Mrs Jones has the preconception of what it would be like to have a child, even though she is barely any longer in touch with her feelings and it is the heightened expectations aroused by Christmas that bring them alive in her again. The bright red doll is a symbol of hope for both of them. Ivy's longing for a doll, even before she sees Holly, and Mrs Jones's response to the sight of the doll in the window, stir them to try to make their wishes real. Mrs Jones prepares her home for a child; Ivy knows what she must look for – 'a house with a tree and no children' – and she is thus able to recognize it when she finds it. The doll is the symbolic mediation which brings the parentless child and the childless family together.

The larger structure of meanings on which the story depends is Christmas itself, with its theme of a child being born and celebrated as a miracle. This hope aroused and fulfilled is enacted through the imagined experience of all the three main participants in the story, Ivy, Holly, and Mrs Jones. The contrast of the girl outside, dressed in a green coat, and the doll in a shop, in a red dress, is resolved when they are both taken into a house by a real couple. Their wishes can be granted when they become the objects of Mr and Mrs Jones's care. For the child reader, the identification is with both doll and child. Mrs Jones at the end makes Ivy a dress just like Holly's, but green, and Holly a coat just like Ivy's, but red. Thus Ivy's and Holly's clothes mark symmetrically their recognized bond with each other; they have become members of a family that each of them helped to create.

The Kitchen Madonna

The symbolic object of the fourth of these stories is a 'Kitchen Madonna' which Gregory, one of two children in a family of two architect-parents, sets out to make for Marta, the Polish Ukranian live-in help whom he knows to be lonely. In this story, which is about a boy of nine and is therefore a little more grown-up than the others discussed in this chapter, the child's feelings about things are described, rather than represented through the life given by the other child characters to their dolls. But common to this and the other stories is the role of symbolization in recreating an absent or lost object in the mind. Hanna Segal's discussion of the relation of the capacity for symbol formation to the 'depressive position', and the recognition of the absence of a mother-figure and the experiencing of a sense of loss, is relevant here.[9] The children, whether through their play with dolls, or through actually making a work of art as in the case of the Kitchen Madonna, are able to give substance and three-dimensionality to their internal worlds. They are able to sustain an idea of possible emotionally vivid and rewarding relationships between family members even when the experience of these in life feels defective to them.

'The children did not like it that Marta was unhappy,' the book begins. Marta is the best live-in help the family have ever had. '"Help! She *is* the house," Gregory might have said.' Gregory has taken an interest in her from the first, though he was not at all interested in her younger predecessors Tove and Babette. Tove could play with him, and Babette was 'so gay'. 'Marta neither played games nor was gay.' Gregory and Marta have something in common. 'She was from the Polish Ukraine, "and no wonder she's sad," said Mother. "Think of the history of her country." But Gregory thought Marta's sadness had nothing to do with her country, it was of now; though Marta was in late middle age and Gregory was a small boy, he too sometimes felt that brooding unhappiness, especially at twilight, "When Mother is still out," he might have said, only he preferred to keep that thought to himself.' Gregory does not understand, either, how his own history has contributed to his present feelings. Marta had been a refugee from her village, 'driven out by soldiers, and had never seen her mother or father or any of her people again.' She tells the children about her own home, about how everyone lived in one room. She doesn't use the sitting room provided for her in Gregory's house. '"I like kitchen," said Marta. "In my home," she told the children, "only one room, and that room kitchen." "Only one room for everyone to sit in?" asked Janet. "Sit, cook, eat, wash, sleep, everythings," said Marta.' She makes the Thomas's house into a proper home for the children, and especially for Gregory who minds its emptiness so much. 'To Gregory it was inexpressibly lovely to come home knowing the house would be lit and welcoming instead of dark, forsaken, with a note telling them to go next door.'

Gregory and Marta share a love of Rootle, Gregory's cat. 'Rootle was called Rootle because Gregory had found him as a starving kitten rootling in a dustbin; he was Gregory's, not Father's or Mother's or Janet's.' But, from the first day Marta came, Gregory let her stroke Rootle, even feed him and pick him up. The story tells us that both Marta and Rootle had suffered from the world. Both had been driven out. Marta limped from a wound – '"They shoot at me,"' said Marta – and Rootle's tabby coat had a bald spot where '"Perhaps someone threw boiling water at him,"' said Mother. Gregory and Marta both feel identified with and protective towards Rootle.

Gregory is in touch with Marta's underlying sadness, for he listens to her more deeply than the others. She is filling up the kitchen with things, but she tells Gregory that 'It empty'.

Gregory remembers this, and later asks her, 'What did you have in your kitchen, Marta, that we don't have in ours?' Then Marta tells them that 'You have no "good place"', and describes the clothed and jewelled image of 'Our Lady and Holy Child' which they kept in the corner of their kitchen at home.

'. . . They faces shine, Mother, Baby, they make happy, warm; everywhere you go, the eyes, they look at you. They look . . .' Marta looked round and once more saw the Thomas kitchen; the glow left her face and she put her head down among the teacups and wept. Gregory's heart suddenly swelled with an unfamiliar feeling so that he wanted to cry too, as he had wanted to cry when he found Rootle in the dustbin. He put out his hand and stiffly patted Marta's shoulder – Gregory, who avoided touching anyone. 'Don't cry, Marta,' he said. 'I will get you an icon.'

Gregory then sets out to find an icon of a Madonna and Child, going to museums and expensive art shops to do so. He is brave and persistent despite confusing and humiliating episodes, but it is painful for a small boy going about such an impossible purpose, and he realizes that he will not be able to buy an icon for Marta. Janet and he are together in trying to find the icon, more than before, and together they realize that maybe there is another way of doing it:

'It was a fool thing to think of giving her one,' said Gregory.
'It wasn't,' said Janet, and Gregory lifted his head. He did not often let his young sister contradict him.
'It was, if I can't make it,' said Gregory.
'You can make it.'
'How can I make it without any money?'
'You can make it with think,' said Janet. It was not what she meant to say, yet oddly it said what she meant.
'How can you make things with *think*,' asked Gregory. He said it scornfully, but now he came to consider it, that is how things are made.

The two children then co-operate in making the icon. Janet is able to think where she could get the materials for the picture – she can ask people for scraps of cloth. Gregory thinks more of his own things, and decides to use the frame of his precious ship picture for the 'Jesus-Mary'. They then patiently and secretly collect and try out materials for the

Madonna, and Gregory makes it in his loft workroom. They ask for help with materials from the lady in their mother's hat shop, and in the sweetshop. The children cannot help telling these older women what they are doing, and their project evokes sympathy and interest. They succeed in making the Madonna (with Rootle sitting by them, and with Janet now free to come in and out of Gregory's previously forbidden room). They are ready to show it first to their parents, and then to Marta.

Gregory is a strange mixture of an English, upper middle-class, inhibited and bookish child, stoical and lonely, and a softer child who finds a way out of this restricting shell through art. He is first in his class but always 'out of things'. For all his remoteness, he is his parents' child. He has been given a drawing board for his attic loft by his father, so it is like his parents' architects' workrooms. His thoughtful and patient experimentation with the picture, trying this material and that, is the activity of someone who can work as an artist, in touch both with his feelings and with shapes and materials. It is important that the Madonna is made of materials, and not merely paint. It becomes literally a three-dimensional, solid object, and the children's relationship to the stuffs they are using is like an infant's feeling for the textures it associates with its mother. Babies hold on to their mothers' hair and clothes as well as skin, and this often develops into attachment to the 'in between' objects, neither mother nor self, which Winnicott calls 'transitional objects'. Janet uses the language of her parents' world to tell them of their work:

'You are invited,' said Janet, at the drawing room door, 'to a private view in Gregory's loft, to see what he has made.'

'Gregory has made something?' asked mother, as if she did not believe it, and Father put down his spectacles.

'Made something?'

'Because of Janet,' said Gregory – and Janet glowed with pleasure – 'because of Janet I found a way to make a picture after all.'

This is an important moment for parents and children, as it will be later for Marta and all the family together:

Mother sat down to look at the picture, poring over it. Now that she looked at it closely she she could see it might have been made by a boy: the Child's crown was slightly crooked, one of the Madonna's cheeks had run, two of the edging papers were out of line, but, 'Made by a boy with imagination and love,' said Mother, reaching for Father's hand. 'Oh Gregory! Gregory!' and she burst into tears.

Gregory stiffens at this point, and feels blamed by his mother's tears. '"Why are you so miserable? What have I done?" he asked almost in a wail. "You let us in, Greg, and you have come out," said Mother, which they did not understand.'

Gregory's self-preoccupied and withdrawn nature – his mother wonders if he has any heart – and his deeper unhappiness don't seem to be explained by what is actually said in the story. Janet his sister after all has busy parents too, and she seems much more resilient and hopeful. Nor are the parents remote or cut off – most of what they learn of Marta's life they learn first from Mother, and she realizes as well as they what Marta has brought to the house. Perhaps Gregory is imagined, consciously or unconsciously by the author, as having been initially hurt by being displaced by his younger sister. This is the special meaning of his not having enough mothering. The starving cat (whose name Rootle calls to mind a baby searching for the nipple), the image of a once close and later disrupted family which he has of Marta's life, and his own rather obsessional care for himself and his room, are metaphors arising from his own situation as the elder of two children with admittedly preoccupied and busy parents.

He has learned to cope with his pain and anxiety by being rather too grown up for his age. The self-contained composure of a cat, friendly only to him (and Marta) is an image of attachment and feeling that is not too disturbing. He responds best to people who are in touch with their or his own sadness, and in an English middle-class way he likes emotional boundaries to be kept in place. His cry, 'What have I done?' when his mother cries is perhaps an echo of his original wounding or stiffening when Janet was born and he thought 'What have I done wrong?'

Marta's very strong impulse to mother the family and make their kitchen into a real home for herself and the children releases in Gregory warmer and less inhibited emotions. Marta's combined simplicity and seriousness make it impossible to deal with her on the everyday sophisticated level of the professional household. Her way of speaking English – 'My little litted lamp' – has a child's directness, while her life has had an adult's pain. In the story the name Marta = martyr = mater. The act of making the Madonna for Marta has many meanings. It is done out of love for Marta, because of her unhappiness and homesickness. It is done out of self-concern by the children, in the hope of keeping her there for them. It is also unconsciously an act of reparation towards Mother, probably for the injury inflicted on her in phantasy by Gregory's coldness and resentment. This is why she responds so tearfully to it and why they are all able to join with love in the gift of the Madonna to Marta. The symbolism of the Madonna itself is obvious enough, and relates to much of what we have said about the meanings of the story. But the particular beauty of the image in the story is that it has brought alive feelings in everyone, and has thus brought together a family which had previously been somewhat lifeless and empty in their shared emotional life.

In this story Rumer Godden succeeds in making vivid and moving the development that can take place in the internal world of a child through the making of a work of art, rather than through play and make-believe as in the earlier stories.

5

The Maternal Capacities of a Small Boy: *The Indian in the Cupboard*

The subject of our previous chapter, the 'doll stories' of Rumer Godden, concerned the relationship between the imaginative play and the emotional development mainly of small girls. Rumer Godden's work thus mostly falls on one side of a conventional distinction between fiction mainly written for girls, which often takes themes of fantasy and make-believe centred around relationships within the family, and fiction written for boys, which is more often about physical and outdoor adventure.

Lynne Reid Banks's *The Indian in the Cupboard* (published as recently as 1980 but in our view of a quality to stand with the very best classic children's books) cuts across those genre boundaries. It is about boys, and it features an Indian and a cowboy, only the Indian and the cowboy are little plastic toys come to life. The intense relationship of the children in the story, Omri and Patrick, to their made-alive toys, is thus similar to the relationship of Rumer Godden's little girl characters to their dolls, while the preoccupations of the children in each case are nevertheless typically defined by their gender. The conventional classifications of gender and genre are also crossed in another way. One of the main underlying themes of *The Indian in the Cupboard* (we will abbreviate this to *The Indian* from now on) is the relationship of its main character, Omri, to his mother – not so much on the surface, which is warm and undisturbed, but in memory and phantasy. The story is able to explore, through a boy's relationship with toys which are conventionally masculine, the more feminine aspects of his character.

Omri is given for his ninth birthday a second-hand plastic Indian, by his friend Patrick. He is disappointed – he has too many plastic figures, and we learn that he has almost given up playing with them. He is also given by his brother Gillon a white bathroom cupboard, probably left out as rubbish, and his mother finds him a special key that will lock it. This key (the key of a jewelry box) was given to her by her grandmother, who had nothing else to leave her, as a remembrance. She stopped wearing it when its ribbon broke, and Omri reproaches her for not getting a chain for it. Mother tells Omri that it is now his. '"Please don't lose it, Omri, will you?"'

Omri decides to lock his plastic Indian in the cupboard overnight. He is woken up by 'a most extraordinary series of sounds. A pattering; a tapping; a scrabbling; and – surely? a high-pitched squeak like – well, almost like a tiny voice.' Omri realizes there is something alive in the cupboard. When he opens it, the plastic Indian is gone. But then he sees him. 'He was crouching in the darkest corner, half hidden by the front of the cupboard. And he was alive.' Omri decides to keep his Indian a secret from his parents and his brothers. He realizes that 'if he was not dreaming and the Indian really had come alive, it was certainly the most marvellous thing that had ever happened to Omri in his life, and he wanted to keep it to himself, at least at first.'

The description and dramatization of Omri's developing relationship with his little Indian are wonderful. The author succeeds in rendering the passionate attachment of a child to the objects of his play, which matches our involvement as readers in her fiction. The apparently boring present becomes the one most alive in the child's imagination. Details of Indian appearance and dress that would normally be dead symbols come gleaming to life, as the figure changes from an ordinary plastic toy into a miniaturized but real Indian. The Indian turns out to be bold and fierce, and insists on *his* definition of self and reality in the strange world in which he now finds himself. He speaks Indian-style, which means tersely but to the point (a style made familiar of course by many Westerns). '"I speak," he grunted! . . . "I speak *slowly*," grunted the miniature Indian at last. . . . "You touch – I kill!" the Indian growled ferociously.' The Indian rejects any condescension by the boy.'Omri suddenly asked, "Were you always this small?" "I not small! You, big!" the Indian shouted angrily.'

Omri realizes very soon that his Indian is a responsibility, not merely a plaything. His first problem is how even to keep him alive. He locks him back in the cupboard before he goes to school, and when he comes back he finds he has turned back into a lifeless plastic toy. He is heartbroken, but when at bedtime he locks him away again in despair he hears noises: his Indian has come alive again. Omri falteringly asks what happened to him, and the Indian's reply is characteristic:

> Happen? Good sleep happen. Cold ground. Need blanket. Food. Fire. Omri gaped. Was the little man giving him orders? Undoubtedly he was! Because he waved his knife, now back in his hand, in an unmistakable way. Omri was so happy he could scarcely speak.

Omri, who is not used to doing such things for himself, then has to find food from the kitchen for his Indian. He is worried that his Indian will be discovered by his brothers or his parents, and has to shield this wonderful secret from the each-for-himself atmosphere of a family which seems to have rather too many boys (three) for comfort.[1] These episodes call to mind the experience of a parent with a first child. There is the same amazement that anything could be so alive and fantastic. There is also recurrent panic that it will die the moment one's back is turned, that it will get the wrong food, that it will fall from a great height, that it will be the victim of some unexpected hazard outdoors. On the other hand, his charge gives him much solid reassurance. Omri's Indian is very much alive, knows what he wants, and has a basic trust that the world (which soon means Omri) will provide it. The baby which appears at one moment so fragile, at the next is a robust little tyrant who demands that all around him serve his needs. This is particularly evident one morning:

> He was awakened at dawn by Little Bear (which the Indian has told him is his name) bawling at him . . . As soon as Omri's eyes opened, the Indian shouted. 'Day come! Why you still sleep? Time eat – hunt – fight – make pictures!'

Parents will remember such mornings.

Little Bear's monosyllabic way of speaking is also reminiscent of a spirited two year old's. His name could be a parent's nickname for a small child, or a child's for a cuddly toy. His beliefs (in his ancestors and in supernatural powers) are like an infant's earliest conceptions of his parents' omnipotence. This inspires Little Bear both with awe, and with greedy desires to turn these magical powers to his own advantage:

> The Indian finished eating in silence, and then stood up, wiping his greasy hands on the sides of his trousers. 'Now. Do magic. Make things for Little Bear.' . . . Omri ranged five or six horses of various sizes and colours before Little Bear, whose black eyes began to shine. 'I have,' he said promptly. 'You mean all of them?' Little Bear nodded hungrily.

An important quality needed in writing for and about children is to avoid the distortions of sentimentality with which adults approach the child's world. The Indian's fierceness and independence is a corrective to any such feelings on the part of Omri (or the reader). Little Bear vehemently rejects condescension. 'You feel better now?' Omri asked. 'I better. You not better,' said the Indian. 'You still big. You stop eat. Get right size.' A plainness and matter-of-factness of description, which *The Indian* shares with E.B. White's comparable *Stuart Little* also establishes this world in its own terms. A realization by these writers that things are different in their meaning depending on one's age and size, is an aspect of this. Much of the pleasure of *The Indian in the Cupboard*, *Stuart Little*, and to take a third case, Mary Norton's *Borrower* stories, is in the exploration of the features of the material world as they might be if experienced on a different scale from our usual one. Another way the author has of making us really see this world is by a continuous experience of the unexpected as Little Bear contradicts the conventional ideas Omri has about Indians. When Omri first suggests a horse, Little Bear seemed surprised. '"Don't you ride? I thought all Indians rode." Little Bear shook his head. "Iroquois walk."' The story is extremely humorous, often through sudden reversals and juxtapositions of what are grown-up thoughts, and what are a child's:

> 'Little Bear!' he shouted. 'It works, it works! I can make any plastic toy I like come alive, come real! It's real magic, don't you

understand? Magic!' The Indian stood calmly with folded arms, evidently disapproving of this display of excitement. 'So? Magic. The spirits work much magic. No need wake dead with howls.'

The humour often arises through recognition of the differences between Omri's point of view and the Indian's. Such flashes of understanding enable the emotional demands of the situation to be coped with more calmly. Omri's own sense of humour is part of his learning to accept the point of view of others, and to bring his thinking and feeling capacities together. Humour often arises, as in the simplest case of puns, when we see that something unexpectedly has more than one meaning. The recurrent upsetting of Omri's preconceptions, but on the other hand the unbelievable and delightful reality to him of what the Indian actually is and does, enables Lynne Reid Banks to convey the sensations of living in the here-and-now. This living-in-the-present is a particularly vital precondition of relationships with small children, and the necessity to do so is one reason why being with them is exhausting for adults.

Fiction for young children has to respect the limits of their factual knowledge and vocabulary, and therefore may appear simple to adults. Nevertheless it can be innovative and complex in its forms. This story makes use of what David Lodge in *The Modes of Modern Writing* calls 'metonymic' or realist conventions.[2] It constructs its characters through the typical features that we associate with them. Their clothes, and accoutrements, and ways of speaking, are taken from well-known conventions brought to life by miniaturization. For example, Tommy Atkins, the toy medical orderly brought to life in the magic cupboard, talks like an English soldier in a war film – '"Keep him warm, that's the ticket."' But the story also has a 'deep structure' which is highly metaphoric, the opposite literary mode to metonymy. One important metaphor, for example, lies in the parallel between Omri's relationship with Little Bear, and his own emotional development in relation to his family and his friend, Patrick. The writer is able to have fun with the boyish conventions, and at the same time to express deep feelings through the story's metaphoric meanings. Perhaps because childhood still gives rise to hopeful feelings in this culture, the authors of some of the modern children's classics we discuss are also able to explore potentially painful and tragic feelings in a containing and non-destructive way.

The importance of parenting and stage of life soon becomes explicit in this story, as the Indian asks Omri where the food comes from. Omri has found him some corned beef, and Little Bear is appreciative:

> 'Very good! Soft! Your wife cook this?'
> Omri started to laugh. 'I haven't got a wife!'
> The Indian stopped and looked at him, 'Omri not got wife? Who grow corn, grind, cook, make clothes?'
> 'My mother,' said Omri, still grinning. 'Have you got a wife then?'

(The Indian's wife is dead.) Their differences become further clarified later. Little Bear realizes that Omri doesn't want a wife:

> 'I'm not old enough,' Omri explained. Little Bear looked at him for a moment. 'No. I see. Boy.' He grinned. 'Big boy, but boy.' He went on eating. 'Little Bear want . . . With Iroquois, mother find wife for son. But Little Bear mother not here. Omri be mother and find.'

The story shows how a child has taken into himself a mental image or memory of his mother looking after him, and how he thus acquires in childhood the capacity to become a parent himself in due time.

Other plastic figures, and other aspects of Omri, are brought to life by the magic key. First, Omri gets Little Bear a horse. (Little Bear is disappointed only to have one, but Omri realizes that he can't have herds of horses galloping all over his room.) Then, after Little Bear has a bad accident and Omri is frightened, he puts the plastic figure of a First World War medical orderly in the magic cupboard, and brings him to life to bandage Little Bear. The medical orderly, who is like a gentle ghost from the trenches, feels he has come from one nightmare into another. But he knows that his job is to patch up the injured, and without complaint he bandages the Indian and is then returned, out of his dream, as Omri has tactfully told him, to the war and his duty.

Omri decides, with mixed feelings, to share his secret with his friend Patrick, who has been feeling hurt at being so obviously kept out of something. He has been disbelieving and envious of Omri's self-sufficient obsession with the plastic toys that they were both becoming tired of. Omri hadn't even seemed to want the Indian that Patrick had given him, so it is all the more provoking that he is now making so much of it, so mysteriously. When Patrick first sees the Indian, and learns about the cupboard which brings plastic toys alive, he is filled with greedy desire. '"Then what are we waiting for? Let's bring loads of things to life! Whole armies –"' Omri has to explain to him the burdensome responsibilities of looking after these people once they are made real. They are not just toys anymore, he says, and he explains how Little Bear is '". . . in the middle of his life – somewhere in America in seventeen-something-or-other. He's from the *past*," Omri struggled to explain as Patrick looked blank.' But Patrick naturally cannot resist locking at least one figure in the cupboard, and he brings to life a plastic cowboy, which he has just offered to Omri as a present and which Omri has refused.

The cowboy, who is called Boone, is the opposite of the Indian in more or less every way. Where Little Bear is resourceful and brave, the cowboy is lazy. He is a drunk who thinks he is suffering from delirium tremens, and he is also inclined to collapse in weeping. However, he has a horse and a gun, and he looks and talks the part of a cowboy. Patrick leaves him with Omri for his first night, under stern threat to bring both Indian and cowboy to school the next day or else have the secret given away. Omri realizes that the Indian and cowboy are likely to be enemies. But, 'a room this size was like a sort of indoor national park to the cowboy and the Indian. It should be easy enough to keep them apart for one night.' The two horses of the Indian and the cowboy hear each other and the cowboy's horse breaks out in the night. Omri 'was awakened just after dawn by shots'.

Omri has to become a sterner parent to his Indian to stop him fighting with the cowboy, and has to issue many threats to keep them apart. Just as the Indian and the cowboy quarrel with one another, so do Omri and Patrick to whom they belong. The day at school is a bad experience, since Patrick hasn't yet learned the responsibilities necessary to look after the Indian and the cowboy, and repeatedly risks exposing them to view. He is expelled from class and sent to the headmaster, and is then terrified into showing him the

Indian, while Omri struggles at the door, beside himself with anguish for Little Bear. This moment at which the live Indian is actually shown to an adult is the least satisfactory episode in the story, since the reality of the figures for the boys, and their reality for adults, are not plausible in the same ways. The author deals with this by having Mr Johnson the headmaster become ill with shock and 'not believe his eyes'. But the interface between child and adult worlds is handled better and more obliquely elsewhere in the story. Omri's parents respect his secret and never know what has actually happened. When Omri has to show the cowboy and Indian to the toyshop owner who suspects him of stealing them he persuades them to play dead: '"Lie still! Don't move. *Plastic!*"' When Boone does a wonderful miniature drawing of his own 1880s town in the art class, Omri has great fun showing the teacher the drawing, but not the cowboy.

The quarrelling between Omri and Patrick, which nearly brings their friendship to an end, is very powerfully and painfully rendered. They fight bitterly over the two live figures. Patrick blackmails Omri to get his way and get his hands on Boone, while Omri feels that Patrick doesn't know how to look after him properly.

> 'Will you shut up?' hissed Omri.
> 'You said I could have them both!' said Patrick, no longer in a whisper. Others in the line began to turn their heads.
> 'Will you shut up?' hissed Omri.
> 'No,' said Patrick, in a loud, clear voice. He held out his hand. Omri felt trapped and furious. He looked into Patrick's eyes and saw what happens to the nicest people when they want something badly and are determined to get it, come what may.

Omri's relationships with his elder brothers are also at times very angry, and his school seems to be a place of mutual persecution held in check by the teachers. Omri imagines bashing his enemies one by one, 'or better still, all at once – a giant knocking down hordes of enemies like skittles. He imagined them all rolling backwards down a long wide flight of steps, in waves, bowled over by his flashing fists and flying feet.'

Just as Patrick and Omri are brought together by their frightening experience at school, so are Little Bear and Boone. Little Bear reproaches Omri for frightening him, and this calls to mind, though with characteristic humour, a child's distress when the adults around it quarrel: '"Big man shout. Give fear!" he said angrily. "Small ears – big noise – no good."' Omri responds like the good parent to Little Bear that he has now become. '"I know. I'm sorry," said Omri. "But it's okay now: I'm going to take you home."' Little Bear hasn't forgotten what he came for, however. '"What about wife?" His promise! Omri had forgotten all about that.'

The cowboy and the Indian express different infantile aspects of the character of Omri, and these become reconciled and integrated with each other as the story proceeds. Omri was only recently inclined to be a cry-baby, the story tells us, like the cowboy. The Indian, on the other hand, is a brave and independent figure corresponding to the strongest part of Omri. In this household of tough little boys, the experience of taking care of his Indian brings Omri in touch with an aspect of himself he has learned from his tender contact with his mother. She is still close to him, and he is sensitive to her moods. 'A movement near the back of the house caught Omri's eye. It was his mother, coming out to hang up some wet clothes. He thought she moved as if she were tired and fed up . . . On impulse, Omri went over to her.' His father, though harassed by the turmoil of his household, is also in touch with his youngest child. When Omri takes his seed tray for the Indian, he lets him keep it, without prying, so long as he will go to fetch him another one. Omri gives him some sweetcorn seeds, which he has learned about through his Indian, as a present. Omri learns to think about his parents as having needs and feelings of their own, and also learns to feel and act as they do when faced with the same responsibilities. He sews the Indian a tepee. He makes Boone wash himself. ('. . . He did consent to rub his hands lightly over the piece of soap, although grimacing hideously as if it were some slimy dead thing . . .') He tells the Indian and the cowboy, who are about to fight, that they must eat their breakfast together, first. '"You can start fighting again afterward if you must."' He adopts his parents' tones. '"First, you must eat while it's hot, I've been to a lot of trouble to cook it for you," Omri said, sounding like his mother.' And he stops them afterward 'in his father's firm, end-of-fight voice. "It's a draw. Now you must get cleaned up for school."' When he loses the key to the cupboard, he tidies up the attic for the first time. Little Bear's practicality and hard work in setting up his beautifully made long-house is a mirror of Omri's growing capacities.

The tiredness he notices in his mother is connected with what *he* now feels: 'the burden of constant worry was beginning to wear him out.' Most important is his passionate devotion to the Indian as a being in his own right. 'It wasn't the fun, the novelty, the magic that mattered anymore. What mattered was that Little Bear should be happy. For that, he would take on almost anything.'

It is relevant that the Indian is a birthday present – the story depicts the birth of a new aspect of himself. When Omri's mother gives him the special key, she remembers her grandmother, but Omri is put in touch with the memory of her early mothering of him. The remoteness of his actual great grandmother to Omri is shown perhaps when the old Indian chief is brought to life in the cupboard and immediately dies, without arousing much sorrow in either Omri or Little Bear. The mirror on the bathroom cupboard suggests that Omri is locking and unlocking reflections of himself and his own past.

Patrick, on the other hand, is less in touch with these more feminine aspects of himself. He doesn't really know how to look after Little Bear and Boone. Omri has to teach him the basics of how to do this. When Omri tells him that it's no good just to leave food in his pocket for them, Patrick replies that '"Cowboys and Indians are used to rough treatment."' Boone's combination of callous bragging about what cowboys have done to Indians, and actual cowardice, is nearer to Patrick's character than Omri's – it is Patrick who breaks down when he sees Mr Johnson. All we learn of Patrick's family is that he is in terror of the headmaster talking to his father, and that his mother has phoned to say he must go home at once. This suggests less sensitive treatment than Omri receives from his parents.

The different aspects of self explored in the relationships of the children and the two little figures are also reflected in what Omri learns of early American history. He discovers that what he knows of Indians is in part white man's myth.[3] He learns that 'the white man seemed to have made the Iroquois and the Algonquin keen on scalping each other, not to mention white men, French or English as the case might be, by offering them money and whiskey and guns . . .' Little Bear, by contrast, wants only to re-establish his way of life, with his long-house, his painting, his hunting, and the wife and other Indians he needs to be a proper chief. Omri (like

Elizabeth and Gregory in the Rumer Godden stories) is brought into touch with a wider human experience by his Indian. For the first time Omri, 'who was not what you'd call a great reader,' finds that he needs to read to find out about the Iroquois. He discovers that you can't believe all that you see in films.

A climax to the story comes when the two boys, and Boone and Little Bear, are watching a Western together on the television:

> Before the ten minutes was up, the Indians in the film started getting the worst of it. It was the usual sequence in which the pioneers' wagons are drawn into a circle and the Indians are galloping round them, while the outnumbered men of the wagon-train fire muzzle-loading guns at them through the wagon wheels.

As the Indians get the worst of it, and 'brave after brave bit the dust', Little Bear becomes upset.

> 'No good pictures!' he shouted.
> 'Watcha talkin' about, Injun?' Boone yelled tauntingly across the chasm dividing him from Little Bear. 'That's how it was . . . mah pah tole me he done shot near 'nuff fifteen-twenny of them dirty savages.'
> 'White men move onto land! Use water! Kill animals!'
> 'So what? Let the best man win. And we won! Yippee!' he added, as another television Indian went down with his horse on top of him.

Little Bear understandably shoots him at this point with his bow and arrow.

While Boone has a crude and decadent outlook in comparison with Little Bear, and the story's sympathies are for the Indians' long-ago threatened way of life, Omri is nevertheless determined to save Boone. He makes Little Bear help him pull out the arrow, and then brings the medical orderly alive once more so Boone can have the attention he needs. When Boone is recovering, after much anxiety about him, Omri tells Little Bear that he's going to make him his blood brother:

> 'It's an old Indian custom,' Omri explained. Little Bear looked baffled. 'Not Indian custom.'
> 'I'm sure it is! It was in a film I saw.'
> 'White man idea. Not Indian.'

'Well, couldn't you do it, just this once?'

Little Bear was silent for a moment, thinking. Then Omri saw that crafty look he knew of old coming into the Indian's face. 'Good,' he said. 'Little Bear give Boone medicine, make him my brother when strong. And Omri put plass-tick in box, make real wife for Little Bear.'

'Not tonight,' said Omri firmly. 'We've had enough excitement.'

But at dawn he wakes up and brings the plastic Indian girl alive for Little Bear.

Little Bear's reluctance to accept Boone as his brother reflects Omri's competitive relationship with his own brothers, of whom at times he would have said, like Little Bear of Boone, '"Not friend. Enemy."' But just as Little Bear is able to feel sorrow for what he has done, so Omri's brothers later on are able to appreciate Little Bear's long-house (which they think their youngest brother has made), and to help him find the lost key. By the end of the story hateful feelings among the brothers are lodged in Gillon's escaped pet rat who is roaming under the floorboards, threatening to eat the little men.

Omri's firm parental concern for Boone and Little Bear enables the Indian, within the limits of sibling rivalry, to forgive and look after Boone. Patrick later wishes they could tell their real brothers about their adventure, and Omri corrects him. '"As for our brothers coming," he said, "all I want of my brothers is to keep that rat in its cage."' Omri had recaptured the rat 'after a long, patient wait with cheese and a fishing net'. The most dangerous and greedy feelings can after all be kept under control.

Destructiveness and violence are important themes in this story, and learning how to manage these aspects of the self is a major part of the process of emotional learning which is symbolized in *The Indian*. Omri and Patrick's friendship nearly comes to an end in moments of bitter hatred; the different stage of emotional development they have reached is revealed in their attitudes to the cowboy and Indian. But through their crisis at school, and Patrick's remorse, they grow together again, and Patrick becomes thoughtful and ingenious in helping Omri to look after them, for example in thinking of a sieve to find the lost key to the cupboard. Boys' play, the author knows, is full of violent fantasies. Omri had been a little frightened by violence, perhaps as the youngest of three brothers. He has a horror of scalping, and returns a fearsome knight promptly to plastic oblivion after he has taken his axe as a tool for Little Bear. But Omri learns to explore the meaning of violence, and its proper limits. In containing the violence of Little Bear and Boone, he learns that the powers to damage of a child are not those of an adult, and thus to be less frightened of the violent feelings in himself. He also learns how losses and damage can be repaired, both with the little figures and in reality. The crucial key is found again, after much searching and risk to Little Bear from Gillon's escaped white rat. Omri develops a compassionate attitude towards war and suffering. He thinks of the First World War from the point of view of a medical orderly. He learns to identify with the world of the Iroquois against the stereotype of the TV Western, reflecting a recent awareness in parts of our culture of the damage as well as the good that western man has done. The psychological meaning of all this is a recognition of the consequences to others, and especially others close to us, of our aggressive feelings when these are acted out.[4]

Omri realizes even before he brings the Indian girl to life that he is near the end of his adventure with his Indian:

> It had been hard enough with one little being to feed, protect, and keep secret. Much harder after Boone came. Now there'd be three – and one a woman. Young as he was, Omri knew that one woman and two men spelled trouble. And what if there should be children . . .

Omri worries as he lies in bed, and realizes that there is no way he can keep his Indian without it ending in disaster of some kind. 'Whatever magic had brought this strange adventure about must be put to use again, to send the little people back to their own place and time.' Once he decides this, 'Omri's stressful thoughts let go their hold on him' and he is able to drift off to sleep.

In the concluding pages of the story, he brings the Indian girl alive for Little Bear, and watches what happens from his bed:

> At once he saw her. His whole body gave a jolt. Omri felt a prickling up the back of his neck. The way they looked at each

116

other. It went on a long time. Then, slowly and both together, they rose to their feet.

The Indian and his woman take care of Boone, and Little Bear expresses his pleasure. '"Fit wife for chief. I pay much for her."' Omri explains that it is best that they all go back home, and the Indian understands. Little Bear and Boone have their blood brother ceremony, and the little people are locked in the cupboard for the last time. 'Omri and Little Bear were staring at each other. Something else was needed – some special farewell. It was Little Bear who thought of it. "Omri give hand!"'. The Indian draws blood from Omri's little finger. 'Then Little Bear solemnly pressed his own right wrist against the place and held it there. "Brother," he said, looking up at Omri with his fierce black eyes for the last time.'

When they open the cupboard door again, tearfully, the figures are just crude plastic figures, the shells of what they had been. But the boys realize that they mustn't bring them back again. 'They're home by now,' Patrick says.

Omri then takes the key to his mother, who sees how upset he is. He tells her that it's better if she keeps the key:

'I'll get a chain and wear it,' she said, 'like I always meant to.'
'You won't lose it, will you?'
She shook her head, and suddenly reached for him and hugged his face against her.

The sadness of the end of their adventure reminds one of the end of a child's holiday, when tears can be shed over a place and people that are not to be seen again for a long time. But it is also a moment of transition for Omri, when he is full of memories of closeness to his mother, and yet also at the point when he feels that this time is passing. Omri's understanding that he can't care both for Little Bear and Bright Star (and their children!) is his recognition of the puberty and then grown-up life that awaits him when he, like the Indian, will marry. While this isn't for him yet, he and his friend Patrick are now ready to give up those kinds of play with little toys in which some of their feelings of caring and being cared for could find expression.

The key that his mother will wear round her neck, which was to remind her of her grandmother, is now also to keep her youngest son in her mind, as he grows away from his

117

infancy and the time of his closest touch with her.

The story is a beautiful realization of how a child takes inside himself his parents' care of him, and becomes able to care for others for their own sakes, in his turn. It is also a moving farewell to infancy, giving symbolic expression to the experience of both a mother and a son.

6

Animals in Reality and Fantasy: Two Stories by Philippa Pearce

This chapter is concerned with two of Philippa Pearce's later stories, *A Dog So Small* and *The Battle of Bubble and Squeak*. Each of these stories further explores the theme of loneliness and emotional need central to *Tom's Midnight Garden*. The contemporary urban setting of most children's lives is more in the foreground of these stories than in the first, and a child's attempted escape from the limitations of this environment is in each case described less by depicting an alternative rural world (though this exists for Ben in *A Dog So Small* at his grandparents' house) than by the children's attachment to the aspect of the natural represented by a pet animal or the idea of one. In these two stories, Pearce shows her profound understanding of the longing and affection that children often project into their relations with animals, and in each case is able to show how such feelings are shaped by the vicissitudes of her child characters' relationships with their families at a particular moment of development.

A Dog So Small was published in 1962, four years after *Tom's Midnight Garden*. It also features as its main character a lonely child, a little younger than Tom. He is involved with two families, his own and his grandparents'. His grandparents are very important to him, as a grandmotherly figure comes to be to Tom. The contrast between town and country, the way of life of the urban present and a more rural past, also reappears, though Ben, the main character of the story, lives in South London, and the urban quality of his life there is carefully described. This story is also about the longings and

119

fantasies provoked in a child by loneliness; it is more sombre in quality than the earlier book, and describes a less magical transcendence of the actual limits of his life. The author seems to have remained interested in some of the themes of the earlier book, but has explored them in a more realist mode.

The story begins with Ben's birthday. He is a boy of about ten or eleven, with two younger brothers, Frankie and Paul, very close in age, and much involved with one another; his two elder sisters, May and Dilys, are preoccupied with May's impending marriage. His mother, Mrs Blewitt, is also very involved with the wedding; his father, a London Underground worker, is trying to live the quiet life he prefers in these difficult circumstances. Ben has been promised a dog, he thinks, by his grandpa in the country, and this is the present he is really waiting for. But the only dog that arrives in the post from his grandparents is a picture of a dog, woven in wool, not at all what he wanted. His disappointment and indignation at his grandpa's broken promise is only slightly softened by the apology he finds in the birthday letter: 'Under Granny's nose, but without her knowledge, Grandpa had managed guiltily, hurriedly, urgently, to write a telegraph-sentence of four words: TRULY SORY ABOUT DOG.' Ben's family try to make the best of his present. The picture is of a dog woven on to the palm of a girl's hand; it has 'Chiquitito – Chihuahua' written on it. Ben's mother remembers that it had been brought back originally from Mexico by Tom's Uncle Willy, who, alone of the eight children of his grandparents' family, had died before making a family of his own. The fact that it is precious to his Granny is small consolation to the boy.

But touched by his grandpa's apology to him, Ben does agree to go to visit his grandparents, and their dog Tilly, in Little Barley, near the Castleford of the earlier book. We see how he loves to be in the country with them, enjoying the settled habits of their household, which nevertheless has a large space for him, and which gives him the freedom and pleasure of roaming about the summer countryside with Young Tilly (no longer young in fact), their dog. Though they have many grandchildren, we realize that the grandparents are particularly fond of this boy, responding to his loneliness and his pleasure in their house, where he feels he has particular place.

On the way home on the train, Ben leaves his woolwork picture of the dog behind in the compartment, where it is crushed underfoot by another passenger. Ben is met at the station by his mother and his brothers, and they are taken to the Tower for a typical London treat. It is only later that he discovers that he has lost his picture. But then, just as he is going to sleep, he sees an imaginary dog, who is to be his companion for many weeks:

> He saw nothing: and then he saw a point – something so small that it had neither length nor breadth. But the point was coming towards him, taking on size as it came. He saw what it must be. 'Chiquitito!' he called softly. The dog was racing towards him, appearing even larger as it came nearer; and yet, when it reached him, it was still very, very small. He realized how small when he stretched out his hand to it: his hand looked like a giant's against such a tiny dog. The dog curvetted round him, knowing its name, knowing its master. . . . This was the beginning of their companionship.

Ben is now mainly occupied with his imaginary dog. He obtains lots of information about dogs from the library, somewhat to the alarm of the adult librarian who vaguely senses that there is something wrong. He imagines amazing adventures, in which his tiny Chihuahua fights several packs of wolves, races about the Underground with him, and dives fearlessly into the Thames from the parapets of London bridges. Though Ben 'was inclined to be rather slow and cautious', he 'perhaps for that very reason . . . took a particular delight in the dog's feats.' Ben's imaginary dog also allows Ben to forget the vulnerable small-boy aspects of himself in its superhuman triumphs. For example, he daydreams of a sleigh-ride through the forests, in which his heroic dog fights off packs of wolves who 'die in hundreds'. (Identification with omnipotent heroes, from Superman to footballers, is a frequent theme of the fiction for children of this age.) His state of mind – his eyes closed so that he can *see* his dog – is observed intrusively by his brothers, and he angrily drives them out of their shared bedroom when they question him. His school becomes worried about him, and calls in his mother. They can find nothing out; his mother fails to connect his trance-like state of mind with his birthday disappointment and his desperate longing for a dog. He won't tell her why he so often sits with his eyes shut, or what is the matter. '"But Ben dear, just tell me *why*." "I've told you." It was Mrs Blewitt's turn to sigh. She gave up; but from now on, secretly and fearfully, she watched Ben.'

Ben and his imaginary Chiquitito roam around in a thick London fog during the autumn. Then, on Christmas Eve, Ben is taken with his brothers on a special trip to see the lights and to have tea out, as it is the last Christmas before May is to be married and leave home, together with her sister Dilys who is going to live with the couple in their new flat. For Ben, the trip is an unbearable intrusion on his now-delusional preoccupation with his dog. He can only 'see' his Chihuahua when he closes his eyes, and he cannot close his eyes on this tiresome trip as he is in sight of his family. But on the bus he does close his eyes for a moment, and when he gets off he follows his imaginary dog across the road. There is an accident, and he is knocked by one car into the path of another. The driver 'could not answer the policeman's questions for crying into her handkerchief and repeating over and over again: "But he walked straight into the road with his eyes shut – *with his eyes shut*."' And the van driver supported her evidence. '"He was walking like a sleepwalker – or like a blind man – a blind man being led – you know, a blind man following a guide-dog."' Ben has been wakened from his trance-like state, moments before being struck, by his mother's screaming his name.

> At this moment he could see three dogs – the 'real' Chiquitito that had been his companion for so many weeks, the Chiquitito that had been worked in wool by the nameless little girl in the white dress; and he also saw no-dog – that is, the no-dog in which the other two vanished like a flame blown out, into nothingness. And the last dog he was master of: no-dog. He had no dog.

Ben recovers from his injuries – broken limbs, ribs, and concussion – in hospital, and is visited there by his grandfather on the day of his sister's wedding, in May. His grandpa tells him that Young Tilly is going to pup again, even though they had thought her too old to have any more. Tilly has got together with Toby, a dog that he has seen her excited by during Ben's last visit. It is arranged that he should go to convalesce with his grandparents in the country, and when he arrives Tilly's puppies have already been born. Meanwhile we learn that Mrs Blewitt has come down with him partly to seek her mother's advice on an important family matter – this turns out to be her idea of moving to North London to be near her two daughters in their new flat north of the river. Ben loves being with the puppies, though this is overshadowed by the pain of knowing that he can't have one for himself. His grandmother comes out for the first time to the former pig-sty where the puppies are kept – she does not have much time for the dogs – and Ben sees her watching him. Before he leaves for home, his granny interrupts his reading aloud to her of the Bible, and tells him: '"Ben, you were promised a dog. That promise ought to have been kept – kept properly. We ought to have done that. So, now, one of those puppies is yours by right."' But there is still a problem – he has nowhere in London where he can keep a dog. '"Yes, but . . ."' said Ben heavily. "Yes," said his grandmother. "That's how things are and I'm sorry for it." As she hated to wrap her meanings in politeness or irony or anything but its own truth, Ben knew that she was truly sorry. "And now, boy, go on reading from the Book of the Prophet Jeremiah."'

When Ben goes home, having a dog yet not having a dog, he finds that the flat to which his parents are thinking of moving is near to Parliament Hill, and he discovers the wonderful open spaces of Hampstead Heath. He sees many dogs, playing freely, and realizes that he *could* have a dog if they lived there. He waits impatiently while his parents decide finally to take the flat, then tells them his thoughts; they hadn't realized the possibilities for Ben of living near the Heath, but they agree that he can now have his dog. Ben goes to his grandparents for the day to collect his puppy, and here he begins to discover the difference between a real dog and the dog he has imagined for so long. He wants to call the puppy Chiquitito, when his grandpa and he had already together named it Brown, and it has been brought up to this name. It isn't at all like his imaginary Chihuahua – it is terrified of its journey, and not at all brave or fierce, yet on the other hand it is bigger than he expected. On the journey back, he has to be told by strangers to be kind to the dog, so unresponsive is he to the dog's distress. Hours later,

he remembered taking the dog into the guard's van of the train at Castleford: he had been about to put on the muzzle, according to regulations, when the guard had said, 'Don't you bother with that. The animal looks more afraid of being bitten than likely to bite.' Ben had been humiliated; for the whole journey he sat at a distance, on a crate of chicken, his face turned away from the dog.

Before going home, he takes the dog on to Parliament Hill, avoiding his younger brothers who have come out hoping to meet them. He is relieved to let the dog off the lead, really wanting to be rid of it. On the Heath, he walks off some of his anger, and sits down in the gathering dusk, the rejected and now nameless dog – neither Brown nor Chiquitito – some distance away from him. He thinks of his imaginary dog:

> No Chiquitito . . . Ben let his head fall forward upon his knees and wept for that minute, intrepid, fawn-coloured dog that he could not have. Other people had the dogs they wanted: the Codling boy and the Russian huntsman and people he had seen on the Heath this very afternoon – and, long ago, in Mexico, the little girl in the white dress with long, white, ribboned sleeves. But Ben – no Chiquitito. He shut his eyes tight, but he could see no invisible dog nowadays. He opened his eyes, and for a moment he could see no visible dog either.[1] So the brown dog had gone at last. Then, as Ben's eyes accustomed themselves to the failing light, he could pick him out after all, by his movement: the dog had got up; he was moving away; he was slipping out of sight . . . Then suddenly, when Ben could hardly see he saw clearly. He saw clearly that you couldn't have impossible things, however much you wanted them. He saw that if you didn't have the possible things, then you had nothing.

Ben remembers the frightened dog's need of him on the journey, and the story ends:

> Suddenly, knowing what he had lost – whom he had lost, Ben shouted, 'Brown!' He heard the dog's answering barks, even before he could see him. The dog was galloping towards him out of the dusk, but Ben went on calling: 'Brown, Brown, Brown!' . . . Then Ben stood up again, and Brown remained by his side, leaning against his leg, panting, loving him; and lovingly Ben said, 'It's late Brown. Let's go home.'

Philippa Pearce shows the same intuitive understanding of the reasons for a boy's loneliness in this story as she does in different ways in *Tom's Midnight Garden* and *The Battle of Bubble and Squeak*. In each case, the emotional context is described in a way which makes the child's imaginative preoccupations intelligible. In *A Dog So Small*, Ben is a middle child located between a pair of older sisters and a pair of younger brothers:

To be the middle child of a family of five may not be as sociable and warm as that sociable position sounds. Paul and Frankie were much nearer to each other in age than they were to Ben, and so were May and Dilys. The two youngest and the two eldest made two couples, and in between them came Ben, alone. He had never been much interested in the girls' affairs, anyway. Paul and Frankie followed more sensible pursuits, and Ben sometimes allowed himself to play with them for relaxation. But, really, their games, their plasticine, their igloos made of eggshells and Seccotined cotton-wool and all the rest – these were things he had done with.

Ben's mother is preoccupied with the plans for his sister's wedding, and with her sadness at the idea of both daughters leaving home. And Mr Blewitt

sometimes felt that his five children and their affairs were almost too much for him: May's wedding plans, and Dilys wanting to leave home with her too, and now Ben's dog . . . Mr Blewitt loved his children, of course, but it was really a great relief, nowadays, to go off to work – to slip down the Underground, where there were hundreds of thousands of people on the move, but none of his business so long as they had their tickets and kept clear of the doors. If some of them wanted dogs and could not have them, that was strictly their affair, not his.

It is pointed out that it is because of Ben's being isolated that he 'needed a mature, intelligent, creature-companion. Nowadays it always came back to the same thing: a dog.' It is because 'Ben somehow seemed on his own (that) his grandparents had often had him to stay with them', in their house that has really only room for one grandchild at a time. And they have a dog, so Ben has his companion there too. The nearly-disastrous loss of the puppy at the end happens because Ben is left alone to cope with something which is almost beyond him: even after his illness and accident the family do not find it easy to stay in good contact with him. Ben's 'blindness' seems an echo of the blindness of his parents towards his real state of mind – his father's wish not to have to think about his children, his mother's preoccupation with the daughters she is about to lose, and with her own anticipated loneliness without them. Because he is not - adequately 'seen' by those around him, he feels there is no point in looking around him, and prefers instead to daydream, even to the point of danger. Yet the effect of this behaviour is to get under his mother's skin, so that she has to watch him all the time to hold him in this world. He forces his way into the centre of her mind. One attraction of his grandparents' home is that they both see him, in their different ways, very clearly.

Ben's disappointment with Brown, who does not stay tiny and entirely in the power of Ben's imagination, might be compared with the disappointment a child might feel in his younger siblings, profoundly hoped-for as perfect little companions for himself, then obstinately turning out to have needs and wishes of their own. There is a parallel here with a common childhood experience of disappointment with Christmas and birthday presents, which is described in Ben's reaction to the dog-picture. The intensely precise image of the desired dog/train/sweater clashes unbearably with the gift that does not match its visualized form. A painful disappointment may then be experienced in the trusted giver, whose understanding was imperfect, so there is a double loss for the child. The imaginary dog is also like the imaginary friend that many children invent, the one who would mirror their ideal, be 'right' in every respect. These common experiences of childhood are vividly depicted in this story.

A more implicit theme is that of pre-pubertal awakening and its states of mind. The impending wedding, which he uncomfortably ('warily') overhears his sisters talking about, makes Ben all the more desperate to have the dog he thinks he has been promised by his grandpa. The fact that the woolwork dog is framed within a picture of a little girl's hand and sleeve – the hand perhaps of the person who wove the dog – enters Ben's imagination. Ben often sees in his mind 'the Chiquitito that had been worked in wool long ago by the nameless little girl in the white dress.' Uncle Willy, the original owner of the picture, has died young, without marrying; Ben seems thus to be associated in both his own and his grandmother's mind with someone who died lacking in something or someone. It is relevant too that Young Tilly is a female dog, and there is a latently sexual quality in the boy's play with her in the water. Tilly becomes agitated by the sight of another dog (the father of her previous puppies, we later learn). 'Ben had not meant to bathe again, but now, seeing Till in the poppling water, he could not resist. He dived in and swam under her, which always agitated her.' The

126

sublimation of incipiently sexual feelings in love of animals is more commonly a theme of stories about girls.[2] Here, and in *The Battle of Bubble and Squeak*, Philippa Pearce has shown how similar feelings can be expressed through a boy's companionship with pets.

The particular role of grandparents in the development of a child is another important theme of this book, as it is, much less directly, of *Tom's Midnight Garden*. The story demonstrates the important role of the extended family as a resource in a child's development, allowing him to explore beyond but also to remain attached to his immediate family. Dilys's choice to move out to live with her married sister points in the same direction. Ben values the place he is given in the lives of his grandparents, all the more because it is so firmly structured by the settled pattern of their lives. He has regular tasks, set by the physical limitations of the old people. He is sent upstairs to put away his mother's letter to his grandmother on its usual pile. He reads to his granny from the Bible, her preferred reading. His grandparents give him a concentrated but circumscribed attention, which gives him the feeling of being held firmly in their minds while leaving him – usually – unintruded upon. But when it matters, his granny knows what is worrying him, where his own parents don't. '"Not interested in stamps now?"' she asks him, insisting on the plain truth when he politely refuses her offer of foreign stamps from a letter.

'No.'
'But in dogs?'
'Yes,' said Ben, quickly and truthfully because he had to, but unwillingly.
'Disappointed you didn't have a live dog on your birthday?'
The clash and splash of washing up stopped in the scullery. Ben was silent too. 'Answer,' said his grandmother.
'Yes,' said Ben.

She then explains the good reasons why the promise couldn't be kept, the weight of the promise (so important to children) contending in her mind with the practical difficulties and with her own antipathy to dogs, about which she and her husband have disagreed for a lifetime.

Ben is made aware of his grandpa's pride in him indirectly, when he realizes that his grandpa has worn his best blue suit to meet him from the train, and from his conversation with the bus driver:

> 'Fine day, Grandpa,' said the driver of the Yellow Salden bus, who was leaning against his vehicle, smoking. He knew that old Mr Fitch lived halfway to Salden, by the driftway beyond Little Barley.
> 'It is, Bob,' said Grandpa. 'Got my grandson with me.'
> 'Wouldn't know you apart,' said the driver, and winked at Ben.

It is clear that this rather lonely boy has a special place in his grandparents' lives, and they in his. Ben thinks of his much-loved grandfather's face when he reads his apologetic message about the dog. 'He could almost see his grandfather's hand writing that, his fingers clamped around the pen, desperately driving it through the curves and angles of the capital letters.' He is able to feel protective about his old grandparents' limitations and anxieties. Grandparents and grandchild have a good understanding of each other, created out of the ordinary routine by the infrequency and specialness of their meetings. The grandparents' acceptance of life as it is makes them able to bear Ben's pain, and still remain available to him. Granny watches Ben's departure with his new dog, and understands: '"People get their heart's desire," she said, "and then they have to learn to live with it."'

But the central issue of the story is the relation of imagination to the loneliness and emotional needs of a child. *A Dog So Small* explores this theme in a more sombre way than the other two stories we discuss in this chapter. Because of its realist form, its descriptions of states of feeling and their objects are less metaphorical in quality. The author makes it explicit *why* this boy wants a dog so much. But in this story, the imaginary object created to fill the space in the boy's life does not magically meet the boy's needs, as the adventure of *Tom's Midnight Garden* seems to do. This is a story about a symbolization that fails. The object sent to stand for the dog Ben wants, and also for the memory of his uncle, is first cracked and then lost. Ben tries to use an ever-diminishing part of the wished-for object – first picture, then memory of picture – to fill this space in his heart. It is consistent with the more realist mode of this story (to use David Lodge's terms[3]) that the imaginary dog is a metonymic (part of a more total reality) as well as a metaphoric symbol. Ben's attempt to

128

create in fantasy what has been denied to him in fact becomes a virtual hallucination, a delusion, and takes the boy so far out of contact with the everyday world as to end in the near tragedy of his road accident. The most truthful and powerful passage of the story is where Ben goes to collect his puppy, and cannot cope with the reality of a dog he had so intensely and omnipotently imagined. Ben's disappointment and feeling of vulnerability make him cruel to the pathetically vulnerable dog. While the story ends happily, and Ben learns just in time to recognize the dog's independent existence and real need of him, and to accept what is possible, it brings the reader close to the tragic experience of the frustration of a profound desire. The author avoids a merely sentimental resolution of the story, by taking her main character, and thus her readers, unexpectedly to the very brink of failure.

Imagination fails as a form of magic transcendence twice over. Not only for the boy, that is, but also for his grandmother. She had imagined that the picture brought by her dead son would have the same meaning for Ben as it did for her. It stood for her as a reminder of her son and the girl he might have had for himself; it was to represent for Ben the 'mature companion' he so much wanted and which his grandparents wanted to give him. But as Frankie rightly says, "'it's a funny birthday present for Ben,'" and his mother's explanation that "'Granny's given you something that was precious to her,'" doesn't help much. Ben's attempt to make something of the largely symbolic present in fact proves too much for him; this boy is not able to hold properly distinct from one another symbol and real thing. The story describes a boy's state of mind when symbolization and imagination cannot cope, a state of mind perhaps related to that which the psychoanalytic concept of transitional object, neither part of self, other person, nor symbol, describes in infancy. The actual picture gets lost, and has to survive as a hope in Ben's mind. It then becomes a magical substitute for the reality, which is the unbearable mental space of no-dog, an almost unbearable absence. It is at the point when Ben sees 'no-dog' that he falls under a car, though this momentary recognition of the truth also marks the beginning of his psychological recovery. Ben and his grandmother come to terms in their different ways with what has happened, Ben through his instinct for survival and by the efforts of his family, Granny by coming to think out, in her own terms, the overriding claims of truth:

129

'It was only that I thought Grandpa had promised . . .' Ben's voice died away. Grandpa was looking at the floor beneath his feet; Granny was looking at Ben. She said: 'And a promise is a promise, as a covenant is a covenant: both to be kept. But, if you're not God Almighty, there's times when a promise can't be kept.' She looked at Grandpa: 'Times when a promise should never have been made, for that very reason.' Now she was looking neither at Ben nor at Grandpa, as she concluded: 'Even so, a promise that can't be kept should never be wriggled out of. It should never be kept twistily. That was wrong.' Granny in the wrong: that was where she had put herself. There was an appalled silence.

The grandmother's strict regard for truthfulness is nicely conveyed in her discriminating attitude to the Bible by which in fact she lives. As Ben reads to her she continually muses over what she is hearing, decides what is true to her experience and what is not. Ben reads:

'And it came to pass after seven days, that the waters of the flood were upon the earth. In the six hundredth year of Noah's life – ' Granny said under breath something which sounded surprisingly like 'Sez you!' 'In the second month, the seventeenth day of the month, the same day were all the fountains of the great deep broken up, and the windows of heaven were opened – ' 'Joe!' cried Mrs Fitch. 'The skylight window – you forgot it!' 'No,' said Grandpa. 'I remembered.'

The point about the grandmother's relation to the truth of the Bible is that even it needs to be thought about, strenuously worked on.

'Don't say it!' Granny interrupted. 'That's what they used to say in chapel. If there was something foolish or downright wicked in a Bible reading, they'd say, "Oh, but of course Sister Fitch it doesn't really mean that at all." But if it was something they fancied anyway, they'd say, "Why, but of course, Sister Fitch, it means just what it says." I know 'em!'

But we also see the confident faith which underlies Granny's awkward independence. Ben has been reading from Genesis, the passage about the rainbow after the flood. (Granny has chosen the reading because it is torrentially wet.) '"I do set my bow in the cloud, and it shall be for a token of a covenant between me and the earth."' The

130

following morning, Granny comes into his room and wakes
him.

His grandmother, in her nightgown, was standing by his bed.
'Look through the window!' she said. It was daylight, but very
early. There were clouds still in the sky, but shifting and
vanishing; and the rain had almost stopped. 'Look, and you'll see
how He keeps His promise, keeps it twice over!' And Ben saw that
the early morning sun, shining on rainclouds and rain, had made
a double rainbow.

The contrast of town and country, hurried present and
more settled past, is a major theme of this story as it was of
Tom's Midnight Garden. London provides both Ben and his
father with a spacious sense of being alone and free amidst
large numbers of people, one of the typical experiences of the
city. Ben's family seem to relate in no particular way to their
neighbourhood in South London. As Mrs Blewitt points out
to her husband, 'that for someone with Mr Blewitt's kind of
Underground job, there wasn't much to choose between
living towards the southern end of the Northern line, as they
did at present, and living towards the northern end of the
same line, as they would be doing.' Ben's freedom to travel
on the Tube, and his conversations with strangers such as the
park keeper and librarian, also demonstrate both the space
that the city provides for self-exploration, and the loneliness
to which it can lead. The park keeper's observations to Ben on
the by-laws concerning dogs are amusingly observed. But it is
also to be noted that these strangers encountered in London
do not take the opportunity to get into real touch with Ben, as
Paula Fox shows can happen in *A Likely Place* with Lewis and
the old man he meets in Central Park. Mr Blewitt's work on
the Underground, tied to no place in particular, contrasts
with Mr Fitch's lifetime of work on the roads in the country,
which seems to have rooted him firmly above ground in a
relationship to a particular space. The family have the
London treats of the Tower and the Christmas lights, little
use as they are at this moment to Ben.

On the other hand, Little Barley is described as a known
community in a different sense. A passenger gets on the
wrong bus at Castleford for lack of personal knowledge – it is
not enough merely to read the destination sign on this village
bus to know which bus to catch. The driver knows Mr Fitch.

131

The young next-door neighbour pops in and out to help Ben's arthritic grandmother. Ben's Grandpa knows the people in the boat that comes by, and Young Tilly knows Toby, the dog. There is the countryside, and the seasons, and swimming naked in the river. And while Ben seems to fall through the spaces of the London family, no-one really noticing him, his grandparents do think about him, allowing him a special place in the routine of their days. The role of the Bible, and of firm moral beliefs in his grandmother's life are another aspect of the more structured and dependable qualities of an older form of life.

Yet the outcome of the contrast isn't simply a nostalgic preference for the old and the country over the new and city. Ben and his father both like London, belong to the capital.

Ben liked to rattle down moving staircases to platforms where subterranean winds wafted the coming of the trains; he liked to burrow along below London. Above ground, he liked to sail high on the tops of London buses, in the currents of traffic. He liked the feel of paving stones hard beneath his feet, the streaming splendour of a wet night with all the lamps and lights shining and reflected, the smell of London. After all, London – a house in a row in a back street just south of the River – was his home.

The river is especially important to Ben, and provides plenty of scope for his imagination. After the event of Ben's accident, people are very kind – even the policeman and the two drivers visit him in hospital. The antithesis of town and country is resolved by Ben's discovery of Hampstead Heath – a real wilderness within the town, where it is possible to have a dog – and by the continuing strength of the link between Ben and his grandparents, Ben's mother and *her* mother.

Mrs Fitch woke with a start and in some confusion of mind, so that – simply and solely, without time for thought – she saw her daughter. 'Lil!' she cried, and Lily Blewitt ran forward into her open arms. Ben hung back in the doorway, watching, feeling forgotten and odd for a moment, as he saw his own mother become the child of *her* mother.

Or as Mr Blewitt puts it, a propos of moving, '"I suppose it all comes down to this," said Mr Blewitt. "You and your ma have made a plan. So it's as good as decided."' During the story, four different journeys take place which bring members of the town and country families together. The plot after all centres on whether or not it will be possible to bring a dog bred at his grandparents' house in Little Barley to live in their house in London. Philippa Pearce knows she is writing books for modern children who mostly live in cities. What her stories attach value to is not the past in preference to the present, or the country in preference to the town, but to maintaining the connections between them, in life and in mind.

The Battle of Bubble and Squeak

This story, published in 1978, twenty years after *Tom's Midnight Garden*, is much simpler in its language and structure than Philippa Pearce's other books. It is intended for younger children, and the author, as in *A Dog So Small*, chooses a working-class setting for the story, rather than her usual more middle-class milieux. While it seems to be the simplest of stories, it shows Pearce's characteristic sensitivity to family relationships, and to states of mind and feeling in children and adults which can best be explored metaphorically. The story has in fact no less emotional depth than the first and best known of her books for children.

Bubble and Squeak are two gerbils belonging to Sid, the eldest of a family of three who live on a council estate. The children's father, David Parker, whose surname they still have, died soon after the youngest daughter, Amy, was born. They now live with their mother, Alice, and their stepfather, Bill Sparrow. Bill works in the nearby warehouses of the General Supply Company, and Alice works in the offices of the same company. Bubble and Squeak have been given to Sid by a boy at school – his friend Jimmy Dean's cousin – who has emigrated to Australia. (Bubble and Squeak is also the name of a dish made of leftover potato and cabbage; this, like the ordinary and homely associations of the name Sparrow, helps to establish the social location of the family.) Sid's sisters, Peggy and Amy, are entranced with the gerbils, and Bill, his stepfather, remembers, sympathizing with the children, the white mice he had when he was a boy. But Sid's mother, Alice, hates the gerbils, and as soon as she discovers them she wants them out of the house. The 'battle' of the title is the family argument about getting rid of or keeping the gerbils, which involves threats of death and a near-fatal accident to one of the gerbils.

The noise of the gerbils (a squeaking treadmill and the gnawing of the bars of their cage) wakes up Mrs Sparrow. Bill is sent to investigate the strange sounds, and finds Sid trying desperately to quieten the little animals. Then Alice comes down too: 'The kitchen lights blazed on; the larder door was flung wide; Alice Sparrow stood in the doorway, like a flaming torch, leaving no corner unlit, catching in her glare her husband and her son. Catching them red-handed.' There is a row there and then in the middle of the night, Mrs Sparrow discovers where they came from, and insists that they go back:

'The Garden Centre isn't far. You can take those rats back.'
'They'll never take them back!' cried Sid.
'As a gift they will,' said his mother. 'They can sell them twice then, to two sets of fools.'
'Please, Mum!' He was almost crying.

Bill ends the quarrel for the moment by saying that he will take them back. Sid is very angry with his mother and stepfather.

But Mrs Sparrow comes back home from work next day to find her children playing delightedly with the gerbils on the living-room table. Bill has brought them back: '"Sid was quite right. The Pet Department wouldn't take them at any price. I had to bring them home again."' Next, Mrs Sparrow advertises the gerbils in a local newsagent: FREE: TWO VERY ATTRACTIVE GERBILS WITH CAGE, FOOD AND BEDDING. Two boys come to take them. This time Sid runs off in rage and despair to hide out in a nearby wood which is used as a local dumping ground. Bill finds him there, and explains, in response to his stepson's accusations of betrayal and cowardice in face of Alice, that he brought the gerbils back from the Garden Centre deliberately, without even trying to leave them there. Bill is able to make friends with Sid, and offers secretly to put back the knife (his real father's) that Sid had taken from his mother's drawer.

The gerbils are again returned, this time by the mother of the two small boys.

She was unpleasantly polite. 'We have come to return your kind gift,' she said. 'In my opinion, parents should always be consulted before children are given presents which parents may not want. We have had animals similar to these in the past. They bred. We don't want them again. *Any more than you seem to want them.'*

The family seems to settle down with the gerbils, who have a brief 'holiday' with their neighbours, the Mudds, in a plan of the children to give their mother time to get used to the idea of having them permanently. But when the gerbils come back, there is a disaster. Their cage is left on the window sill, behind Mrs Sparrow's best scarlet curtains, and they eat large holes in them. Mrs Sparrow again resolves to get rid of them once and for all, and leaves the cage out for the dustbin men, but her new plan fails too:

> Later, nearly at breakfast-time, there was a ring at the doorbell. She answered it. One of the dustbin men stood there. He held the gerbil cage in front of him. 'Missus,' he said, 'you can't do this. There's something alive in here.'

Her youngest daughter Amy has seen what has happened, and is very upset.

> Amy looked past her. She saw the dustman and the cage he held. She looked past him. She saw the huge van that had drawn just past the front gate. She saw the open back of the van and the great fangs that closed slowly and opened . . . and closed . . . and opened . . . She began to scream.

The gerbils are again reinstated, and this time catastrophe strikes them by accident. The family is becoming more relaxed about the animals, and Amy disobeys Sid's instructions and plays with them out of their cage one day before school. In the rush to leave, she fails to close the cage door, and they escape. Sid spends the day in the house recapturing the missing gerbil, and keeping it from the attentions of the next door cat whose services as a rat-catcher have been kindly offered by their neighbour, Mrs Pring. Philippa Pearce shows her observant way with animals as well as people when Sid flings Ginger out of the window to keep it away from the gerbil:

> Ginger landed neatly on all four paws, but was displeased – one could see that. He sat down at once and began cleaning himself, as though he had never really meant to go gerbil-hunting. What

he had always really intended was to clean himself in the fresh air.

But Ginger returns in the evening, springs on the cage while the family are watching television, and catches one of the gerbils in his mouth. It is Mrs Parker who has the presence of mind to rescue it, hauling on Ginger's tail until he drops the gerbil, but getting scratched quite badly in the process. Mr Sparrow reassembles the cage, and the gerbils are restored to their home. All seems well, but next day Bubble, the gerbil who has been in Ginger's mouth, seems very ill. Bill Sparrow is pessimistic:

> Then he looked at Bubble, held cupped in Sid's hands. He looked long, and then he cleared his throat. 'I had a white mouse. A cat mauled it. The mouse had to be put out of its misery. It was kinder. It had to be destroyed . . .'

But Mrs Sparrow is now concerned about the gerbils' well-being for the first time. 'From her chair, Mrs Sparrow, hearing him, groaned.'

Sid and Peggy take Bubble to the vet, who, while holding out little hope and offering to 'keep' the injured animal, prescribes an antibiotic which the children can try if they wish. But holding the gerbil still while Sid administers the drops proves too difficult for Peggy, and the medicine won't go down. She despairs:

> Peggy let Bubble go and burst into tears. Sid lifted him by his tail and put him back into his hay. Then he sat down at the table again. He was trembling. Mrs Sparrow came in from the kitchen. 'Have you finished?'
> 'No,' said Bill Sparrow.
> Peggy wept and wept. 'I can't – I can't!'

But again Mrs Sparrow takes a hand.

> Peggy sobbed: 'I'll go and fetch Dawn.'
> Mrs Sparrow said, 'You'll do no such thing. Show me, Sid.'
> Peggy hushed suddenly. Bill Sparrow put his newspaper away. Sid got Bubble out again, and showed his mother where her grip should be.
> 'Right!' said Mrs Sparrow. She had never touched one of the gerbils before, but all her mind and will concentrated on taking hold of this one.

The gerbil is cured, and when finally a boy of Sid's age appears at the door to take back the gerbils ('"Please," he said, "I'm Jimmy Dean's cousin. We've come back from Australia. It didn't suit. Please, I'd like my gerbils back again"), the whole family is united in persuading him that this is now the gerbils' home, and that he should use the money he has offered to buy some new ones instead. Amy and Peggy console him with the idea that he can now get a male and a female gerbil and let them mate. Let them have babies.'

'Babies! Babies! Babies!' cried Amy.

Jimmy Dean's cousin was very much taken with the idea. 'But I don't know what my mum and dad would say,' he said.

'Pooh!' said Mrs Sparrow. 'They'll just have to put up with it won't they?'

When her husband in the final pages of the story plays a Christmas joke by giving them all sugar-mice, 'Mrs Sparrow gave a wild screech of laughter that drowned everyone else's'.

This story works so well in its apparently simple and literal terms that explanation or interpretation of its moving force may seem unnecessary. It is, at one level, a story of a family argument about keeping pets. Since child readers will naturally identify with both the gerbils and their would-be owners, and will be satisfied by an outcome in which the parents eventually relent, the story's success with children may not seem to require much interpretation.

Yet it is worth noting how subtly the story renders a working-class milieu, both through its characters and in its language. Both Mr Sparrow and Mrs Sparrow are people who have learned to endure, Mr Sparrow with irony, Mrs Sparrow with determination.

But there seemed no doubt that she did not feel as badly about gerbils as she had once done. She put up with them. She did not love them – any more than she loved other things she had put up with. She put up with the draught through the back door, and old Mrs Pring's cats, and Bill Sparrow's gardening boots. She loved none of these things, but she put up with them. Now she had begun putting up with gerbils.

Her son takes after her: 'Sid now stood up in front of the

137

gerbils' cage, meeting his mother's gaze, enduring it.' There is an assumption in the family that the children must do what their parents tell them, without too many explanations being given. When they don't, there are rows. Mrs Sparrow tells Sid, '"How many times have I got to say that we're not having animals in this house. You've roller-skates and a camera and a transistor: what more do you want?"' Much of the linguistic vitality of the story comes from its use of everyday phrases taken from a shared habit of speech, but given real force by the particular moment and manner of use. Mrs Sparrow is especially vivid in her comments on her neighbours.

It is also important that the author tells us that this is a family in which a stepfather, Bill Sparrow, has taken the place of the children's real father who has died some years before; the story gives some emphasis to this. The older children think about their father. Sid steals his father's knife from his mother's drawer, and threatens Bill with it in the pitch-dark wood (though he does not, perhaps, know for certain that it is Bill). Peggy answers her inquisitive friend Dawn's question about her real father:

'Was he nicer than Bill Sparrow?'
'Yes. Well, really, I suppose I just don't know. Bill's not bad. My real dad – I remember he used to give me his finger to hold, instead of his hand . . . She brooded. 'Sid remembers him properly. Amy doesn't remember him at all.'

But the reader already knows that Amy and Bill have the special way of holding hands that Peggy has described as her real father's. In some way, the memory of the dead father is still in everyone's mind.

In her quarrel with the children and with Bill over the gerbils, Mrs Sparrow is continuing a disagreement with her first husband:

On the other hand, she didn't like animals, had never liked animals, and never would like animals. It was bad luck that the three children had not taken after her in this. They were like their father, who had died soon after Amy was born. No doubt, if he had lived, the house would have swarmed with cats, dogs, rabbits, guinea pigs, hamsters, budgerigars and canaries in yellow clouds. What would she have been like then? Alice drank her tea slowly, and thought all kinds of things.

Bill, her second husband, remembers the white mice he kept when he was a boy, and would like to help the children keep the animals. But he doesn't want to upset his wife, and will only intervene by stealth. He seems dominated by Mrs Sparrow. In the matter of his liking for pets, as perhaps in other respects, he is not being allowed fully to take the place her first husband would have asserted for himself in the house. Bill is a reparative man, who clears up the coal, goes to search for the angry son, makes a new cage, massages his wife's back when she is upset – even his warehousing job implies looking after things.

Amy, the youngest child, is entranced with the idea that the gerbil couple might have babies. It is this idea that new gerbils might mate that persuades Jimmy Dean's cousin (known by his family, not by his name) to leave Bubble and Squeak with the Sparrows. Babies are being thought of at the end, even though they will be those of other gerbils, and not Bubble and Squeak's. It seems that the gerbils stand for new babies in the Parker-Sparrow family, and are a focus for conflict because of what imaginary babies mean for the various members. The noise of the gerbils woke Mrs Sparrow, 'as the crying of her children would have woken her'. The gerbils have to be cleaned and fed all the time like young children, and the visit to·the vet and the antibiotics that are prescribed are another reminder of infancy. Amy was only a baby when her mother was widowed – she did not know her real father. Mrs Sparrow seems to feel that she has been left with too many children to look after. This comes out in her scorn for other neighbouring families with children who have come late: 'Mrs Sparrow had once said sarcastically (of Dawn) that she ought to have been Sunset Mudd: she was the last – after a long gap in time – of a very large family.' And of Peter Peters, Amy's friend, she says, 'They must have been at their wits' end for names when *he* was born.' These gerbil babies seem to have been abandoned too, like her real ones, by their owners going away to Australia, so far away. Babies mean the dirt, demands and confusion that she spends her life keeping under control. We see that she has managed her bereavement and her being left with the children in this controlling way, and by never giving way to her feelings of anger and despair. When the gerbils are brought back by Bill from the Garden Centre, she sees her family playing with what seem like twenty gerbils:

Everyone was laughing, not loudly, but softly, affectionately. And Bill stood over them, laughing too. Mrs Sparrow stood in the doorway, and looked. They never noticed her. She backed out and slammed the door – but perhaps they never noticed that either? She went into the kitchen and sat down. She felt like screaming and screaming; but she knew that she never screamed.[4]

For the somewhat bullied Bill, the gerbils bring back his own boyhood, and enable him to identify closely with his stepchildren. But the gerbil-babies that are not allowed by Mrs Sparrow also suggest the new babies that he and Mrs Sparrow do not have together, and whose absence seems to leave him as something less than a real father in the household. Bill has to make a point of raising his voice for his remarks about the gerbils and his white mice even to be heard by his wife. Bill can only dream of 'the garden: monster marrows, and runner beans that towered over their apple tree.' The Bubble and Squeak couple (Dawn thinks they are both male) who are not able to have children are perhaps like the Bill and Alice couple who don't have any children in *their* marriage.

The story is perceptive about the different feelings of the children, who have experienced at different ages the loss of their father and their mother's re-marriage. Sid, the eldest, is both closely tied to his mother, yet also trying to establish a distance from her, and from intense feelings in general. The gerbils are important as something for which a boy, much given to football and fighting with his friend Jimmy Dean, is able to express love, though even so he doesn't show his feeling for them as his sister does. ('"Why does he want them then, when he seems hardly to bother with them?", his mother asked his stepfather. "I remember my white mice," said Bill Sparrow.') Sid's anxiety about the gerbils when they escape – 'It was extraordinary how nervous he felt' – is a state of mind similar to that explored by Lynn Reid Banks in *The Indian in the Cupboard*, in which she describes a boy's experience of caring for a quasi-infant. Sid imagines the gerbils in their natural habitat – the hot desert – and at risk in the world, just as he begins to think of being independent himself. 'He imagined Bill Sparrow riding along with the gerbil cage in his bicycle basket, the gerbils keeping their footing with difficulty, like tiny sailors in a rough sea.' All the older children are fascinated by the gerbils' natural habitat.

140

The animals for these children like Omri in *The Indian in the Cupboard*, are a way of imagining life beyond the confines of their housing estate. Peggy 'wondered what it was like to see everything through bars, to have beneath your feet a little sawdust-covered metal floor instead of the vast Mongolian desert. To have bars above you, and above the bars a white ceiling, instead of blue infinity.' The author cleverly has the gerbils express feelings for the family, within the bounds of plausibility. '"That's one of those gerbil-things," Mrs Sparrow said in the voice of a sleepwalker. The gerbil seemed not to like her tone, for it withdrew into the tube again.' And when they are first discovered by Mrs Sparrow, 'The only indication of their presence in the cage was the drumming of tiny feet on the floor of the bedroom. The gerbils were drumming the alarm for extreme danger.'

It is Sid and his mother who are woken by the gerbils, as if by a shared preoccupation. When his stepfather comes down and offers a complicit joke about the gerbils, Sid is more concerned about his mother's reaction. 'But Sid rarely smiled at his stepfather's jokes. He asked, "Did Mum hear?"' Sid understands his mother. The night after she has left the gerbils out for the dustbin men, he explains to Peggy what was in her mind: 'Sid said carefully: "I don't think she really knew herself what she meant to happen. She was a bit off her head. She still is, a bit. All right: she promised. But she only needs some cast-iron excuse."'

Sid feels betrayed when Bill takes the gerbils back, and reproaches him bitterly for his subservience to mother:

'Well,' said Bill. 'I hadn't much choice in coming. Your mum sent me out.'
Sid was furious. 'Can't you do anything on your own? Do you always have to do what she says?'
'No,' said Bill. 'But mostly.'

Sid cannot identify with a father figure who is so dominated by mother. His gerbils may be seen as an oedipal bid to produce *his* babies for mother, which leads to rage and despair when his precious offer to the family is rejected. Sid is pushed back into a despairing identification with his dead father. The wood in which he hides is, as Dawn Mudd tells Mr Sparrow, not a nice place, 'somewhere to feel awful in.' It is full of rotting, dumped things. Bill stumbles in terror, when a tree gives way in his hand. 'It was supported by its companions, dead on its feet, the corpse of a tree.' Sid threatens Bill in the darkness. 'Then, much closer than he [Bill] could ever have expected it, came Sid's voice. It sounded thin and hard. Very unpleasant. "I've got a knife," said Sid.' But when Bill explains that he had earlier brought the gerbils back from the Garden Centre of his own accord, Sid is softened. Bill offers to help him:

'You might get two more.'
'You mean, in spite of Mum? *Against* Mum?'
'She'd have to be talked round.'
'And who'd do that?'
'Well, I'd try.'
'Why?'
'I'm' – Bill Sparrow hesitated. 'I'm your stepfather. And, when I was your age, I had white mice.'

Bill thus resolves the rivalry between them, by his identification with Sid's wishes. Sid is able to tell Bill he has got foul stuff on his shoes on the way into the wood, and Bill tells him in his matter-of-fact way to clean it off. Bill can now be trusted to know about the murderous and messy parts of Sid, and can help him to sort them out.

Amy is the youngest child in the family, and the nearest to being a baby herself. She is the recipient of tender feelings which are generally repressed in the family, and which are even expressed towards her in a rather secret way. Her mother embraces her when she is asleep in her bed: 'Her mother knelt by her bed, put her arms round her, hugged her. There was little fear of disturbing Amy. She hugged her, kissed her, buried her face in the warmth of sleeping little girl. She knelt there for minutes.' Amy and Bill also seem to be closest when Amy has him to herself: 'She followed him while he put his bike away. She touched his left hand with her right one – it was her signal. He stuck out a finger. She wrapped her hand round it and they walked indoors together.' Amy is the most upset by her mother's hostility to the gerbils, perceiving it as a hatred of babies that *she* feels identified with. It is Amy's distress when the gerbils are nearly put in the dustcart which makes Mrs Sparrow relent and agree to keep the gerbils. Mrs Sparrow tries to explain to the crying child:

'Amy,' her mother said. 'Listen, Amy. I didn't mean them to go in the van. Truly. I put them on top of the dustbin, not inside. Truly. I thought one of the dustbin men might have a little girl that liked gerbils.'

Amy wailed, 'I'm a little girl that likes gerbils! I love Bubble and Squeak!' She still cried, but she was beginning to allow her mother to cuddle her. This was as her mother talked to her, coaxed her, promised her. Mrs Sparrow found herself promising that – No, she wouldn't send Bubble and Squeak away. She would never send them away.

Mrs Sparrow has to agree to tolerate the gerbil-babies in response to the feelings of her own infant daughter. Amy has a nightmare about the gerbils, and both parents have to comfort her again. 'Bill Sparrow carried her downstairs to look at the gerbil cage, quiet and safe, and then carried her back to bed. At last everyone was in bed again, free to sleep again.' Amy expects both her mother and her father to share her love of babies, and this is the first time the parents have been together in their acceptance of the gerbils.

Peggy, the middle child, is a little less involved in the family crisis than her siblings. She has a good friend, Dawn, with whom she can stay overnight, and whose easygoing and welcoming household is in contrast to the over-controlled Sparrow family. Dawn is the last of many children; Mrs Mudd is knitting placidly for an unborn grandchild, one of many, and Mr Mudd keeps pigeons, whose droppings are in demand among the estate's dahlia-growers, which include Bill. They have an easier attitude to mess than the Sparrows. Peggy is less upset by her mother's hostility to the gerbils than Amy and Sid. She wants to believe her mother's promises, but when she realizes that Sid is probably right about them, it is she who thinks up the practical idea of giving the gerbils a holiday at the Mudds'. Peggy is also the only child who can actually tell the two gerbils apart. Whereas Sid is lonely, and angry with his substitute father, Peggy talks to Dawn about both him and her real father without reproach. In their enjoyment of the gerbils, and especially when Bubble becomes ill, Peggy and Sid are able to get closer together, boy and girl in better contact with one another. As they are taking the gerbil to the vet on the bus, 'Tears of hopelessness rolled down her cheeks. Sid had been watching the passengers reflected in the glass of the bus window. He watched Peggy. He did not turn his head towards her, but his hand picked up her hand and gripped it.' Just as Mrs Sparrow has earlier responded to Amy's distress, so her maternal feelings and capacities are awakened by Peggy's misery when she cannot manage the gerbil's medicine, and she takes her place holding the gerbil, supporting her son and daughter's parental efforts for their injured pet.

The development of the story shows the members of the family brought together by their conflict over the gerbils. While at the beginning they were able to function only by closing off many painful feelings, by the end Mrs Sparrow is better able to accept the more needy and passionate aspects of her children. Whereas she consoled herself at one point with the thought that gerbils live for only three years (the limited time she feels she can cope with children, perhaps), by the end they are to be cared for like members of the family. The curious and playful gerbils allow the children a scope for playing happily together which does not seem to have been otherwise easy within the family. Alice comes not to mind it when the gerbils' adventures untidy the house. The infantile qualities of the feelings evoked by the gerbils are revealed in the oral associations so frequent in fiction for young children. The gerbils eat everything in sight – including Mrs Sparrow's curtains, perhaps a metaphor for her feeling of having holes eaten into her by her children after her first husband died. Feeding them is a great pleasure for the children. 'But, they wouldn't get peanuts anywhere but in that cage. That's for certain,' Dawn Mudd tells Peggy. Ginger, on the other hand, wants to eat the gerbils, and the dustcart is seen by Amy as having cruel fangs. Bill's concluding joke with the sugar-mice makes public within the family his childhood love of white mice, when earlier Mrs Sparrow had told him sharply, 'You keep quiet about that.' It may perhaps be a sexual allusion in Bill's joke (as there may be in the gerbils' love of tunnels and ticklish trips from sleeves to trouser-legs) which makes Alice laugh so much. She originally regarded the gerbils as 'smelly little rats' and wanted to hear nothing more of her two husbands' love of animals; now she can enjoy his joke about mice sweet enough to eat. The family at the end get together to persuade Jimmy Dean's cousin, now returned, that he doesn't want *these* gerbils, whom only they know how to look after. They all sit down together to bubble and squeak for tea, once Bill has explained to Amy that they won't be eating fried gerbil.'Bill explained to Amy, and she said happily: "Not Bubble and Squeak. *Never* dear Bubble and Squeak."' The animals are no longer symbols of internal confusion, for any of the family.

The author has succeeded in finding a metaphor for an intense experience of conflict and development within a family, in terms which remain wholly within the understanding of young children.

7

The Poetic Power of Ordinary Speech: E. B. White's Children's Stories

Re-reading and thinking about E.B. White's books for children during a year's recent stay in the United States brought us in contact with the extraordinary place his work occupies in that part of children's cultural experience that is shared with adults. *Charlotte's Web* is a book people remember having listened to in school, and these recollections include the class's tears over Charlotte's death. In local library surveys of 'most popular' books amongst today's American children, it regularly tops the list. It has also achieved a prominent place in children's reading on the British side of the Atlantic, perhaps loved not only for its remarkable engagement with universal emotional experience – love and dependence, loss and death, growth and change – and the way in which White brings fundamental, often unconscious, childhood anxieties into the realm of thought and imagination, but also for its distinctively American qualities. The hero and heroine belong in a tradition of triumphant optimistic individualism, in which the individual is nourished by family and community and his or her identity acquired and sustained through intertwined living with others. This is a pattern of life ideally attuned to the younger child's vision, and an ideal of personal and social integration which remains powerfully attractive long after childhood ends.

Charlotte's Web is in our view one of the very best children's stories to be published since the war. Our discussion of this story, principally understood by us as a fable of the ordinary processes of the development of an infant, follows a brief

146

summary of the narrative. The story begins with the discovery by an eight-year-old girl, Fern, that her father is about to kill one of a newborn litter of pigs, because 'it's very small and weak, and will never amount to anything.' She is upset, and her father lets her raise the little piglet with a bottle. When the pig, whom Fern has named Wilbur, has grown to five weeks, Fern's father says he must be sold. This time Fern's mother, Mrs Arable, comes to the rescue, with the idea that the pig can go to the farm belonging to Fern's Uncle Homer if Fern will telephone and sell it to him.

Fern visits Wilbur every day in the Zuckermans' barn. There it turns out that there is a community of animals – sheep, geese, a rat called Templeton, roosters – who talk to Wilbur. Wilbur is nevertheless feeling lonely and bored in his pen, but is offered friendship by Charlotte, a spider. He at first finds her way of life – catching and eating flies in her web – cruel and distasteful, but he comes to find that she is a kind and good friend to him.

The most dramatic events of the story happen when it is revealed that Wilbur is soon to be killed for ham and bacon by Mr Zuckerman. Charlotte decides that she will save him, and using all her skill in web-spinning she creates a sensation in the district by one night writing the words SOME PIG in her web. With the aid of Templeton the rat's foraging for pieces of writing, she follows this with TERRIFIC and RADIANT, with the object of making Wilbur so famous and precious to his human owners that they will not want to kill him. Finally, Wilbur is taken to compete at the local fair and Charlotte, again with Templeton's help, writes HUMBLE in her web to win him a prize and the certainty that he will not be killed.

By now Fern, whose earlier preoccupation with the animals and their conversations has worried her mother, has become more interested in riding on the Ferris Wheel with a boy, Henry Fussy. Charlotte is meanwhile preoccupied not only with saving Wilbur through her writing, but also having her own babies, something which we gradually understand is going to exhaust her strength, and, in the natural life cycle of spiders, end her life. She spins an egg sac, her 'magnum opus' as she calls it, and Wilbur enlists the help of Templeton to bring it to him so he can take it safely back to the barn. In the spring, Charlotte's babies hatch out, and to Wilbur's dismay begin flying away. But three of them decide to stay and make friends with Wilbur. The story ends with life in the barn revolving happily through the seasons for Wilbur, who never forgets Charlotte, and a remarkable closing statement: 'It is not often that someone comes along who is a true friend and a good writer. Charlotte was both.'

This memorable story succeeds at the same time in being both playful and serious, while remaining within its convention of detailing the adventures of animals and a child in a farmyard. It begins with the threat of death, and a little girl's outraged reaction to it, and ends with the memory of the dead Charlotte. The successful saving of Wilbur from the axe provides the main action. This story does not bear out the unfavourable comparisons often made, for example by Bruno Bettelheim in *The Uses of Enchantment*, between modern children's fiction and the classic fairy tales from the point of view of confrontation with painful reality; in *Charlotte's Web* these matters are handled with grace and subttety, but without evasion.

Like most modern children's fiction, and, however, unlike most fairy tales, *Charlotte's Web* is written mostly from the point of view of children – the little girl, Fern, and her brother Avery – and the child-pig Wilbur. It is in fact a fable describing a benign but far from painless process of development. There is on the one hand Fern's development from concern with babies to interest in boys, and on the other Wilbur's development from a helpless and dependent newborn piglet to an independent creature able to take responsibility for others. The narrative is unusual in facing up to and representing the anxieties and pains of this process, and its demands on the adults – notably Charlotte, but also Fern's family – who make it possible.

The story centres on its depiction of the great love and sacrifice of self required of 'mother' (Fern and Charlotte) to bring up Wilbur, the baby, particularly when the baby is a runt, an especially vulnerable baby needing extra-special care to survive (in this case to avoid slaughter). In E.B. White's two other children's stories, *The Trumpet of the Swan*, and *Stuart Little*, unusual difficulties (Louis's lack of voice and Stuart's being born a little mouse) are also overcome by special qualities. This theme, unusual in children's literature, must have had immense personal significance for him, to which his letters and other writings bear witness.[1] Fern devotes herself completely to her baby, and her devotion saves him a second time when he gets to the age of weaning.

Wilbur's active mothering is then taken on by Charlotte, the spider, while Fern sits and watches events unfold in the barn. The milking stool on which she sits evokes her now indirect relation to the feeding of Wilbur, which nonetheless holds a prime place in Wilbur's thoughts. While Charlotte offers herself as a friend to Wilbur, her role as a mother for him is hardly in doubt; the scenes of Wilbur being told stories as he goes to sleep, and of Charlotte bearing his anxieties of abandonment and death while she tries to think out how to save him, are delicate transformations into this fantasy-form of the relationship of mother and infant.

The story shows the total dependence on a mother's unqualified devotion of her infant, and the life-preserving function of its specialness for her. This is brought out where Charlotte is about to write TERRIFIC in her web. 'Wilbur blushed. "But I'm *not* terrific, Charlotte. I'm just about average for a pig." "You're terrific as far as *I'm* concerned" replied Charlotte, sweetly, "and that's what counts."' Charlotte's inspired word-weaving is a way of making the world share her own feeling for her friend. While she is aware of her own achievement in this ('"Your success in the ring this morning was, to a small degree, *my* success"') her object is to bring attention to Wilbur, not to herself, to make *him* a star. The irony of this is brought out where Mr Zuckerman tells his wife: '"A miracle has happened and a sign has occurred here on earth, right on our farm, and we have no ordinary pig." "Well," said Mrs Zuckerman, "It seems to me that you're a little off. It seems to me we have no ordinary spider."' But the miracle remains Wilbur's, in human eyes, for Charlotte's creative intervention was only seen for the gift it was by Wilbur himself.

The story gradually explores the preoccupations of infancy, through, for example, the little pig's love of his food, of his warm bed, the narrow confines of his world, his inclination to dirt and the sudden irruptions of bathing. And, just as in Beatrix Potter's stories, the infant's anxieties are the obverse of this, of being lost, killed, abandoned or eaten. Many of these themes reappear in *Stuart Little* – Stuart's tiny stature gives rise to very acute anxieties about getting lost (down the drain, or in the garbage, for example) for both him and his parents. But it also shows in a more profound and unusual way the emotional dimensions of the weaning process, as one in which the infant learns to give up the primary possession of his mother's mind to someone other than himself. This is on the basis that what has been given to the baby (Wilbur) is really enough to nourish him well: life within has been established. The baby can thus love a mother who is not him, but separate and individual.

When Wilbur first goes to the barn, he can't make friends with the other animals, and is a butt for their cruel warnings about his impending fate. But through Charlotte's care he becomes more independent, and at the end can make his own deal with the formidable Templeton. He is able to face going to the fair without Charlotte, even though he is longing for her to come. He can bear the idea of something else growing in her mind which is not him, a preoccupation which she does not at first divulge, but which gradually turns into his understanding that she will bear babies:

> 'What are you doing up there, Charlotte?'
> 'Oh, making something,' she said. 'Making something, as usual.'
> 'Is it something for me?' asked Wilbur.
> 'No,' said Charlotte. 'It's something for *me*, for a change.'
> 'Please tell me what it is,' begged Wilbur.
> 'I'll tell you in the morning,' she said.

And in the morning it is revealed with her usual careful explanations as her masterpiece, her egg sac. '"It's a perfectly beautiful egg sac," said Wilbur, feeling as happy as though he'd constructed it himself.' Charlotte's precise, simple explanations are offered without condescension to Wilbur, moments of learning imparted from teacher to pupil in an ideal way. It is Wilbur's right to gain understanding with her help, just as White's calm and gracious use of his literary gifts and scientific knowledge seem very lovingly offered to his readers. Facts are respected and are shown to be most relevant in facing the anxious moments in life.

Just as Wilbur has received special care from Charlotte, so he takes exceptional pains to protect her babies and thus her memory after she dies. The necessity to share with siblings is brought out vividly in his agreement with Templeton to exchange for ever the first choice of food in his trough for Templeton's help in bringing him the egg sac, so that he can take it back with him to the best place for them, Charlotte's barn. His decision to carry it in his mouth is another symbolic renunciation of oral gratification for the sake of the other babies. He nearly falls into despair (crying himself to sleep, a reverse echo of being lulled into sleep by Charlotte) when the babies hatch and start to fly away like the balloonists in Charlotte's bedtime stories. He fears that he will have no continuing link with Charlotte, and will not have been loved by the spider babies for what he has done for them. What a relief when three of them decide to stay, and appreciate the barn and Wilbur himself. It is not an illusion that he has helped, not a fantasy which drifted away in the air like the baby-spider dreams. The sense of dying and being reborn is important to the story, which spans a year on the farm from spring to spring. The ecological balance of the farmyard world is very carefully portrayed: a pig can be well fed on the kitchen leftovers, garbage dumps have their use, even a rat can be an essential link in the chain of life.

The author's choice of a pig and a spider for hero and heroine is worth pondering. Pigs are not such unusual characters in childhood nursery rhymes and tales, from Beatrix Potter's *Little Pig Robinson*, to A.A. Milne's character 'Piglet' and Nina Bawden's *Peppermint Pig*; but a spider is a real original. E.B. White's pig is undeniably charming, both as a baby and as the courageous little-boy pig he grows into, yet 'little pig' is most often used as a derogatory name for a child. It is sometimes used lovingly by a mother for a hungry baby, but also with hostility amongst children themselves. Pigs are ordinarily thought of as greedy, fat and dirty, just the attributes often given by older children to a baby, who can seem to be forever feeding at milk or sloppy food, like Wilbur's slops, and forever dirty: babies have faces messy from food, dirty bottoms, and like to crawl around on the floor. Wilbur's love of food is very sweetly described, delineated not as greed, in contrast to Templeton's boundless greed, which leads him to eat absolutely anything with a preference for the slightly rotten, but as his baby pig-nature: he has a lot of growing to do, like a baby, and he needs a lot of food. Wilbur is quite clean and fresh when anyone cleans him – actually the account of the buttermilk bath is positively lyrical, as it is a delightful realization of an infantile phantasy of being bathed in mother's much-loved milk – and his liking for rolling in the mud is shown to involve his search for a soft warm place where he can feel enveloped and protected, and one is reminded of a baby's panic and dislike at being undressed and exposed. There is also another respect in which Wilbur expresses an infantile characteristic: he is horribly afraid of dying, and faints when confronted with the idea of death; although this may seem much less obvious, some acute anxieties in babies seem linked with an overwhelming fear of being separated from the sources of life and goodness, and such a separation may feel like a kind of death. The love and concern which Wilbur's baby-needs draw forth in Fern and Charlotte is thus a profound acceptance of the often despised or even hated aspects of our infantile selves. Given such consideration, Wilbur becomes capable of growing and maturing to the point when he can sacrifice his own immediate interest, which is that Charlotte should live for his sake, to concern for Charlotte herself and for her unborn babies. He has become capable, through identification with his psychological mother, of enduring grief and loneliness without despair and while retaining his loving impulses; this is in contrast to Templeton, who has never got to the point of any altruistic concern, but is swallowed up by narcissism.

Now what about the spider heroine? Many children, and indeed many adults, are really frightened and repelled by spiders, and Charlotte's nature and habits are very fully described. At first Wilbur, too, is horrified by her: he perceives the cannibalistic entrapping spider, sucking the blood of her victim in vampire style. This nightmare vision is a fundamental fear in the human infant too; the soft-voiced loving mother holding out her arms, offering food and comfort, might turn out in our worst dreams to be drawing us into a deathly trap. These overwhelming paranoid anxieties are transmuted in the story into a recognition that the Charlotte who may be a terror to flies is also capable of selfless devotion to Wilbur the pig. The integration of a loving character with unlovely aspects acknowledged and accepted is remarkable. Wilbur, however, does not really deal with another aspect of Charlotte's spider nature: the many legged spider, specially feared under the bed and in the dark, often seems to serve as a symbol to the child in us of a frightening conception of uncomprehended parental intercourse, a mingling of bodies not seen as loving but as hostile and dirty.

Wilbur seems able to imagine himself as a father or at least an established older sibling for Charlotte's babies. However, the spider whom Charlotte's child admirers learn to love probably does evoke and contain, through her continuing loving concern for Wilbur, even while exhausted by her egg-laying, primitive anxieties about sexuality.

While Charlotte is seen as producing her babies without a mate, in the human world E.B. White offers us rather a rich portrait of male and female interactions. Mr Arable may have intended to kill the runt pig, but he is almost moved to tears by Fern's passionate remarks about this 'terrible case of injustice' to the weak. Mr Zuckerman may be almost overcome by self-important pride about his miracle pig, but he can also keep alive his belief in Wilbur at the fair when he seems displaced by the pig next door – Mrs Zuckerman is in tears and Fern wants to run away to ferris-wheel oblivion, but he pushes on with the buttermilk bath. Fern's earlier distrust of boys and men, her 'heavily-armed' brother Avery and her farmer father, grows into her excited interest in Henry Fussy. Charlotte, who calmly accepts the aggressive aspects of her nature, has perhaps helped Fern to live with her own passions too.

Charlotte's final achievement is not the laying of the eggs, but her acceptance of dying alone. This is a very poignant moment in the story: she has sustained Wilbur through his sad renunciation of her, she has poured her strength into her progeny, but she also then has to endure on her own, giving up her living importance for her babies, both literal and psychological ones. This is an echo of the mourning process for the nursing mother when a baby is weaned: together with the pleasure in the infant's growth and development, is the pain of becoming less essential to his or her health and welfare. The special one-to-one closeness of the nursing couple ends when the baby is ready for life in a larger world. Wilbur was psychologically ready to be weaned when he returned to the farm without Charlotte, but it is Charlotte who has to experience being abandoned and alone. Charlotte's death is also a true delineation of the experience of death for parent and child: Wilbur, the child, cannot help her with her agony, but Charlotte, the parent, protects and prepares him so that he has the resources to live without her.

The story of Wilbur's growth from infancy is paralleled by Fern's growth away from her little girl preoccupation with mother and babies, which is hostile to father (Mr Arable and Mr Zuckerman are the ones who would kill Wilbur), towards the pre-adolescent excitement of being with her brother Avery at the fair, and with Henry Fussy high up in the Ferris

Wheel. Not without a lump in the throat for her mother, she moves out of the maternal spaces of kitchen and animals feeding in the barn to the wider world where there is a different sort of adventure and where sex exists.

Perhaps it is the co-existence in the story of different stages and kinds of development – Avery's aggressiveness as well as Fern's tenderness, Fern's growing away from Wilbur just when he does for Charlotte's babies what Fern has done for him – which enable the tenderest aspects of infancy to be registered without sentimentality. For the reader's attention and identifications are drawn towards many different figures and feelings. The natural indifference and jealousy of outsiders towards the extreme claims of the mother-baby couple are thus also vigorously present inside the story. While there are these contrasts of feeling, there is also a Russian-doll like enclosure of one nurturing relationship inside another. Mr and Mrs Arable understand Fern's feeling for the little runt pig, and help her to care for it. She has an uncle and aunt nearby where she can find private space for a more day-dreamy experience of her feelings about families. There is a pastoral abundance of attention, food, warmth and community in this world, and the Arables, the Zuckermans, Dr Dorian, Fern, Charlotte, and finally Wilbur all take their share in nurturing others. It is the conjunction of this with the acknowledgement of loss and death which give the story such an unusual depth of feeling.

Another distinctive attribute of this story is its fore-grounding of the practice of *writing*. This interest in the fundamental importance of words, speaking and writing recurs in another White story, *The Trumpet of the Swan*: Sam Beaver's diary records his private observations of and relationship with the swans and his self-inquiring musings, and Louis's whole quest revolves round the search for a voice. The school episode in *Stuart Little* has some of the same interests, for Stuart shows the children how words can be used to think with rather than imitate. This provides of course the central point of the narrative of the story – Charlotte saves Wilbur through her writing – and we are reminded of this by the testament to her in the last lines of the book. But the book plays with and reflects on the properties of language in subtle ways throughout. It is thus amusing and thought-provoking in its detailed texture, as well as in its overall conception and narrative.

Charlotte's achievement in writing SOME PIG, TERRIFIC, RADIANT and HUMBLE in her web succeeds brilliantly in dramatizing the problem of writing, and more generally of language, for a young child. Where to get the words from, what they mean, the problem of literally *writing* them, are wonderfully transformed into the physical and mental work and ultimate achievement of the spider. The sense of bricolage – words collected from soap-flake packets and newspapers, tried out and rejected for their imagined meanings – has to be connected with the meaning of writing to the age group for whom the story is intended. Charlotte's search for words to copy, with uncertain knowledge of their meaning, is expressive for a child who starts to read and write in just this way.

But as is the way with words, these inventions of Charlotte then take on a life of their own, and begin to define the reality which one might naively have thought they merely re-presented.

> 'O K, Templeton,' said Charlotte, 'the soap ad will do, I guess. I'm not sure Wilbur's action is exactly radiant, but it's interesting.'
> 'Actually,' said Wilbur, 'I feel radiant.'
> 'Do you?' said Charlotte, looking at him with affection. 'Well, you're a good little pig, and radiant you shall be. I'm in this thing pretty deep now – I might as well go the limit.'

So Wilbur lives up to his descriptions, and the human beings around are also deceived by Charlotte into believing the pig to have these miraculous properties. There are amusing passages in which they describe him in all seriousness in Charlotte's words, as 'some pig' and the rest, much as they might come to use the phrases of the original advert. The writing in the web convinces the world that Wilbur is extraordinary, and the world's opinion then convinces the Zuckermans. Charlotte is thus able to use her writing by conscious contrivance to make the world see Wilbur differently, a fortuitous selection of words which only acquires truth, so to speak, after the event. It is a diverting refutation of a realist theory of writing as a mere reflection of what already *is*.

Much of the interest of the writing throughout the book depends on exploring the meanings of expressions and the intentions that they convey for different characters. On the first page, for example, Fern is outraged by grown-up euphemism:

> 'Well,' said her mother, 'one of the pigs is a runt. It's very small and weak, and will never amount to anything. So your father has decided to do away with it.'
> 'Do *away* with it?' shrieked Fern. 'You mean *kill* it? Just because it's smaller than the others?'

Or later where Wilbur asks Templeton to play with him:

> 'Play?', said Templeton, twirling his whiskers. 'Play?, I hardly know the meaning of the word.'
> 'Well', said Wilbur, 'It means to have fun, to frolic, to run and skip and make merry.'
> 'I never do those things if I can avoid them,' replied the rat, sourly. 'I prefer to spend my time eating, gnawing, spying and hiding. I am a glutton but not a merrymaker. Right now I am on my way to your trough to eat your breakfast, since you haven't got sense enough to eat it yourself.'

In a number of classic books written for children, such as Beatrix Potter's and Lewis Carroll's, the adult reader's interest is held by multiple levels of meaning in particular expressions or turns of phrase. In *Charlotte's Web*, as in *Alice*, these implications are often explored in dialogue between the human characters. The author aims for a more naturalistic quality in his dialogue between the human characters, than between the animals in the barn. White assumes powers of thought and imagination in his readers and the animals are permitted longer and more literary speeches, in pursuit of the meanings of language or character. For example, when Wilbur asks one of the lambs to play with him, the text proceeds thus:

> 'Certainly not,' said the lamb. 'In the first place, I cannot get into your pen, as I am not old enough to jump over the fence. In the second place, I am not interested in pigs. Pigs mean less than nothing to me.'
> 'What do you mean *less* than nothing?' replied Wilbur. 'I don't think there is such a thing as less than nothing, nothing is absolutely the limit of nothingness. It's the lowest you can go. It's the end of the line. How can something be less than nothing? If there was something that was less than nothing, then nothing would not be nothing, it would be something – even though it's

just a very little bit of something. But if nothing is nothing, then nothing has nothing that is less than *it* is!'

'Oh, be quiet!' said the lamb. 'Go play by yourself! I don't play with pigs.'

Thus Wilbur learns the limited powers of rational argument, and tries out his own talents with language.

Charlotte, the writer, is especially given the facility of speaking in rounded and finished sentences. She values composure, and understanding, and though she is tender towards Wilbur she doesn't like emotional excess. '"I am going to save you and I want you to quiet down immediately. You're carrying on in a childish way. Stop your crying! I can't stand hysterics."' We get a sense of her descriptive powers after her brief interview with the rival pig Uncle, to whom she says little, but of whom she gives this report: '"One thing is certain, he has a most unattractive personality. He is too familiar, too noisy, and he cracks weak jokes. Also, he's not anywhere near as clean as you are, nor as pleasant. I took quite a dislike to him in our brief interview."' She is also a magnificent story-teller, for Wilbur. Five chapters end with Charlotte lulling Wilbur to sleep, an artful homology for adults reading aloud to their children. She is able to describe her own way of life as a member of a trapping species with the excitement of a sports commentator, but also philosophically: '"Way back for thousands and thousands of years, we spiders have been laying for flies and bugs."' She is able to bear the anxiety of waiting until she has an idea for saving Wilbur, much as a writer has to wait for thoughts to evolve. All in all, her composed qualities of thought and speech convey the impression of a professional woman for whom responsibility for Wilbur and her own babies have come late, when she is well settled in her life.

There is some play in the story with literary genres, which even children can respond to. Wilbur is horrified to learn about her diet of insects. '"Do they taste good?"' he asks. '"Delicious. Of course, I don't really eat them. I drink them – drink their blood. I love blood," said Charlotte, and her pleasant, thin voice grew even thinner and more pleasant."' To this evocation of gothic-horror fiction can be added the echoes of the gangster novel in the character of Templeton, the rat. '"A rotten egg is a regular stink bomb"', he is told, as he collects the one unhatched egg of her clutch. '"I won't break it," snarled Templeton. "I know what I'm doing. I handle stuff like this all the time."' He is a convincing hedonist and tough guy, willing to press home the advantage when he has one:

> 'I guess you're licked, Wilbur. You might as well relax – nobody is going to hang any medal on *you*. Furthermore, I wouldn't be surprised if Zuckerman changes his mind about you. Wait until he gets hankering for some fresh pork and smoked ham and crispy bacon. He'll take the knife to you, my boy!'

By this time in the story, however, Wilbur is able to stand up to Templeton's cruelty, and tells him in reply that Charlotte is going to become a mother:

> 'For your information, there are five hundred and fourteen eggs in that peachy little sac.'
> 'Is this true?' asked the rat, eyeing the sac suspiciously.
> 'Yes, it's true,' sighed Charlotte.
> 'Congratulations!' murmured Templeton. 'This *has* been a night.'

It is a second major virtue of *Charlotte's Web* (besides its emotional depth and truthfulness) that its language is so continuously alive, and so actively registers the relationships and conflicts of its characters.

Finally, let us make a few points about the social meanings that are condensed in this narrative. It is, in its own way, a very American story. It has an atmosphere of plenitude (even extending to the pig's diet of kitchen slops), yet also of ordinariness and equality of status. Just as in one of E.B. White's other books, *The Trumpet of the Swan*, Louis the swan likes to play *all* music, classical and jazz, so in *Charlotte's Web* the spider's writing is made out of popular bits and pieces, and yet regarded as a miracle. The farm is a pastoral frame, an ideal setting for children, and the existence of a single farmhand among two families suggests a community without over-many levels of status. There is a wry observation that, to Lurvy the farmhand, Wilbur's 'miracle' means more work.

There is also, in *Charlotte's Web* a healthy respect for the principle of self-interest. Even Charlotte partly likes Wilbur because 'his smelly pen and stale food attracted the flies that she needed.' While Templeton the rat is feared and disliked, even a scavenger and predator such as he has his place in the scheme of things, and it proves possible to exploit his sense of self-interest by pointing out the advantages to him of having Wilbur around.

Learning to deal with Templeton's meanness and gross sensuality, as well as being nourished by Charlotte's love, are necessary to Wilbur's survival. The earthy material realism of the story – the importance of food and making a living – whether in the manner of the human being, or in Templeton's or Charlotte's ways, is another American feature. The glowing descriptions of Charlotte's agility in spinning her webs evoke not only an admiration of nature's mysteries, but also of sheer practical skill. Whatever is done well is worth admiring, is an implicit moral of this democratic story, just as in the movie *The Hustler* the character played by Paul Newman celebrates the excellence of a skill such as brick-laying when it's performed well. Writing for children in an English context does not usually celebrate manual skills in these ways.

Dialogue is also more plain and direct than would be likely in an English story, as characters assert their views of the world forcefully against one another. Realities have to be faced (Charlotte's diet), disagreements stated (Fern defending the truth of Charlotte's stories), self-interest put first ("'Let him die,' said the rat, 'I should worry.'"); the claims of reputation sarcastically put down ("'Just watch what you're doing, Mr Radiant, when they get shoving you in.'") Language is for stating facts, for asserting opinion, and for elaborating an individual's way of seeing the world, and social conventions have little inhibiting effect on its forceful use. Language is for bargaining, too, as when Stuart Little arranged to buy the five drops of petrol required for his car. This greater abrasiveness and inventiveness of dialogue also seems an American quality.

Charlotte's Web has, of course, a rural and pastoral vision of American life. In *The Trumpet of the Swan*, Louis makes his fortune in the city – on the swan-boat lake in Boston – and returns to the lake nature reserve to raise his family. In *Stuart Little*, the mouse-child grows up in the city, a child's New York delightfully glimpsed, but then seeks his love on the open road. *Charlotte's Web* never leaves the farm; qualities that can just about be managed in the control of a face-to-face community – like Templeton's greed – could hardly be coped with outside. The fair is imagined to be about the limit of the world which a child reader, identified with Fern and Avery, can be expected to think about.

Yet, as so often in literature, the figure of the writer also enters and influences the moral standpoint of the narrative, as it does by transformation into musician in *The Trumpet of the Swan*. Charlotte, the spider and writer, understands more than the human folks, and her 'fictions' become facts for them: Wilbur, made memorable, will survive. With the same spinnerets, she creates writing, and also her other work, her egg sac and 'magnum opus' (the subject of a lengthy conversation with Wilbur) which thus become comparable acts of procreation. Through her achievements of writing, she herself becomes remembered, though this is not her motive.

Charlotte's outstanding success – credited by her stratagem to the pig – is also revealing as an American theme. Individuals, the story implies, can achieve success from quite ordinary qualities, given dedication. Louis also has this experience through his trumpet playing, in *The Trumpet of the Swan*, and Stuart Little has his particular moments of triumph too, besides his daily accomplishments as a child-mouse. But E.B. White returns his characters, after their moments of glory, to the place where they were brought up, where familiar surroundings, love and family matter most. By transforming the achievements of a baby for its mother, and the devotion of a mother for her baby into these animal miracles, *Charlotte's Web* is able to celebrate common human feelings. The potential for creative human achievement is in everyone, the stories imply, and are found in the everyday process of development. White's three stories depict this development at different stages. Wilbur grows up as a baby, in a close relationship to mother figures. Stuart Little appears from the moment of birth as an independent adventurous person, and, as a mouse, is able to represent infant, child, and adolescent all in one. His disappointing romantic outing on the river with Harriet Ames, a composed young lady of his own size, shows amusingly what he is not yet ready for. Louis, the trumpeter swan, helped by his Dad's intrepid devotion, achieves success and finds a wife, only to return from the fame of the city to the peace of the lakes. This emphasis in the stories on both the exceptional creativity which is manifested in individuals (but springing from the natural capacities of their kinds, and from the parental care they give or receive) and the stress on the virtues of friendliness, neighbourhood and family, seems to represent a particularly American and democratic dream. But the central concern with family also relates to the fact that these are stories for children, and to the author's understanding of the deeper preoccupations of his readers, the child-in-the-adult as well as children themselves.

Charlotte's character and way of life also disrupt the conventional division of labour between genders which is otherwise strongly represented by the differences between Fern and her brother Avery, and between the adults of each sex. ('What fantastic creatures boys are! Why did I let myself in for this?' comments Templeton when he encounters Avery's exuberant play-acting.) Charlotte is female, but she also hunts and traps. She cares for Wilbur, but she thinks coolly, and is unsentimental and realistic. She is the exceptional figure of the story – a twentieth-century heroine, in truth, by virtue of her ability to respond through creative mental effort to the needs of her infants. She embodies vigorously the qualities of maternal reverie which have particularly interested psychoanalysts working in the tradition of Klein and Winnicott.[2]

The story celebrates the centrality of fantasy and imagination in the development of children. As so often in writing for children, parents are shown to be less in touch with imagination than children themselves, and indeed Mrs Arable goes to consult the doctor to see if Fern's absorption with the barn and its conversations are a sign of ill health. Fern reports Charlotte's stories with down-to-earth certainty:

> 'Fern dear, how would a fish get into a spider's web?' said Mrs Arable. 'You know it couldn't happen. You're making this up.'
> 'Oh, it happened all right,' replied Fern. 'Charlotte never fibs. This cousin of hers built a web across a stream . . .'

Soon Fern almost interests her mother in these adventures, and her father and Dr Dorian are both able to accept them. It may be that the conversations that Fern overhears between Charlotte and Wilbur also represent the unspoken communications between mother and baby, which are so important to their developing relationship.

The love of nature, of imagination, and of childhood in *Charlotte's Web* are a classic and recurring combination of themes in children's fiction. E.B. White's exploration of the links between love, nature, thought and words is, however, outstandingly original.

The last lines of the book are very direct. 'It is not often that someone comes along who is a true friend and a good writer. Charlotte was both.' It is hard to believe that there was not a beloved figure in the author's inner life being commemorated in these words.

8

Who Believes in 'Borrowers'?

Mary Norton's *Borrowers* have inspired a classic five-volume series. They are tiny people-like creatures whose natural habitat is in secret places in the houses of human beings (or 'human beans' as they call us), and they live by 'borrowing' the tiny objects and minute quantities of food needed to support their lives. Even their names are borrowed. They have nothing of their own at all, but 'they thought they owned the world'. Those human beings who become aware of the Borrowers' lives in Mary Norton's stories are characteristically struggling with a sense of what they do not have, and the manner in which felt deprivation is dealt with is one of the themes of these books. This is relevant both in matters of historical setting – the British war and post-war preoccupations with lost family members, evacuation, rationing, 'making do,' improvising, sharing and 'pulling together' to tackle things pervade these books – and in Norton's sensitive psychological grasp of the inner problems of character and development to which deprivation and loss give rise.

The complexity of the structure is considerable, since throughout these volumes the worlds of the Borrowers and of the humans they meet are both kept in mind, as in the relation between an old lady, Mrs May, and a child, Kate, to whom she tells the story, who come to share a great deal through its significance for them. Mrs May is a widow, living in Kate's parents' house, and, like the Borrowers, she seems to have no place of her own. She is lonely and enjoys the company of Kate, who is 'wild, untidy and self-willed,' inclined to 'stare with angry eyes', but not when with Mrs May. Mrs May teaches her how to crochet and other domestic arts. The first story begins when a crochet hook goes missing, for Mrs May introduces Kate to the Borrowers, who might be making use of all our unaccountably lost domestic items. We are soon to learn how a Borrower house is furnished:

> Homily was proud of her sitting-room: the walls had been papered with scraps of old letters out of wastepaper baskets, and Homily had arranged the hand-writing sideways in vertical stripes which ran from floor to ceiling. On the walls, repeated in various colours, hung several portraits of Queen Victoria as a girl; these were postage stamps, borrowed by Pod some years ago from the stamp box on the desk in the morning-room. There was a lacquer trinket box, padded inside and with the lid open which they used as a settle; and that useful standby – a chest of drawers made of matchboxes. There was a round table with a red velvet cloth, which Pod had made from the wooden bottom of a pill box supported on the carved pedestal of a knight from the chess set. (This had caused a great deal of trouble upstairs when Aunt Sophy's son . . . had invited the vicar for 'a game after dinner' . . .) The knight itself . . . lent that air to the room which only statuary can give.

Kate is upset by the loss of the crochet hook which she needs to pursue their shared hobby (they are making a blanket). Mrs May tells her hesitantly, '"I had a brother . . . he was killed . . . a 'hero's death' on the North-West Frontier. He told me so many things – my sister and me,"' for brother and sister had shared a cabin on a boat to India, and he had told her all about the Borrowers he had met in Great Aunt Sophy's house, where he had stayed for weeks when recovering from rheumatic fever. In the house lived his bedridden great aunt, Mrs Driver, the cook, and Crampfurl, the gardener. Behind the grandfather clock in the hole lived the Clock family, (named by their social location, in a particularly English fashion,) Pod, Homily and Arrietty. The hidden recesses of the house turned out to contain a whole life unknown to the busy managers of the household's everyday existence, but there was space in the boy's mind for imaginative experience, and in Great Aunt Sophy's, as now in Mrs May's and Kate's, so they could gain access to the secrets of the house's history and of the inner world of the imagination. We penetrate behind clock time to memory, past time, a child's Proustian adventures.

Arrietty is thirteen, a child who has an education achieved through literacy and a solitary sheltered existence. She is full of desire for a wider world. Pod is the practical working man who goes out on his borrowing work when it is necessary; he sees borrowing as 'a skilled job'. Homily, the stay-at-home houseproud wife, is full of lower-middle class snobbery and status anxiety, but she approves of culture for Arrietty, who is to be the first generation to benefit from a better education (this a post-1944 British Education Act setting). In some ways, Homily is braver than Pod in facing the fact that their daughter has to be inducted into the dangers of the world beyond the carefully constructed grating entrance to their home under the floorboards. A crisis gathers when Pod is 'seen' by the boy visitor, the ultimate danger for Borrowers, who believe they must live unknown to their host family in order to stay safe; Arrietty is then told the truth of their mode of existence, but knowledge of 'the boy' is kept from her. She reveals to her parents her passionate hatred of being 'cooped up'. '"I don't think it's so clever to live on alone, for ever and ever, in a great, big, half-empty house; . . . no one to talk to, no one to play with. . . ."' The sense of life-destroying imprisonment, a theme which is to recur in the stories, echoes war experiences, the narrow cultural opportunities of British class-stratified society, and the despairing loneliness of a child who knows there is something to be found in life which she cannot grasp. As she says in *The Borrowers Afield*, when they have left their first home, 'This is what I longed for, what I have imagined, what I knew existed.'

Homily is able to acknowledge her lack of freedom, comparing Arrietty's lonely life with her own wider social world as a child in a house lived in by many Borrower families, and Pod is persuaded to take Arrietty beyond the grating. Arrietty's passionate capacity for love of the natural world blooms as she encounters sunlight, birds and growing plants, and her intelligence and attentiveness focus with delight on a world rich enough to fill her mind, which was starved in the half-light of the cellars. She notices the moss growing by the grating, and realizes that the slops thrown out by her mother provide the damp medium. She meets up with the boy in the grass and they talk. Arrietty is not fundamentally frightened but fascinated by him, giant as he is from her point of view. When the boy says, 'Don't move or I shall hit you', she asks 'Why?' – she has an enviable capacity for creative curiosity. For both children, their meeting has a magical quality: the boy establishes that Arrietty can read, and would be willing to read to him, and she can thus become for him a living link with the sisters he so much misses. They have overcome the problems of his bilingual life – the inheritance of the British child brought up in imperial India – which, he explains, makes it hard for him to learn to read. The pain of the child's life divided between two languages, two cultures, the time together and away from his family in India, is all touched on at this moment. For Arrietty, the boy is her first friend and he offers her all kinds of exciting if indigestible information about the world she does not yet know:

> 'Listen!' he said. And he told her about railway stations and football matches and racecourses and royal processions and Albert Hall concerts. He told her about India and China and North America and the British Commonwealth. He told her about the July sales. 'Not hundreds,' he said, 'but thousands and millions and billions and trillions of great big enormous people. Now do you believe me?'

Arrietty's intense optimism is an important element in her character, and stands in contrast to the cautious and easily-disheartened attitude of her parents. The gift of book-knowledge, which they have helped her to acquire (Pod borrowed miniature books for her to read) seems linked with a much larger confidence in her own perceptions, doubts about received Borrower wisdom, a love of language which perhaps makes her believe that those who share her language must be comprehensible and interesting creatures.

The children's encounter is profoundly moving for each of them – it allows for the exploration of their shared need to enter a wider world, the pre-adolescent stirring of the growing child's realization of how much there is beyond the embedded assumptions of one's own family culture. They quarrel about whose life is to set the standard, Arrietty assuming that human beings exist in order to make the Borrowers' way of life possible, and the boy assuming that the world belongs to human beings, and trying to throw back at Arrietty the disquietening uncertainty her appearance causes him by threatening her with the idea that the Borrowers are a dying race. Their pleasure in each other serves to restrain their potential rejection of the strange new questions they are now faced with, and they join forces to sustain their investigation of the new worlds they now apprehend.

The boy agrees to help Arrietty try to make contact with the Hendreary family, relations who emigrated to the fields beyond the house, for in the light of his perception that there are no other Borrowers, it has become imperative for her to make sure the Hendrearys are alive. Mary Norton's understanding of this crisis between the children is brilliant. The boy says, 'You'll be the only Borrower left in the world' and smiles triumphantly, attempting to project his pain and loneliness, which arise from the separation from his family, into Arrietty, for whom he constructs a desolate future. At first he's satisfied to see that he has made her cry, but as she struggles to defend herself from these overwhelming anxieties and announces she will go home, he is filled with panic at the idea of losing this potential big sister – emotionally she is seen thus, despite her diminutive size, for she can stand being lonely, angry, and hurt better than he can, and she could help him to learn to read; this represents not only the richer world that reading would offer him, but also the potential understanding of himself through thought made possible by language. Arrietty can bear to say of the Hendrearys, 'We don't see them because it's too far,' but the boy's sense of dazed loss in relation to his distant family has undermined his conviction of a future reunion. Her capacity to bear the mental pain and uncertainty he has evoked in her allows his sympathy for her and for the suffering part of himself to emerge: he will deliver a letter which may re-establish a link with other Borrowers, and implicitly he thus assents to the idea that she has a future. Arrietty may have 'adventure and safety mixed,' as she hopes.

We have earlier in the story been introduced to other members of the human household who are to pose a threat to the Borrowers. The central character is Mrs Driver, the cook and household manager, whose ruthlessness is heralded by her name, in Dickensian fashion, and whose ally Crampfurl also has a name redolent of painful restriction. She takes care of the boy (perhaps his lack of a name reflects the failure of the adults in the house to think of him as anything but 'that boy') with loveless efficiency, her ugliness contrasted in his mind with his mother's remembered beauty: 'She's fat and has a moustache and gives me my bath and hurts my bruise and my sore elbow, and says she'll take a slipper to me one of these days . . .' Arrietty saw his lip tremble. 'My mother's very nice . . . She lives in India. Why did you lose all your worldly riches?' he asks hurriedly. Arrietty explains about the burst boiler which had disrupted their life beneath – here again the boy needs her to be able to deal with her losses and perhaps help him by her example with his own unbearable feelings about his mother's absence. The nine-year-old boy's experience is dominated at such moments by the passions of babyhood – the ideal mother of infancy who offered him 'worldly riches' has been replaced by the harshness of Mrs Driver, who causes him pain, both physically and emotionally. Arrietty's greater emotional resilience is supported by the ongoing relationships with her parents. She may be itching to explore beyond the confines of the home, but she can always go home in sadness and feel comforted. While she can practise small deceits on her parents in pursuit of her secret concerns – she pretends to practise 'getting a feeling' for the approach of human beings, a crucial Borrower skill, by listening to Driver and Crampfurl in the kitchen, while her real interest is the content of their conversation – she can rely on their continuing concerned involvement with her. Homily, for example, feels for her developing need for privacy: when Arrietty angrily says, 'Let me be!' Homily comments soothingly to a ruffled Pod, 'It's the Spring. Used to take me like that sometimes at her age.' And Homily summons reserves of courage when she persuades Pod that Arrietty must be introduced to the world above the floorboards, sensing Arrietty's need to move beyond the home.

Mrs Driver's opportunity to wreak havoc arises when the boy and the Borrowers become so excited that the caution which normally characterizes human-Borrower contacts is abandoned. One day the boy removes the floorboards, their roof, exposing the whole Borrower house. At first the little family is terrified, and this motif of horror at total exposure, the invasion of their private space, is further explored in a later volume when the mercenary Mr Platt captures them and attempts to wall them up behind glass for display in a model village – the most awful aspect of this is felt to be the totally public display of every intimate detail of their family existence. There is perhaps a somewhat parallel anxiety touched on in the relation between Mrs Driver and the boy, where her intrusive assault on his private world, on the playful activities of his imaginary world, is equated with a penetration of his inner self and his mind which threatens his personal integrity. Phantasy and dream need a protected inner space unless we choose to share them with others. But the essential protective boundaries are breached when the family lay aside their habitual fear and prudence under the stimulus of greedy desire for possessions – the boy brings wondrous furniture from the dolls' house and persuades them to accept more. '"I've got more things upstairs," he said. Homily nudged Pod. "Ask him what kind of things."' Her petty bourgeois ambition is spurred: to be able to change for dinner into a satin 'Grecian' gown, for her sitting room to become a salon. Pod's anxiety grows as the grandeur increases – he feels Homily 'should call a halt' – but greed unleashed is difficult to control. The boy begins to bring valuable items from the drawing room cabinet and Mrs Driver notices that things are going missing. The roof lifted off the house describes also the lifting of repression and the bursting into consciousness of alarming, unfamiliar, but exciting emotions. The Borrowers are living a 'golden age,' but the sense of danger gathering is immanent: Mrs Driver's 'little black eyes became slits of anger and cunning . . . It was, she calculated, as though someone, suspecting her of dishonesty (pilfering of Aunt Sophy's madeira) were trying to catch her out.' The blind denial of danger and immersion in a consumerist fools' paradise perhaps recall the uneasy mindlessness of sections of the British middle class during the 1930s, prefiguring an appalling disaster which is allowed to grow inexorable by neglect.

Mrs Driver discovers the 'nest' by spying: the Borrowers' home in her eyes is a nest of vermin, fit only for extermination. The World War II echo is unmistakable as the gassing rat-catcher is called in to dispose of the vermin and Mrs Driver prepares to enjoy a sadistic triumph. The Borrowers face the knowledge that only emigration through the iron grating can save them. Mrs Driver combines a paranoid fear of the Borrowers, who are perceived as thieves taking everything valuable from her, and whose murder requires the mobilization of large resources, with a cruel excitement in wounding the boy who begs, 'Don't hurt them' and allies himself with his friend when he defends himself against her accusation of theft by saying 'No! I'm a borrower'. The passions unleashed are primitive and powerful; she sees her chance for a double revenge, on the child whose lot in life is materially much more privileged than hers, a representative of the soft despised upper classes who do not deserve what they own, and on the Borrowers, who represent the hated unconscious dependent aspects of her character and her social position. The boy experiences the 'nest' as a source of imaginative life and love and becomes able to cry: 'Something fell hot on his hand: it was a tear from his eye.' The image of the healing tear is recurrent in children's fiction, as in Hans Andersen's 'Snow Queen', where the poisoned vision of the child pierced and possessed by icy arrogance and cold-heartedness is cured by tears. The boy's tear is a moment of experienced integration – his sympathy for his own loneliness and neediness is united with his concern for the Borrowers, who have enabled him to hope and care about himself again through his relationship with them. It reminds one of the lost 'worldly riches' he asked Arrietty about, for the nest so exquisitely refurbished via his depredations on the house represents the reconstruction of a beautiful interior world peopled by a happy family, by which he himself feels nourished.

At this point in the story the listening child intervenes: Kate's passionate liveliness, 'wild, self-willed and all the rest of it', is stirred by tragedy, and she cries as the boy did. We are reminded that just as Arrietty and the boy are dealing with their unhappiness together, so Mrs May and Kate feel their isolation and difficulty rendered bearable by their intense intimacy in relation to the story.

All is not lost, for the boy is able to evade Mrs Driver's custody and undo the grating which will allow the Borrowers to escape the gas and emigrate, as homeless refugees. This terrifies home-bound Homily, but allows Arrietty to leave the cramped below-floor quarters and emerge into full light. Her goal of moving out has been achieved, albeit unconsciously. Mrs Driver is humiliated, in a wonderfully comic dénouement, by the local policeman, who gives her an 'old-fashioned look', and by Great Aunt Sophy, who has all the madeira brought up to her room, suspecting drunken sightings. Thus Mrs Driver, who does not believe in make-believe and the life of the imagination, is made fun of because she does believe in the Borrowers as 'nasty, crafty, scurvy squeaking little thieves' who are persecuting her.

Over the years, Mary Norton added four further volumes to the original story, following the Borrowers in their life in the world beyond the big house. They have many adventures before finally establishing themselves in a new home, which is secure by virtue of its being secret from the human beings who inhabit the host house. Arrietty continually tests out the Borrowers' way of life and mode of thought through her particular interest in the humans with whom they come in contact, and Pod and Homily struggle to draw her away from her fascination with what they perceive as so dangerous to their existence. The 'otherness' of humans is for Arrietty a source of great interest; for her parents it mainly evokes fear. Just as the Borrower family we get to know best – we do meet others, relations and strangers – is divided in its response to new experience which may prove alarming and dis-orienting, so the human characters include some who can enjoy even the confusing results of exploration of the imagination and others who are out to control the unexpected at all costs, by various means, as we shall see. How many layers and levels of experience can be kept fruitfully in mind? This is the issue which Mary Norton is addressing in stories which show us the greater richness of a world peopled by phantasy and the anxiety which has to be tolerated to achieve this. As Mrs May says to Kate of Borrowers, 'Some houses are more apt to have them than others,' and here the metaphor of house as the scope of the mind is unambiguous, for she has told Kate, 'Don't be so literal . . . anything we haven't experienced for ourselves sounds like a story.' Literal-minded truth is one-dimensional, too tightly defined by the external facts of perception, whereas the truthfulness of the imagin-ation is inherently linked to emotional commitments and discriminations, and contact with potential selves, not just the already actualized.

The Borrowers Afield opens with Mrs May's inheritance of a house in the country. This house has been inhabited by Tom Goodenough, an old countryman who is described by Mr Beguid ('Be Good,' the man of relentlessly strict conscience in contrast with the man who can live with himself more easily, 'Goodenough'), the lawyer, as 'the biggest liar in five counties'. His lies, of course, concern his unconcealed belief in little people, Borrowers. When Kate and Mrs May go to visit the house, Kate and Tom exchange a secret smile of understanding, perhaps characteristic of certain special links possible between children and old people – one is reminded of *The Secret Garden* and the children's sharing of their secret life in the garden with the old gardener who can tell them so much they need to know in order to make sense of the puzzling present. Tom gives Kate access to the further adventures of the Borrowers. There is an important contrast here in Norton's way of setting the wisdom of the old and the country-loving, like Tom and Mrs May, in opposition to the narrow rationalism of the town man, Mr Beguid, too busy with facts to attend to phantasy. This echoes the implicit generosity of spirit in Great Aunt Sophy in contrast to the greedy and manipulative Mrs Driver, and Kate's need for Mrs May's company and sense of her own awkward character might also suggest an absence of an adequately live link with her own parents. (The old and the young come together in a similar way in some of Rumer Godden's stories, and in *Tom's Midnight Garden*.) This idea need not be taken as a literal comment on modern mores, although it may be so intended in part, but it also tends to draw our attention to the crucial nature of the time spent by child and adult where their imaginations can reach each other, in play, in stories, and in all the activities where there is room for phantasies. Writing seems understandably to be regarded with special affection by writers for children and the activity of writing often features in their stories. E.B. White's *Charlotte's Web* is the outstanding example of this, and another is Arrietty's taste for writing in her diary. She says of her pencil and tiny book, '"each to his hobby and the tools of the craft he loves" (and hers she knew to be literature.)' Tom and Mrs May are also characteristically full of common sense and realism, giving the child's imagination secure boundaries within which to wander, and this they share with Pod and Homily, who serve Arrietty well in a similar way.

In the family's wanderings in the field they set up home in a boot; Homily worries about its origins: 'I wish I knew who'd worn this boot' and is later delighted to learn that it was a *gentleman's* boot; 'Oh, thank goodness for that.' Her house-wifely and snobbish anxiety is relieved, for this news seems to render it a tolerable setting for a home. Meanwhile Arrietty is enchanted by 'the golden suns (which) were the lace-holes of the boot.' Pod protects Arrietty's wonder and excitement in the field by down-to-earth practicality; they encounter a crow, gigantic to them, and Pod manages a showdown with steady courage and then remarks, 'Size is nothing, it's the talk that gets them.'[1]

There is an ultra-conventional division of physical and emotional labour between Pod, the determined man of the family who deals with the outside world, and Homily, the homemaker, but whatever the limitations this might imply in terms of sex roles, we can observe Arrietty's enchantment with her widening horizons, facing a world she had imagined but can now make her own. The adaptations to their new outdoor life involve all kinds of inventive making-do, and this is also an important feature of their later settling-in with their relations, the Hendrearys, all highly reminiscent of wartime evacuation and housing shortages. Homily comforts herself with the reflection that 'at least (we have) a separate entrance.' The sometimes grisly determination to put up with things is very much relieved by the humour, both conscious and unconscious, and this is another way in which Arrietty is freed from the strain of their circumstances.

Norton's ear for the cadences of working-class speech is splendid and the private life of the family is enlivened by conversational exchanges which capture the speakers' characters and amuse both child and adult reader because of their layers of reference. Pod announces one day, '"We better become vegetarians . . . and make no bones about it." Homily remarked grimly, "There won't be no bones to make, not if we become vegetarian."' Later, she muses '"Leeches might be all right stewed,"' a remark which plays with the child reader's mingled curiosity and abhorrence for strange foods. The potentially alarming complexities of everyday survival are domesticated, and Homily becomes much less frightened herself, but she is also helping Arrietty by her struggles; we learn that Arrietty is much impressed by Homily's transition from terror at the sight of her first worm to the efficient handling like 'the professional casualness of the experienced snake-charmer' to which she swiftly progresses.

The little family are having to cope at high speed with profoundly confusing questionings about their basic categories. They are indoor creatures, now having to forage in the outdoors. They are used to cooked food and now have to eat raw food; they had furniture and separate rooms and are now all bundled up together. Such disorienting changes touch on fundamental ways in which human beings (and Borrowers) organize their lives, in contradistinction to the non-human, non-linguistic animal world. Mary Douglas's formulations concerning symbolic boundaries enable us to appreciate the heroic efforts that the Borrowers have to make at this point and that the threat to their civilized identity which Homily feels so keenly is indeed real.[2]

They are helped in this transition by a new character, a half-wild solitary Borrower called Spiller, who epitomizes in his grubby skin and clothes and unpredictable comings and goings the loss of what Homily treasures as respectability. Spiller could be described as 'street-wise' in the fields, knowing how to forage, what dangers to take seriously, how to interpret the clues of the outdoor world. He loves his outdoor life, and Arrietty and he share each other's pleasure in nature. He is as bold as she is in disregarding the Borrower commandment not to reveal oneself to human beings, and he has a child friend, Tom, whom we have already met as the old man Tom Goodenough. Tom saves them from capture by a gypsy, Wild Eye, whose intention is to cage the Borrowers and sell them. 'Fetch a pretty penny, that lot would – cage and all complete.' Wild Eye, the thieving gypsy, like Mrs Driver, is enraged by the domestic life of the Borrowers, which they have achieved by making a home out of a boot that he had once had in his possession. His own sour relation with a gypsy woman who jeers at his story of midgets only intensifies his determination to possess and exploit the fellow-feeling and fragments of comfort he has discerned in the Borrower family life. There are two characteristic responses which follow an encounter between human beings and Borrowers – either the humans feel themselves filled with wonder and privileged to share and protect the Borrowers' vulnerable lives or they seem impelled to crush the independent liveliness of these creatures, by death or imprisonment, which feels to the prisoners like a living death, hardly to be preferred: '"Better the cage than the ferret," breathed Pod. "No," thought Arrietty, "better the ferret."' For the Borrowers represent dangerous possibilities that the world is not quite as we thought, that the imagined or magical element might break through, and when change is feared as catastrophic it has to be resisted with every available tool.[3] Arrietty says, 'It's so awful and sad . . . to belong to a race that no sane person believes in.' The human viewpoint is that one has to face feeling mad if one believes in Borrowers, in the life-power of the imaginary.

The last two volumes, *The Borrowers Aloft* and *The Borrowers Avenged* concern the epic confrontation between the Borrowers and Mr and Mrs Platter, who want to possess them just as if they were food to be dished up on a platter. Mr Platter is a builder and undertaker. Mary Norton implicitly links the market-exploitation of the shoddy builder, the tasteless factory-food teas provided by Mrs Platter in their tea-room, with dealing in death, physical and emotional. 'As villas fell vacant and funerals became scarcer, Mr Platter had time on his hands. He had never liked spare time. In order to get rid of it, he took to gardening. All Mr Platter's flowers were kept like captives – firmly tied to stakes . . . . It was said of a daisy plant that, realizing suddenly where it was, the pink-fringed petals turned white overnight.' The bottom has fallen out of the new housing development market, so the Platters turn to building an imitation of an original model village created by Mr Pott, a railwayman retired after injury, and his friend Miss Menzies. Mr Pott and Miss Menzies have found comfort in their shared project – Mr Pott had lost a leg and is supported by the Railway Benevolent Fund for which he had always worked hard. He used to say sadly when he opened up a pilfered collecting box 'Fox been at the eggs again,' for the gifts to the charity indeed represented creative nourishment for its beneficiaries. Following his accident, he built an entire miniature railway modelled precisely on his old patch, and then he recreated in miniature the surrounding village. Miss Menzies is a lonely spinster; we learn that she loved a cousin who married someone else, and now she sustains herself by art and craft work and writing children's books. She is sad, but alive to everything with imaginative possibility, and 'she also believed in fairies'. She helps Mr Pott's patient recreation with her deft capacities to model and together they make an exquisite rendering of their village world, which is opened to the public.[4] Miss Menzies notices one day with great happiness and very little surprise that tiny living creatures have come to inhabit the village in addition to all her model-people, and she and Arrietty become friends.

Mr Platter lacks inspiration of his own, but by careful spying he is able to wrest the secrets of Mr Pott's more popular village and copy it, adding various technological wonders; but when he observes the live creatures he is dumbfounded and depressed. He decides to steal the Borrowers and build a cage-house in which they can be displayed forever behind plate glass, and make his fortune because of all the paying visitors they will attract. The Platters launch a night-time foray by boat and succeed in capturing the

Borrowers and confining them in the attic of their house while the cage is being completed. The Clock family gather their resources together as they gradually comprehend the Platters' plan – they successfully conceal their capacity to think and talk, while fuming at being treated like domestic animals, fed like cats in saucers. They achieve a magnificent escape by air balloon (technology put to good use); Arrietty, reading in old magazines left in the attic, finds a description of how to build it, Pod's practical improvisation reaches its apogee in the construction, and Homily's faith in Pod combined with 'feminine intuition,' 'feelings' (hunches) and 'wild ideas' carry them through moments of despair. Just in time, they escape into the air through the attic window from the 'living prison' in which they felt they would 'shrivel up under (people's) stares'.

The excitement of the adventure-story escape and the joyous delight evoked in the reader can perhaps be linked with primitive human emotional experience: they bring to mind anxieties linked to infantile phantasies arising from impulses to possess and control whatever is passionately desired, and to do so by imprisoning the desired objects inside the body of the desiring infant where they can be totally controlled and manipulated. In the infantile part of the mind, Melanie Klein has shown that this psychic process can be experienced concretely and confused with bodily processes, so that the imprisoned objects are felt to be equivalent to bits of faecal mass.[5] The almost magical use of gas to fill the escape balloon from the attic prison gloriously reverses the anal connotations of the prison as they sail forth into the fresh air. Only when objects of desire can live and breathe in their own right can life really be lived with joy.

It is fascinating to notice that at this point in the stories Arrietty is clearly emerging into adolescence; the idea of marrying Spiller crosses her mind, she is ashamed of the clothes she is wearing but has grown out of, and terribly depressed when the air balloon bursts as they land and thus ruins the elegant return to earth she had imagined. Pod has a strong conception of a Borrower way of life, but Arrietty is more and more questioning the rightness of it. Why cannot she talk to human beings? By whose authority is she to live? So the escape from incarceration by the repressive Platters is also the backcloth for Arrietty's puzzling over finding her own way to live. She admires the 'One for all and all for one' ethic

176

of the Borrowers (a sense of community frequently contrasted with limited human capacities for mutual identification – Arrietty can barely comprehend that man could kill man), but she is powerfully drawn to make contact with humans. Her love of words and talk makes conversation such a pleasure, and her loneliness is assuaged by the loving recognition and appreciation she receives from Miss Menzies. Like the boy in the first volume, the link with Miss Menzies seems to grow from her curiosity, wish to understand more, and conviction that words are a good tool for this.

In the final volume, the Borrowers are 'Avenged' on their persecutors. The Platters pursue them to their new home, determined to recapture them. The Hendreary family have set up house in the church vestry, and the dénouement takes place in the church itself. Mrs Platter has observed the Hendreary child, Arrietty's beloved cousin Timmins, who dashes round the church building with scant caution but huge pleasure. All this occurs while the church is being lavishly decorated for Easter with spring flowers by the three ladies who take care of the church – Miss Menzies, who continues to mourn the lost Borrowers and has even tried to alert the village policeman to this group of 'missing persons'; Mrs Whitlow, the Irish caretaker who believes in fairies; and Lady Mullings, who has a reputation for unusual capacities for faith-healing and finding lost objects. This trio represents one conception of human social life – they all combine an involvement in the traditions of village life, here epitomized by the life of the village church, a sense of life as in part mysterious, full of elements not accounted for by over-literal rationality, and a pleasure in their shared work which offers them companionship mitigating the loneliness and difficulties of life. For Miss Menzies, the Borrowers had symbolized a recovery of her own vitality and creativity, rescuing her from a depressive preoccupation with the babies she had not had: 'How could I make them?' she puzzles, in response to Mr Pott's questions. 'These creatures are alive.'

The Platters are placed in opposition to this evocation of 'organic' community. Their driving ambition is for themselves, their link with other people is through making money out of them, and their attitude to the Borrowers is totally exploitative. They do not marvel at the aliveness of these tiny creatures but are dominated by a desire to own and control this 'gift' of nature. The church setting elaborates a metaphor:

the Platters' life values involve a sacrilegious attitude. In fact, the attempt to take possession of the Borrowers becomes interpreted as an attempted theft of the church silver when the Platters are discovered in disarray in the church in the middle of the night. The human actors in the drama are thus divided between those able to celebrate new life, beauty, creativity, possibilities of restoration and to live in awe of the wonder of the world, and those dominated by a vengeful desire to assert mastery.

There is no doubt a powerful political statement here – an idealized version of the old order of the countryside in which rich and poor can co-operate without envious hostility is contrasted with a version of bourgeois selfishness associated with town and money-making. The social and historical oversimplification may offend, but the contrast can also be seen as focusing on a different and primarily psychological feature; the 'old order' just like old houses (imagine the perils of house modernization for Borrowers) allows for changing elements because of the confidence in continuity derived from a degree of external and internal structure; the world of the Platters is so lacking in roots or any rich relatedness that encountering anything unexpected is a cause for acute disturbance, stirring up the omnipresent greed which characterizes their relationship to their neighbours and tortures them personally. Such tormenting desire is only assuaged by the swallowing up of its source.

The recurrent importance of village policemen in these stories is significant. Mrs Driver has been laughed out of court by one, who punctures her paranoid and hate-filled delusions by his hilarity. P.C. Pomfret, even though he cannot comprehend Miss Menzies' story of the Borrowers' disappearance from Mr Pott's village, listens with concern to her distress, pondering behind his 'wistful' face and 'soft brown eyes', and later he embodies the moral authority of the law as he deals with the dishevelled Platters caught in the act. The policemen stand for the assertion of a reality principle; those driven out of their senses by destructive omnipotent wishes can be appropriately controlled, and the law can uphold justice in a just way, without vengeance. The child-reader is offered both the traditional delight of the unmasking and punishment of the villains, and a differentiation between the pseudo-morality of the Mrs Driver-type, full of repressive dislike and denunciation, and genuine moral judgement based on accurate observation, not projection and prejudice.

In this final volume, there is an interesting shift in the perception of human and Borrower worlds. In the first four books, the human world is represented in terms of extreme alternatives; there are idealized human beings who can help to preserve Borrower life (the boy of the first story, Tom Goodenough, Miss Menzies) and there are pernicious rather monstrous enemies who threaten it (Mrs Driver, Wild Eye, the Platters). By contrast, the Borrowers themselves are presented in the round, with the detail of their characters finely shown, and as the stories progress and Arrietty meets more Borrowers (the Hendreary family, Spiller, the 'wild boy' borrower, Peagreen, the lame intellectual aesthete) this is extended. But in the final volume, the human world too takes on more ordinary proportions in the events which take place in the church. The process of Arrietty's maturation, shown so touchingly in her increasing capacities to observe the complexities of people's character including her own – when she realizes, for instance, what a 'rotten snob' Peagreen is, in full awareness of how much she shares his love of books, poems, paintings and how this separates her from her own family – and in her adolescent uncertainties about what sort of Borrower she is going to be, is structurally parallel to the resolution of the final volume. The sequence of stories ends as human beings become perceived as ordinarily good and bad, not as the ideal or horrific types of interior phantasy or fairy tales. The Platters go off to live in Australia and this distancing seems less on the basis of their continuing to represent the unassimilable nastiness of human nature – they are even given relations out there – and rather more to imply the possibility that these utterly awful parents of our childhood imaginations can be relegated to a less central position in our minds because of the growth of richer capacities for experience and relationship. The reader can imagine various possible futures for Arrietty, but in a less totally imperilled context. There is space to live, not just survive.

While Mary Norton's version of the social context which nurtures this is one of an idealized village community, the characteristics she draws our attention to have a psychological accuracy which may help to explain why her ideal vision of a good place to live is one so frequently shared, particularly by young children. The resonance of the 'small is beautiful' theme arises from the human requirement for personal identity to grow from an experience of knowing and being known.

9

Making Out in America:
The Mouse and His Child

The Mouse and His Child is something of an American epic novel scaled down for child readers. It provides a double point of identification for its reader, both through the fantasy of a toy come to life (a theme shared with many earlier stories such as *Pinocchio* and *The Little Wooden Horse*[1]) and through the toy mouse's being characterized as a child, with a child's primary preoccupations. The mouse child's longing and hope is to reconstitute a home and a family, remembered from his earliest days of consciousness in the dolls' house in the toy shop, where an elephant sang him a lullaby and where there was a seal whom he later chose to be his adopted sister:

> 'Maybe we could look for the elephant and the seal and the dolls' house that used to be in the store with us,' said the child. 'Couldn't we, Papa?'
> 'What in the world for?' said the father.
> 'So we can have a family and be cosy,' answered the child.

This mouse-child's longings have the power to remake the world of this story, bringing about the marriage of his father, the adoption of a sister and three uncles (Frog, the kingfisher and the bittern) and the redemption of their main enemy, the gangster king of the dump, Manny Rat, and his eventual adoption as the fourth uncle. The potency of the child's longings and dreams is a powerful realization of a child's view of the world, made universal through the story, by constant reference to the main characters not by names, which they seem to lack, but as 'the father' and 'the child'. In the context of this story, the moving force of the child's hopes for his family also carries a specific social meaning.

As the mouse father reminds his child, they encounter in their adventures bank robbery, war, a theatre company (Crow and Mrs Crow's 'Caws of Art'), a philosopher (the deep thinker and author C. Serpentina, a turtle), the entrepreneurial dam-making beavers and the less successful intellectual and teacher Muskrat, who makes his own splash in the beaver pond. Above all, there is the gangster Manny Rat who pursues the mouse and his child throughout the story, and his burning garbage-dump world. A real tramp frames the story, finding and mending the wind-ups at the beginning, setting them on their journey ('Be tramps'), and rediscovering and blessing them ('Be happy') in their restored house and family state at the end. This world of animals each with their different occupation and disposition is linked by a form of mass communication, the blue jay's telegraphic news bulletins: MUSKRAT, WINDUPS ACTIVE IN WINTER SPORTS. While the particular value to the plot of this device is to keep Manny Rat informed of the whereabouts of the wind-ups (his pursuit of them in order to smash them is the negative counterpart of the mouse couple's search for elephant, seal, and their house), it also makes Manny Rat's humiliation at the hands of the wind-up toys a public fact. Reputation is power in his world, and he is therefore impelled by fear of public discredit to seek his revenge. Unusually, therefore, for an animal story for young children, *The Mouse and His Child* represents the life of the city as well as the country, and describes the encounters of the inexperienced father and child with the impersonal and violent hazards of the modern world. Its happy ending describes the success of the mouse family in their new world too, as they establish a hotel for travellers like themselves and then make it the respected centre of their community.

The weight of allegory of this story makes it, from our experience, a somewhat difficult one for its intended child readers. It shares this presenting difficulty with adult novels of a corresponding social range and complexity. Attempting to encompass a whole modern world in a novel, as Dos Passos or E.L. Doctorow do,[2] requires authors to explore many characters, locations, and modes of expression. Though this children's story is very finely crafted and scaled-down to keep within the terms of its animal allegories, (it is no surprise to read in the author's note that it took him three years and four re-writes to complete), there are nevertheless many references beyond the child reader's possible understanding. These multiple levels of reference are probably a little over-indulged, pleasurable as they are for the adult reader. They lead, in our experience, to some loss of intensity of response to the narrative in younger readers, as they cope with the diversity of the story. And by the time some of the more sophisticated references and comedy (for example concerning theatrical and gangster genres) become available to young readers, they may be embarrassed about children's stories and unlikely to be reading animal fables at all. There is thus a problem in the remarkable extent to which *The Mouse and his Child* stretches its basic form to encompass such a range of cultural and social references. Where great psychological depth and intensity can be achieved in children's fiction through specific transformation and symbolizations of a process of development, as in E.B. White's *Charlotte's Web*, for example, the aim of sociological depth runs more quickly up against the limits of the child reader's knowledge of the world. Intensive depth in regard to the child's internal world is perhaps more readily available to writers for children than the possibility of exploring extensively the qualities of the social world. The most distinctive requirement of children's fictional genres, namely their narrowing of the objects of fiction to what a child might know, fantasize, or have feelings for, sets natural limits to what they can say about societies.

In *The Mouse and His Child* everyone has a place except the protagonists. They begin their existence in the story as transients, waiting to be sold in a toy store. They have five years in a family home, kept in store through the year until they are brought out, by convention, to play under the tree at Christmas time. Then the mouse child's exceptional longings to have a home of his own and his memory of the elephant he had wanted for a mama lead to their undoing. He breaks the rules of wind-up toys and 'cries on the job'. This unsettles the family cat, who knocks a vase over and breaks them as a consequence. They are cast out, and their homeless adventures begin.

This theme of homelessness is elaborated in the narrative in terms of a concept of territory which is really a controlling metaphor in this story. The term connects with the scientific understanding of animal behaviour brought about by ethological and ecological studies, and imagines the mental states of animals engaged in a struggle for survival in their environment. The mouse and his child come to realize what it is to be without a specific territory of one's own. At first, the mouse father does most of the reflecting about their situation, while the mouse child impels them through his passionate longing to recover the territory – the dolls' house in the store – that he thought they once had:

> 'But what is a territory?' asked the mouse child again.
> 'A territory is your place,' said the drummer boy. 'It's where everything smells right. It's where you know the runways and the hideouts, night or day. It's what you fought for, or your father fought for, and you feel all safe and strong there. It's the place where, when you fight, you win.'
> 'That's your territory,' said the fifer. 'Somebody else's territory is something else again. That's where you feel all sick and scared and want to run away, and that's where the other side mostly win.'
> The father walked in silence as a wave of shame swept over him. *What chance has anybody got without a territory!* he repeated to himself, and knew the little shrew was right. What chance had they indeed! He saw now that for him and his son the whole wide world was someone else's territory, on which he could not even walk without someone to wind him up.

'Territory is both a concept of natural history, giving some basis in reality to the story's fantasy explorations of the natural world, and a social idea. Such links between readings of nature and readings of society are a persistent feature of Western science, each area of study having influenced the other through its dominant paradigms and metaphors of understanding. Social Darwinism[3] and the more recent fashion of sociobiology[4] are only two examples of this reciprocal connection. In the case of *The Mouse and His Child*, a Darwinian idea of the natural competition of species for survival is softened, as it has been more generally under the recent impact of ecological ideas of a less individualist and more 'social' kind, to include a concept of social equilibrium, in which each species, including the mouse and his child, could find its appropriate niche.

The resonances of this territorial metaphor are considerable in the story. The issue of 'eat or be eaten' seems well adapted to the infantile preoccupations of young readers, and occurs in many fairy tales and young children's stories.[5] The story effectively evokes the anxieties of the young about being lost and away from home, for example in the description of the frightened young soldier shrews, whose battle has both the qualities of play and of struggle over life and death. The finding and defence of one's own territory, both in the literal sense of land, and in the symbolic sense of economic and social space, seem particularly evocative in the historical and social imagination of the United States.

Against the more or less ordered world of nature in the story, the dump provides a contrasting negative image of society, consisting of rats, vermin, and rubbish, and evoking hell through its recurring image of burning fires. Where the mouse and his child imagine family and brotherhood, and obtain the friendship and co-operation of other creatures in their adventures, Manny Rat's dump is a ruthless struggle for power, in which all are competitors or subordinates, and in which the wind-up equivalents of the mouse and his child are enslaved:

> Who's that passing in the night?
> Foragers for Manny rat!
> We grab first and we hold tight –
> Foragers for Manny Rat!

This malign place is the underworld aspect of the city:

> Manny Rat snickered and pushed the mouse and his child along through an evil smelling huddle of gambling dens, gaming booths, dance halls and taverns, all crudely built of scraps of wood and cardboard boxes. The bonfires in the alleyways threw moving shadows of the revellers large on walls of open stalls; the dance halls thumped and whistled savagely with tin-can drums, reed pipes, and matchbox banjos, while the dim light of candles through the doors and windows sent bobbing rat shapes dancing blackly on the snow.

Manny intends to be master of the dump:

> He came closer, and bared his slanting, yellow teeth. 'Notice my teeth, if you will,' he said. 'Pretty, aren't they? They're the longest, strongest, sharpest teeth in the dump.' He swept his paw round the dark horizon. 'All this will belong to Manny Rat one day,' he said. 'I'll be boss of the whole place. Is that so or isn't it,

185

Ralphie!' He leapt suddenly at the youngest rat. 'You're the boss, Boss,' said Ralphie, stepping back quickly. 'Don't get excited.'

There is much black comedy of this kind in the genre of gangster dialogue, which the story adapts to its audience and its purposes in a way not dissimilar from *Bugsy Malone*, though in this case through allegory with animals rather than by casting children in adult roles. The moment of Manny's electrocution on the power lines as he tries to destroy his rivals and their house suggests a familiar, somewhat black climax of such stories:

> As he connected the wires there was a blinding flash, and every hair on Manny Rat stood up and crackled with blue flame. He felt a shuddering thrill as the full voltage of the power line coursed through his body and sent branching lightnings into his brain.

But in this case the outcome is not fatal, and leaves space for Manny's redemption. His humbling and defeat, and his acceptance by the mouse family as the child's 'Uncle Manny' marks the triumph of a benign form of community and family over the violence and depravity of the dump.

The theme of territory and the plight of those without one has a number of specific referents in this story. The mouse and his child lack a home. Together with a home, the child wants a mama for himself and a wife for his father. This is the most direct point of identification with the feelings of the child reader. There is also the situation of two other wanderers, the tramp, shunned by passers-by outside the toy shop, but joined by a stray dog and with kindness enough to spend a day mending the wind-up toys and setting them on their way. The frequent references to the railway tracks, passing freight cars, and life on the road evoke the importance of the railroad to older stories of hoboes and wandering in America,[6] where more recently (and in E.B. White's *Stuart Little*) the open road would be more likely to symbolize the expanse of the United States. The tramp's reappearance at the end (he drops from a freightcar) confirms that wanderings can after all end happily.

But perhaps the most important level of allegory is in the idea of creatures without a home who have to make their way in a strange and frightening world. The trajectory of the wind-up mice, from their elaborate and socially pretentious house at the beginning of the story (where they are objects of condescension for the 'established' residents), to their success-ful transformation of this stately dolls' house into a hotel (whose sign says 'Migrants Yes'), suggests a story of European immigrants to America. These ill-equipped wind-ups, full of social rules and conventions and ill-adapted to living in their new world, encounter a metaphor for the worst of the American city in Manny Rat and the dump. But they later encounter other more positive and helpful elements of American life. Apart from the energetic Beavers, who are examples of successful American enterprise and have no time for them, nearly all the creatures they meet are themselves struggling for a living but find time to help them along the way. Frog, for example, in the character of a travelling quack and fortune-teller, reminiscent of a preacher, narrowly escapes death on several occasions but finds himself taking risks for the mouse couple. The shrew soldiers are hapless conscripts in wars they do not understand. Muskrat is a failure, with only a jarful of young firefly admirers, and only the most limited capacity to think out problems through his 'Much in Little' formulas. Crow and Mrs Crow run a struggling theatre company, and escape being eaten by their audience of weasels only through the intrepid intervention of the mouse and his child. The mouse and his child have to achieve self-winding (or autonomy) and also learn to move in a straight line instead of dancing round each other in a circle: 'The whole secret of the thing, they insisted (after their triumph) was simply and at all costs to move steadily ahead, and that, they said, could not be taught.' But they found not only a home for themselves, but also a hotel and centre of many activities for all their friends. They become, by allegory, the founders of a thriving business and community, designed especially for other travellers (migrants) like themselves. The wind-ups move from an artificial world that seems like an echo of polite European society, into the new self-reliance and sociability of the United States: '"One does what one is wound to do,"' says the elephant early on. '"It is expected of me that I walk up and down in front of my house; it is expected of you that you drink tea. And it is expected of this young mouse that he go out into the world with his father and dance in a circle."'

At first these artificial creatures do not understand feelings, with the exception of the child:

'Do be quiet,' said the elephant to the mouse child. 'I'll sing you a lullaby. Pay attention now.' The mouse child stopped crying and listened while the elephant sang:

'Hush, hush, little plush,
Mama's near you through the night,
Hush, hush, little plush.
Everything will be alright.'

'Are you my mama?' asked the child. He had no idea what a mama might be, but he knew at once that he needed one badly.

'Good heavens!' said the elephant. 'Of course I'm not your mama. I was simply singing words I once heard a large teddy bear sing to a small one.'

'Will you be my mama?', said the child, 'and will you sing to me all the time? And can we all stay here together and live in the beautiful house where the party is and not go out into the world?'

'Certainly not!' snorted the elephant. 'Really', she said to the gentleman doll, 'this is intolerable. One is polite to the transient element on the counter, and see what comes of it.'

But they all have to learn to go out into the world. By the end, the mouse and his child are self-winding, and the battered elephant has put her sense of style to new use. 'Wearing a black eyepatch over the missing eye and a bright kerchief knotted over the missing ear, she achieved a look both charmingly rakish and surprisingly chic.' Even her sense of domestic order and cleanliness plays its part, and she contemptuously sweeps up the gunpowder sprinkled by Manny Rat to blow them all up. 'Men simply won't clean up after themselves – that's what it amounts to. Wind me up please and attach my broom.' So her old-fashioned habits become adapted to her new life. In the end she lends 'the whole establishment a raffishly patrician flavour that was irresistible'.

This optimistic, active way of making out in a new world is expressed in two other important aspects of the story. Characters are particularly defined by their modes of action and the vigour and energy of the writing is contained particularly in its dramatic action, rather than through descriptive language. The 'picaresque' movement of the main mouse characters through so many worlds, literal and figurative – toy store, family hearth, fields, 'swamp and pond', garbage dump, and dolls' house again, – enables the author to dramatize their adventures using dialogue and action as his principal devices. Suffering and disadvantage are expressed in inability to act, for example in the wind-ups' problems of dependence and mobility, and in their period of submergence under the water. The description of Manny Rat's captive squad of wind-ups conveys the contrast of the aggressive, active rats, and the helpless toys who have lost their former modes of action:

The mouse and his child heard the singing again, and in the dim starlight they saw, dark against the snow, an ugly young rat driving a group of battered wind-up toys ahead of him. There were more than a dozen of them, all staggering under the weight of the bags they carried on their backs. They had been salvaged from the dump by Manny Rat and Ralphie, his assistant and rat-of-all-work, and whatever mobility they possessed was due to the mechanical skill of the two rats. Once they had been kicking donkeys, dancing bears, tumbling clowns, roaring lions, baaing goats – all manner of specialities were represented in the group – but few of them by now had all their faculties. And most of them had lost a limb or two along with fur and clothing, eyes and ears. All their trades and tricks were gone; the best that they could do was plod ahead when wound, and that not very well. They tottered up the avenue, led by a mouldy goat, both lame and blind, who with the others feebly sang:

Who's that passing in the night?
Foragers for Manny Rat!
Make your move and take your bite
After us or stand and fight
Manny Rat!

The wind-ups are defined by what they do, or can no longer do. Virtually all the characters in the story – the mice, Manny Rat, the Crows, C. Serpentina, Euterpe the parrot, Miss Mudd the dragonfly larva, the drummer boy, fifer, and other soldier shrews, the blue jay reporter ('avid for disaster and eager for a headline') are defined, in an American way, by their characteristic forms of activity. The mouse and his child have the most passionate commitment to action, like their enemy who is drawn to them by an identification he doesn't understand.

The dramatic qualities of this story make it well adapted to being experienced as a form of play by its child readers. The element of make-believe of its animals learning the difficulties of real life, often with the same ironic self-awareness as the spider in *Charlotte's Web*, allows the child to enter and learn about these various situations in imagination. The make-believe of the animals taking quasi-human roles allows the child reader to think about pursuit, violence, and passionate longing in ways which are both powerful and sufficiently distanced from their own lives. The element of learning from the experience of a strange place is evocative of learning about a new world, as well as learning through growing up.

Another aspect of the story which evokes the experience of immigrants is the leading role given to the mouse child as the sustainer of the family and its fortunes. When they find themselves Manny's prisoners, the child is supported by his father: 'His father's hands were firm upon him, and he resolved to see what next the great world offered.' But it is the son's innocent desire to constitute a family that gives purpose to his father's resilience, and which also leads others, such as Frog, to be more helpful to them than their helpers themselves expect. In the longing to establish themselves in a territory like other animals, the wind-up mice depend on the child's naive hopefulness.

In their improvised intervention in the Cawa of Art's experimental play, *The Last Visible Dog*, the child and his father are already equal partners in inventiveness and courage. It is the young who have the hopefulness and spirit to make out in the new world and the old learn from and are moved by them.

The coin which brings them good luck throughout the story (and becomes the weapon with which the father knocks out Manny's teeth) has on one side *Your Lucky Day*, and on the other *You Will Succeed*, an apt combination of appeals to fortune and determination. The story is a story of deserved modest worldly success as well as a story of a family reconstituted.

The intensity of the child's need in this story to find a mama (a new one, and a wife for his father) and to become part of a proper family suggests another point at which *The Mouse and His Child* corresponds to contemporary experience. The story evokes a world in which families are now often broken and children often find themselves with one available parent rather than two.[7] The tramp wishes them well in their wanderings, but recognizes their good fortune when he sees the family home restored as *The Last Visible Dog* – in the end, valuable though the journey is, a place of one's own is best.

It may only be against the background in which families are fragile and liable to break-up and separation that the lack and need of one can become so convincingly the moving impulse of a children's story. Whereas in earlier fictions, *The Secret Garden*, for example, premature death is the reason for a child's being left without parents, in this story the mouse and his child just are that way, joined together as a couple when the child thinks there should be three, with a sister too. To put it directly, this is a fiction about a one-parent family, and this seems to be part of its contemporary appeal. In only a limited way is the story even about growing up. The mouse child's passion is to be a child in a proper family – for the elephant who once sang him a lullaby to become his mama. Perhaps it is a contemporary fragility of home and family which is able to invest this hope with such passion.

So far we have most emphasized the social and cultural connotations of the story, and its evocation of a variety of ways of making out in the world in allegorical terms which are accessible to children. The humour of the dialogue must often be partially lost on child readers (for example, the reactions of audience and critics to the Caws of Art's experimental play, with its allusions to Beckett – '"The meadow isn't ready for this yet," said the fieldmouse critic to his wife'). But the child reader can become involved in the variety of social scenes depicted in the story. There are also unconscious emotional dimensions to *The Mouse and His Child* which are psychic correlates of the social alternatives and choices described in the story. The idea of a territory and a family has to be real in the mouse child's mind before it can be brought about in action. The child's exceptional quality is imagination mingled with hope. The mouse child's confidence that there must be a mother and a sister for him is like an innate knowledge, corresponding to the psychoanalytical notion of the baby's object-relatedness as an endowment at birth.[8] There is an implicit reference to what is innate in the child's earliest experience in the lapse of five years between the loss of the original dolls' house and the elephant mother he wanted, and the beginning of the mouse couple's adventures. It is as if the period between this formative first experience, and the moment when the mouse can actively begin to look, is frozen. His later life thus becomes a project to realize his earliest desires. An implication is that without this state of psychic hopefulness emigration would not be possible, since the hopeless ones would not take the risk or would perish, like the captive wind-ups, in the attempt.[9]

There is a psychic as well as a social contrast between the hospitable house that the mouse family establish, and the counter-world of the garbage dump. Physically, this is an antithesis between the providing, containing breast, the welcoming house high up on its pole, illuminated and cared for by both sexes, and the all-male, anal dump below which contains pain, the filthy remains of food and carrion matter, and death. The dump is a society of greed and vice – the red light district is another association to its glowing embers and fires – whose feverish pursuit of pleasure and power is not however without its fascination. A society in which characters try without sentiment to care for each other is juxtaposed in the story to a fascist world of tyranny and sadism. Its pleasures depend on denying the weaknesses of the self through crushing them without mercy in others. The dump is also a parody of industrial organization, in which Manny Rat exploits his mechanical ingenuity to enslave the wind-ups and casts them aside when they are no longer productive. The rats from the dump invade the lofty world of the dolls' house in a perverse way, turning into a place of orgy what the mouse family wants for a home and a place of shelter. The dump has a characteristic sexual organization, in which sexuality is subordinate to power, and in which there are few women except, at Manny's party, 'lithe young beauties of vaguely theatrical connection'. Manny's name conveys, among other things, the delusion of the dump world that its exploitation and survival of the strongest is manly. For the mouse child and his father, hope lies in finding a mother and a sister, and regaining contact with the feelings absent from the dump. The elephant is early on split off in her complacent identification with being inside the house from the anxieties of the outsider mouse-child, and it is only when she shares their suffering that they are able to get together. This is a psychic comparison of the state of mind of insider haves and outsider have-nots, and suggests a division on which the sadism of the rats can thrive. The struggle of the mice to become self-winding also has both social and unconscious dimensions. Socially, it signifies the possibility of finding one's own direction in the modern world, compared with the set patterns of the old world where everything is pre-ordained. The adaptation of the tin seal to her earlier life with the kingfisher suggests such a successful adjustment to autonomy, which clearly requires a capacity to abandon preconceptions and accept what comes. There may also be a reference to the particular difficulties of the one-parent mouse couple, for whom learning to move in a straight line is an improvement on dancing round each other in circles. While they become 'self-winding' as a couple, one motor reciprocally winding the other, they never do become separate from one another, but then the story ends with the constitution of a family in which the mouse can take his place as a child of two parents.

The most emotionally complex aspect of the story is in the relationship of Manny Rat to the two wind-ups. He, like Frog, is unexpectedly disturbed by them. Frog, who has survived through his wits ('he had attained his present age, however, by paying closer attention to not being eaten than his enemies could bring to bear on eating him . . .') finds himself moved to tell the truth to Manny and to risk his life for the wind-ups for reasons he doesn't understand at all. Manny's relationship with his wind-up captives – the predecessors of the father and child – is sarcastically intimate. He mocks them through his understanding of their terror, seeking to raise their hopes of comfort only to smash them down more cruelly.

> 'Where are you taking us?' asked the father.
> 'To a ball' said the rat. 'To a jolly, jolly ball at the royal palace, where we shall all drink champagne and dance till dawn. How'll that be?' He laughed softly. His voice, half pleasant, half repellent, was oddly mild and persuasive.
> 'Are we really going to a palace?' asked the child.
> 'I don't think so,' said the father. 'He's teasing us.'
> 'Yes,' said the rat. 'I'm a dreadful tease – famous for my sense of humour. And here we are home again, safe and sound.'
> They were off the highway now, and at the dump.

But we learn that there is a more frightened and anxious part of Manny Rat too, which is stirred up by Frog's prophecies of doom for him. He comes to fear the weak and helpless wind-ups, and his self-respect depends on his destroying them. He knows that this is an irrational and self-destructive quest:

> But Manny Rat had no choice left; some choice beyond himself was pulling him whichever way his quarry turned. He wound the

elephant, cursed forlornly at the now empty provision bags she carried, and shuffled on as if at the end of an invisible chain by which his prey would drag him to his doom.

Manny Rat's need to destroy father and child can best be understood as the need to destroy the vulnerable parts of himself. His wind-up slaves serve not only as his labour force in his struggle for supremacy over the dump, but also as his alter egos – their suffering enables him to feel strong. His confiding tones with them are the means by which he manipulates and keeps at a distance his own vulnerable feelings. He ruthlessly punishes any weakness:

> 'Him,' said Ralphie, pointing to a one-eyed, three-legged donkey. 'He's got a lot to say.'
> 'It's nothing,' said the frightened donkey as he heard Manny Rat approach his blind side. 'I was just feeling a little low – you know how it is.'
> 'You're not well,' said Manny Rat. 'I can see that easily. What you need is a long rest.' He picked up a heavy rock, lifted it high, and brought it down on the donkey's back, splitting it open like a walnut. 'Put his works in the spare part can,' said Manny Rat to Ralphie.[10]

It is this sense of interior weakness which begins to disorient and torment him when he leaves the dump in pursuit of the toy mice. Finally, in the story's happy ending, Manny is able to experience his softer feelings, and accept his weakness. As with the Frog, it is the magical appeal of the child's love which brings about this redemption. The sadistic empathy with and dependence on the weakness of others of Manny Rat provides the most subtle characterization of the story. Manny, having exploited as a form of cruelty a falsely reassuring and avuncular manner, is finally moved to be accepted as a real Uncle Manny by the child.

The Mouse and His Child is able to use conventions of a story about animals to represent great cruelty and danger as well as the ultimate attainment of safety and happiness. The ecological scheme of a feeding cycle or pyramid, with predators at the top and lowly creatures at the bottom, both serves as a metaphor of worldly competition and as a way of dramatizing anxieties about eating and being eaten which seem, to judge from psychoanalytic discoveries, to be universal unconscious phantasies of childhood, related to the primary importance of food and bodily security. The animal allegory enables Hoban to represent a much wider range of feeling than could readily be coped with by children in a more realistic mode. The mouse and his child are, after all, mechanical toys, and the convention of the story even allows them to experience death and re-birth at the hands of the reformed Manny Rat when he makes them self-winding:

> With an odd little questioning smile he picked up his screwdriver and touched the mouse father's tin with it.
> 'Go ahead,' said the father, and felt his senses leave them as he and the child were taken apart.
> They returned to consciousness to find themselves walking, the springs inside them buzzing and clicking as they alternately expanded and contracted their coils.[11]

In this engagement with the extremes of fear and happiness, life and death, *The Mouse and His Child* shares qualities with the classic fairy tales, though it is more literary and sophisticated in its methods. It makes many references to other familiar writings; Manny's entry on the stage as 'Banker Ratsneak' echoes Shylock, for example, and his cry of defeat evokes a memory of one of Beatrix Potter's stories (these also, in their gentle way, treat of life and death): '"No teef!" wept Manny Rat. "I am finished! I am done. No teef at all! No teef at all!"'

This story succeeds in representing and integrating an extraordinary range and depth of feelings, concluding with a happy outcome which is perhaps especially appropriate for young readers considering the extreme fears that this demanding story is likely to evoke in them. An important criterion of exceptional quality in children's fiction, as in other literature, is success in integrating powerful conflicts of feeling into an emotionally truthful narrative.

10

Inner Implications of Extended Traumas: *Carrie's War*

Nina Bawden is a writer greatly enjoyed by children, and admired by adult readers of children's fiction. Her work is full of themes that have also interested other good children's writers: childhood recalled (as in Philippa Pearce's *Tom's Midnight Garden*), the impact of moving house, especially town and country contrasts (as in E. Nesbit), wartime experience (as with Mary Norton's *Borrowers*), the impact of family separations (also central in Bawden's delightful book *The Peppermint Pig*); the meaning of magic and myth for children (also explored with varying success for example by Ursula Le Guin, Susan Cooper, and Alan Garner); the frightening aloneness of a child with a belief or fear which cannot be shared. In *Carrie's War*, Nina Bawden tells the story of the wartime evacuation to a Welsh mining village of a child, Carrie, and her brother Nick. She attempts to show the way in which Carrie's experience there is woven into her imaginative life and personality. Carrie revisits the place twenty years later with her own children; the story is set in the context of 'la recherche du temps perdu'. The framing of the story is not wholly successful, but the intensely remembered events of the months of evacuation provide a moving and compelling encounter with twelve-year old Carrie, and repay a detailed reading.

The book opens with a rendering of Carrie's recurrent dream, which ends in a nightmarish way with her twelve-year-old self running away, frightened:

The yew trees in the Grove were dark green and so old that they had grown twisted and lumpy, like arthritic fingers. And in Carrie's dream, the fingers reached out for her, plucking at her hair and her skirts as she ran. She was always running by the end of this dream . . .

So we understand that her return is concerned with this dream which is pressing for some resolution. Her children see the overgrown wood which they walk through to reach the Grove as like the forest surrounding the Sleeping Beauty, but Carrie is returning not as a pre-pubertal child but as a recently-widowed woman with four children. However, some part of herself is trapped in the dream and her journey may enable her to find a way through the thickets and to re-establish contact with this. She is mourning the loss of her husband, and this has opened her mind to thoughts about earlier losses. Alone and vulnerable, her dream can no longer contain for her some lifelong confusions and anxieties: we see her talking to her children about herself in ways they cannot understand, exposing her fears and her need to be taken care of, to which her oldest boy responds protectively. She is both a mother telling her children a story about her childhood (one of the great delights of family conversation), and a woman talking to herself, with a 'remembering smile, half happy, half sad':

After all, what happened wasn't my fault; *couldn't* have been, it just didn't make sense. That's what I've been telling myself all these years, but sense doesn't come into it, can't change how you *feel*. I did a dreadful thing, the worst thing of my life, when I was twelve and a half years old, or I feel that I did, and nothing can change it . . .

Telling her children about the sudden evacuation of whole schools from the cities, hearing their amazement at the idea of children being sent away without parents, she confirms, 'Oh, quite alone. I was eleven when we first came here. And Uncle Nick was going on ten'. The troubling undercurrent which now draws her back to Wales is an aspect of that experience by which she felt shattered. Her children have lost their father; she brings them with her to the place where she learnt about being without parents, perhaps unconsciously hoping that she can solve something for herself which is now

197

additionally urgent because of their need for her to understand their experience of loss.

Carrie introduces her children to 'Druid's Bottom', smiling with them at the ambiguity of the phrase, with the same confused mixture of down-to-earth facts and 'queer' feelings that she had felt as a child: 'Oh, Johnny Gotobed and Hepzibah were real all right . . . But they weren't *ordinary*. Any more than Albert was. Albert Sandwich. Our friend who lived with them.' Carrie frightens herself in beginning to recall these childhood events, though she is also stimulated to want to remember. Her children ask her to go on with the story – she is 'good at stories' – but her eldest boy sees her 'ironed out' and 'crumpled up', crushed by a glimpse of the ruined house which she had hoped to find otherwise. Wishing his father were there, he closes his eyes tight in a half-belief that he can summon his father back to life to deal with his mother's distress. It is like Carrie's experience as a girl, when she felt the responsibility to look after her younger brother; the pressure of anxiety draws each of them into an omnipotent mode of thinking, a resort to magic.

The scene thus set, we enter the world of Carrie's childhood stay in the village. It begins with a beautifully precise delineation of Nick and Carrie, Nick the baby brother, a greedy child over-eating to comfort himself on the train journey from London (and being sick), and Carrie, cross and superior. They are leaving their mother for the first time, and the children have been left to face their uncertainties, as their mother is committed to making the best of things:

> 'Oh, it'll be such fun,' their mother had said when she kissed them goodbye at the station. 'Living in the country instead of the stuffy old city. You'll love it, you see if you don't.'

There is a division of labour between the children, in which Carrie struggles to be calm and competent, and in fact allows Nick to rely on her, and Nick expresses for both of them the feelings of desolation and confusion. Carrie's character is the one most fully explored in the book, and we become aware from the start that mixed with her affection and protectiveness towards Nick is a good deal of unconscious hostility: he is the 'greedy pig', the 'garbage can', and it enrages Carrie to see him 'always let people do things for him, not lifting a finger'. His capacity to show his neediness openly arouses her jealousy, and Carrie's conception of him as a 'garbage can' is connected with her own use of him as a container for her own more infantile feelings. She takes care of him and of her own baby-self in him. Carrie both denounces Nick's anxious clinging to her and loves him for keeping her in touch with her own vulnerablilty. (Bawden's interest in children's relations with each other and in particular their unconscious interdependence is a recurrent theme and strength in her writing.)

The evacuees arrive in a Welsh mining village, and the bewildering impact of this on the children is beautifully evoked: the children smell the coal dust, hear the unfamiliar Welsh voices, walk along a steep cinder track to the village hall, where they are to be assigned to families. It feels to the children like a 'cattle auction' as they stand around waiting to be chosen, though the sense of community responsibility is tangible. Albert Sandwich reads a book as if without a care in the world, but Carrie 'had already begun to feel ill with shame at the fear that no-one would choose her, the way she always felt when they picked teams at school'. Almost suffocated with panic, she turns on Nick, needing someone to blame for the unendurable torment. But once Miss Evans takes an interest in her, her generosity to Nick resurfaces; she is a child particularly capable of identification with adults who care for her, which is to prove a source both of strength and difficulties. Her thin-skinned ultra-sensitive awareness of other people's feelings is a profound capacity in her but also a burden.

So Carrie and Nick go to live with Miss Evans and her brother Councillor Evans, the local grocer, a 'particular' man, with a large sense of his own importance. On their bedroom wall, a notice announces 'The Eye of the Lord is Upon You', and Miss Evans nervously explains how good and quiet they must be and makes it clear that Samuel Isaac Evans is a god to be appeased. Louisa Evans is terrified of the children's effect on her highly ordered existence, and the children are amazed at the contrast between their 'warm muddly house' in London and the astonishingly clean and tidy Evans's house. They are mutually embarrassed when Auntie Lou suggests that they put on slippers to go upstairs and Carrie explains that they have none; the children realize that she thinks they are too poor to own slippers, while they are in fact recalling their comfortable middle-class life at home where Milly the maid tidied up after them. When she explains that they should use the outdoor earth-closet during the day to save wear and tear on the carpet, Nick is outraged, humiliated and frightened at the thought of spiders in the closet. But Carrie rushes to comply and suppress his complaints, terrified that they might lose their new home. Nick both turns to her for comfort and puts into words for both of them his homesickness and fear of Mr Evans who he thinks might be an ogre. Louisa's nervousness about her brother has of course stirred up the children's worries, adding to their own natural anxiety.

Gradually, Carrie and Nick absorb and adapt to their new circumstances. They perceive that the ogre of their imagination is a thin cross man who bullies anyone who is afraid of him, and by using their intelligence to ridicule him – 'You can't really be scared of someone whose teeth might fall out,' Nick tells Carrie – they avoid becoming victims. They learn that Louisa was 'taken in' by her older brother when her mother died, and that their father had been killed down the pit. Mr Evans is a widower with a son in the army. The harsh realities of the mining village become familiar, and the rhythms of domestic life and the life of the shop, where Carrie likes to help, serve to draw the children into a sense of belonging and gradually detach them from their 'other life'. Carrie and Nick's father is a naval officer; their mother has become an ambulance driver in Glasgow, their maid a munitions worker; when mother sends a photograph of herself, they put it on the wall but feel 'she didn't belong in the Evans's house'.

Nick is caught stealing biscuits from the shop and is threatened with a beating. In the wake of finding their way through this totally unfamiliar situation (Nick avoids the beating by saying he will tell his teacher he was hungry, and to avoid this disgrace, Mr Evans prays over him instead) the children realize that they now feel in some sense at home: 'it seemed, in fact, as if they had lived there all their lives long'. Nick hates Mr Evans, and espouses Auntie Lou, smugly confident of his own righteousness. Carrie is more troubled: she observes Auntie Lou's masochistic passivity which invites her brother's bullying attitude, and Nick's greedy exploitation of Mr Evans's desire for a good reputation in the village. Carrie's wish to be 'fair' as regards Louisa and Samuel Evans is perhaps linked to an ongoing unspoken preoccupation with how to put together in her mind the memories of parents and family home with the absorbing immediacy of her foster home. When mother comes on a brief visit, bewildering them with a new haircut which makes her look unfamiliar, the children find themselves defining a new 'we' – the 'we' of the village community – using Welsh expressions their mother does not understand; Carrie is afraid that Nick will complain and that this will hurt Auntie Lou's feelings. There is a very painful sense of mutual incomprehension in this meeting: their mother needs the reassurance of an idealized version of their new lives, and is thus unavailable to them for any serious reflection. This intensifies their turning towards their new home and family, and this thereby wounds her. Nick tells her: "'I like it here very much. I don't ever want to go home again. I simply *love* Auntie Lou. She's the nicest person I've ever met in my whole life.'" And Carrie, though she sees her mother's sadness, is more involved in Auntie Lou's need of them.

At Christmas, the children are sent to fetch a goose from Samuel's sister, who lives at Druid's Bottom. She has married an English mine owner, betraying both Welsh nation and class, and remains unforgiven by her brother. Walking through the dark grove, Nick and Carrie are frightened and blame each other for their panic; the fear of the dark and unfamiliar place reverberates around and grows into something monstrous, connected in Carrie's mind with the legendary reputation of the place and with strange footsteps and mysterious sounds she cannot make sense of. Tumbling into the kitchen, they meet Hepzibah Green, the housekeeper, who introduces them to Johnny Gotobed, the spastic whose jumbled sounds terrified them in the grove. Also living here is Albert, another evacuee child whom they had first met when they arrived in the village. Hepzibah's kitchen, full of warmth, wonderful food, and emotional liveliness, is a new world for the children. They see her as a wise witch, with her knowledge of herbal medicines and her special quality of seeing into people's hearts. This is the very thing that is lacking in their lives with the Evanses and that they were not able to re-establish with their mother on her short visit; it is there for them in Hepzibah. (There is perhaps an echo of the fairy story of Hansel and Gretel in the image of the 'abandoned' brother and sister stumbling out of the dark woods into this magical house.) Hepzibah observes them with loving perspicacity, seeing Albert's 'know-it-all' nature, Nick's little-boy longings – he finds his way on to her lap in no time – and Carrie's passionate intensity.

But the house has other things besides: a library, in which Albert the would-be scientist can wander, the invalid Mrs Gotobed whose life is fading, and the mentally handicapped Johnny. Hepzibah's qualities of care make manageable for the children an encounter with all kinds of frightening aspects of life. On their first visit she tells them a story which illustrates her maternal story-telling role (Carrie's story-telling comes to be appreciated by her children in the next generation – what a powerful theme for a children's writer this is). This role can render accessible some of the deeper feelings of the children: the story tells of an African slave-boy brought to the house who did not survive the winter; he cursed the house of his exile and demanded that his skull be kept in the house forever – otherwise disaster would ensue. There is a skull in the house which is supposed to be his. The practical and observant Albert is more interested in investigating the real origins of the skull, but for Carrie the story's power lies in its evocation of the despair of the child transplanted from his home, and the complex way in which the skull is to serve as a vengeful reminder and source of dread to the household. The slave-boy of the story brings alive the anger and fear which Carrie works so hard to control in herself.

The happiness of their visit is marred afterwards by Carrie's realization that Mr Evans is very jealous of Nick's delight in Hepzibah. Alerted to the danger that he might want to spoil their pleasure, she conceals her actual feelings behind a mask of indifference, and this leads to a quarrel with Nick who denounces her faithlessness. Carrie, however, is terribly troubled by how to be loyal to Hepzibah and Johnny without arousing Mr Evans's envy and suspicion, and this is added to when she overhears Samuel and Louisa discussing how Carrie could give them access to what is 'really going on' in Mrs Gotobed's house. Mr Evans believes that his sister is in Hepzibah's 'power', and that Hepzibah is exploiting her position to feather her own nest – he hopes to use Carrie as a spy. Carrie's miserable discomfort in being caught up in this bitter family quarrel is intense, for it echoes her own unresolved problem about how to put together the fragments of her own experience. If she likes the village, is she betraying her old home and her parents? If she keeps her distance, is she lacking in appreciation of the Evans's concern, particularly Auntie Lou's tender efforts to make the children feel at home? The conflict of loyalty is now being played out in a fresh arena, and she feels impaled by it.[1]

Carrie's own complex personality renders her very vulnerable in certain ways. Her unusually developed capacity for empathy with adults (not at all an uncommon feature in sensitive first children, and echoed in this story by Carrie's own eldest son's relation to her) involves an over-anxious preoccupation with what adults are feeling and a sense of precocious responsibility for keeping them happy. For Carrie, this is linked with a feeling of having to try and fill the gap left by a missing partner – Mr Evans's dead wife, their mother's husband absent at sea, Auntie Lou's spinster condition – all concern her. The fine adjustment of her own moods and wishes to take account of others' needs is a traditional version of ideal femininity; we are made aware that Carrie finds out what others need at the expense of her own personal integrity, for she enters so closely into their mode of being that she loses touch with herself at times. This is why she is so susceptible to the accusation of spying for Mr Evans: she does in fact feel herself a very proficient spy, finding a way past the ordinary barriers of individual identity – ostensibly in order to take better care of people she loves, but perhaps also so as not to feel excluded by the individuality of other people. The way in which she herself ends up deprived is particularly clear when she overhears Mrs Gotobed's tears, and cannot accept Hepzibah's comfort, for she feels Mr Evans's hostile suspicions of Hepzibah alive in her, and feels controlled by his wish that she should spy on his behalf. Gone is her own experience of Hepzibah's generosity – '"she likes to feed people,"' Albert had said, and she knows this to be true – and in its place is the fear of Hepzibah's unusual emotional clear-sightedness. Instead of pleasure in feeling acknowledged and understood, she dreads an encounter which might make transparent her divided heart. She feels doubly uncomfortable, fearing to reveal to Hepzibah and Mr Evans her attachment to the other. She is driven to imagining Hepzibah as an untrustworthy witch and Mr Evans as a torturing inquisitor, losing contact with the reality of her good feelings for each. Perhaps Carrie's own circumstances make her especially open to invasion by Mr Evans's paranoid delusions about usurpers: she is in a sense, as a foster-child, usurping the position that might belong to Mr Evans's own children. (The hostile episode when his son Frederick returns on leave underlines this possibility). She may also be worried about being usurped in her mother's affections. Her mother has in effect chosen to put her husband, her own mother, and war victims before her children in deciding to work as an ambulance driver in Glasgow, near her mother's home and her husband's port. None of this is even half-conscious in Carrie's mind, but her rigorous turning away from thoughts about mother is matched by preoccupations in her new life which seem shaped by important aspects of her relation to what went before.

Meanwhile, the children's presence has been stirring changes in Samuel and Louisa. Carrie's anxiety about Mr Evans's jealousy of their happiness at Druid's Bottom is exaggerated – she confuses her own jealousy at seeing Nick's easy intimacy with Hepzibah, Louisa, and Johnny, with Mr Evans's reactions. (She finds it especially hard to bear as she sees that Nick's enjoyment is greatest when she is excluded.) But nevertheless, Mr Evans has been provoked into a more intense preoccupation with his sister's household by the children's comings and goings. Louisa, in contrast, seems to grow visibly in self-confidence through her care of the children who are fitting recipients of her hitherto thwarted capacity for maternal affection. Her own pitifully limited child-self begins to flourish again through identification with Carrie and Nick. After a bad winter cold, she goes to visit a friend and returns palpably happier: 'she sang while she worked in the kitchen'; her brother comments sourly on this. The atmosphere of new growth is echoed in the birth of a calf at the farm, by which Nick is entranced. 'It's my *best thing*,' he says, a typical example of Bawden's ear for children's speech. Less divided and complex than Carrie, Nick can throw himself into the delights of the moment and discern the happiness of others too – he becomes aware of Louisa's involvement with an American serviceman with cheerful and conspiratorial smugness, for he is altogether set against Mr Evans.

Life is harder for Carrie. The in-between time spanning the shift from childhood into adolescence leaves her without the easy support the younger child Nick can take unself-consciously from Louisa and Hepzibah. Nick can still suck his thumb and nestle on Hepzibah's lap, but Carrie's sentimentality, brought out for example in her reaction to the story about the slave-boy – 'a lovely *sad* story. Poor little African boy, all that long way from home!' – in fact obscures from her the forlorn sense of something lost which she cannot get a grasp of, and also cuts her off from the archaeologically-minded Albert who knows the difference between human and other skulls, and does not sympathize with Carrie's romantic story-making. Carrie is frightened by the talk of Mrs Gotobed's impending death, and her 'horrible, spooky' clothes, (twenty-nine ball gowns given her by her husband, and now eerily different from the workaday clothes of war-time). When her mother sends her a dress for her twelfth birthday which is too small, ('too tight in the chest') Carrie's distress is a compound of feeling how out of touch her mother must be, and how painfully insulted she is when her pre-pubertal womanliness is ignored: 'her mother should have guessed how much she had grown.' But when Albert gives her a birthday kiss, she does not know how to respond, any more than she understands the meaning for Mrs Gotobed of her ball gowns. Albert gave the old woman something to live for in suggesting she wear them again, for her sexual attractive-ness was a core without which her self could barely cohere.

The joy of her birthday party at Druid's Bottom – Hepzibah's cake, the crown of wild flowers, Albert's kiss, which is an overture to the young woman in her – have, however, left Carrie 'silly with happiness', and she provokes Mr Evans with her bubbly liveliness which seems to take no account of Auntie Lou's birthday preparations at the Evans's house. Carrie's inner problem of sustaining loyalty to her various parental figures meets up at this crisis in the story with a raw conflict between Mr Evans and Hepzibah Green (whose relationship with his sister makes him envious and paranoid) and the beginning of a bitter parting of the ways between Samuel and Louisa. Living with the children has helped Louisa to want something more for herself: when she ventures to appear in a frilly blouse and lipstick her brother's repressive and sadistic moralizing pour out vituperatively – his own fear of loneliness and abandonment lie behind his efforts to control his sister, and any awareness of her sexuality terrifies and enrages him. Earlier on in the story, we have been able to observe his capacity for perverse excitement when he threatens to beat Nick with his belt – 'on your bare bottom' – for stealing biscuits. Welsh puritanism and religiosity is mixed in his character with class distrust and envy of Mr Gotobed, the mine owner, and of the American soldiers who seem so rich.

When Carrie tries to understand this hostility to the American serviceman in talking to Hepzibah, she learns something of how hard a life Mr Evans has had, made more bitter by his sister's privileged existence as a 'lady'. Like many an evacuee, Carrie is learning some of the social and historical realities of the wider world, enlarging her capacity for imaginative empathy and for understanding. For Hepzibah comprehends the integrity of Samuel's world – the narrow 'fear of the Lord' and distrust of 'pleasuring' are part of his colossal effort to save himself and his family from the dangers of pit life: 'He saw his dad die down the pit, and he couldn't save him. He came up and swore he'd never go down again, it was no life for an animal! . . . Mr Evans had had a hard, lonely fight and it's made him bitter against those who haven't,' Hepzibah explains. In the book, we hear nothing of the children's experience of school, but we watch them learning, and Carrie's encounter with these other families and vastly different cultures (of the mining village, of Welsh Protestantism, of the decaying country house, and of farm life) comes at that particularly sensitive moment for children when they are ready for something beyond their family-defined world, intrigued by the possible differences they observe, beginning to wonder how they themselves will live in the future; this is the moment when things are no longer taken for granted. This state of mind contributes to children's enthusiastic immersion in reading, since stories can extend our conception of the possible.

Bawden's title expresses beautifully the layered complexity of the story: we are to be concerned with the war months Carrie spent in Wales and the war Carrie was simultaneously experiencing internally. The images of the two arenas intertwine: Carrie's conviction is that Mr Evans wants her to *spy* at Druid's Bottom; the power of the notion of spying must derive also from the national war effort, from nationalistic sentiments and from extreme hostility to 'spies'. Carrie's very painful sense of conflict revolves around feeling trapped into making exclusive choices – she feels Mr Evans wants her to choose him in preference to Louisa and to reject Hepzibah altogether. There is no way she can find in which she can be comfortable with *both*. It is the small girl's complex of contradictory oedipal feelings, re-lived at the pre-pubertal moment; this is made intensely difficult to manage by the mixture of feelings that are really her own and the intrusion of Mr Evans's desire to win her affection and loyalty for himself. When Louisa's American soldier boyfriend comes to call and finds only Carrie at home, Carrie sends him away, consciously, because of the anger she fears in Mr Evans, and Louisa's distress when her brother bullies her.

> She was afraid Major Harper would be angry but he only smiled, blue eyes twinkling. 'I'm a very respectable American soldier,' he said. He *was* nice, Carrie thought. So nice that it would be quite awful if Mr Evans were to turn up and start shouting at him. It would upset Major Harper and it would upset Auntie Lou, and all to no purpose because Mr Evans would never let her see him again. She said, 'There's no point in your staying, really there isn't. It wouldn't be any good at all. Even if you did see her, Mr Evans wouldn't let you go out with her, to a dance or the pictures or anything. Mr Evans says dance halls and cinemas are haunts of the Devil and a frivolous woman is an abomination in the sight of the Lord.'

Carrie is overwhelmed here by an unconscious stirring of feeling for Major Harper, whose uniform must remind her of her own father, and she cannot bear to imagine Louisa and Major Harper together, a couple happy with each other when she herself is deprived of both mother and father. As she explains to Nick, (who sees immediately that Carrie's interference is profoundly selfish and in no way motivated by concern for Louisa), '"I can't bear it when she cries."' Nick responds: '"*You* can't bear it? What's that got to do with her?"' Carrie's confusion arises from the match between Louisa's helpless and masochistic response to Samuel's bullying tactics, and her own inner division between a bullied, submissive self and an overweening sense of duty which continually spoils her chances of happiness. Nick's generosity – rushing off to fetch Louisa – perhaps arises from the earlier emotional context he has found (plenty of mothering from both Louisa and Hepzibah) which seems as yet uncluttered, in a classic latency fashion, with preoccupations about the sexuality of mothers. By contrast, Carrie seems to need the two-ness of the parental couple, the presence of father as well as mother, and to be exposed to a great deal of distress when the external world does not provide her with a firm framework which can withstand her divisive impulses, and thus renders her terrified of the omnipotence she secretly attributes to her wishes.

Another aspect of Mr Evans's tragedy is revealed when his son Frederick comes home on leave. Samuel imagines that he is nursing the grocer's shop as a 'sound business' for Frederick to inherit, but the children learn that he has no intention of resuming life at home. The war has widened his horizons too. His abusive treatment of Mr Johnny also shows someone perhaps coarsened by experience of the army. The children's dislike of Frederick is another example of complex mixtures of feeling at which Bawden excels as a writer. Frederick is greedy and lumpish, but also offends them by his behaving as if he belongs in the house – his own house – making them re-experience their temporary visitor status:

> Frederick ate his meals with Mr Evans in the parlour and they were both fond of meat, liking it juicy and rare. Nick saw them one day. . . 'Blood running out of their mouths,' he told Carrie. 'They're carnivores, that's what they are.'
> Frederick was on leave for a week. He slept a lot of the time, either in bed or sprawled in the most comfortable chair in the kitchen, snoring loudly with his mouth open.

The children do not get much meat to eat, nor are they allowed to lounge around. While harvesting the hay, Frederick's callow taunting of Mr Johnny leads to Mr Johnny's attacking him wildly. After Albert and Nick have intervened to stop the dangerous fight, there is a complicated sequence of events which concerns the question of where the 'vicious lunacy' attributed by Frederick to Mister Johnny rightly belongs. Bawden's subtlety is considerable. The children are committed to their picture of Mr Johnny as a beloved member of their intimate world, and they have been shamed by their initial reaction to him. At the same time, they have now seen him go berserk and attack Frederick with a pitchfork and have had to take responsibility for stopping this. Is it Frederick who is a mad beast, with his brutalized provocation? This is a tempting resolution for them, but they had enjoyed Frederick's company on the way to Druid's Bottom and had admired his prowess at hay-making. As they puzzle over this, Mrs Gotobed emerges from the house, and Carrie observes her contempt for Frederick and the grocery shop.

She notes that 'her eyes remained cold as winter' behind the condescending smile. Here is a different source for the cruel mockery which Frederick had directed at Mr Johnny, and it has two generations of family hostility behind it. But Carrie is also dealing at this moment with the shock of seeing Mrs Gotobed in her 'last' dress, the last of the twenty-nine to be worn; and she feels faced by a woman about to die. She is appalled, hardly able to keep her eyes on such an image. Mrs Gotobed sees her terror and understands it, showing the kinder side of her nature to Carrie, just after the revelation of the part that she had played in the drama of brother's and sister's enmity.

When Mrs Gotobed does die, Carrie is frightened, and also bruised by the crossness which both Mr Evans and Albert vent on her as they cover up their own distress. Albert accurately senses Carrie's self-pity, but is not in touch with the fact that any death evokes afresh the anxieties of war-time. They are watching an ant-hill Albert has disturbed, and Carrie speaks of the loss of their home as being like a house with its roof blown off by a bomb. (In *The Borrowers*, the Clock family also suffer the experience of having their roof lifted off their house.) This is a good metaphor for the whole experience of evacuation for this child, and this underlying area of distress in her·makes her especially vulnerable to worry about loss of home. This vulnerability is crucial in understanding both Carrie's actions at this stage in the story, and her way of construing her departing vision of the fire at Druid's Bottom.

Carrie has to take action on the message which Mrs Gotobed had given her for Mr Evans, and this becomes entwined with the idea she and Albert share of a will which would give Druid's Bottom to Hepzibah so that she and Mr Johnny can continue to live there. Excitedly believing she now understands the mysterious message, she buries her uncertainty, upset, and fear in an inflated view of her own vital role as messenger. 'It'll make him so happy,' she claims, confusing her own wish to make everything all right and everyone happy with Mr Evans's possible reaction. Blurting out her message in the guise of comforting him, though in reality more taken up with how comforting she finds all this, she is horrified to face the consequences of her action. She has in fact revealed that Mr Evans's sister had confided in her, that Carrie had deceived him as he feared, and that she is unable to be in touch with his mourning because of her self-centred complacency. She is carried away with her melo-dramatic role, and only begins to get a grip on her own feelings and anxieties as she tries to imagine her brother Nick dead. It is the more down-to-earth Nick who sees that something quite mad has got into Carrie at this point.

Carrie's life-long guilt about throwing away the slave's skull is based on a confusion between those actions she had taken which really did have damaging effects, at least in the short run, and those events which only omnipotent delusions could make Carrie responsible for, but which in internal reality did precisely that. There is unreal innocence in the claim that she 'only passed on a message' – it could not have had the overwhelming excitement for her if it were an unimportant 'only' – and the hurtful bickering between Albert and Carrie is based on a wish to find someone else to blame. Beneath the puzzle about the will, is also the hovering question of how to see their own position, as evacuees – are *they* to blame for being sent away? Carrie's exaggerated desire to please speaks of fearful worry about being displaced afresh, reopening the sense of rejection and unworthiness. Earlier on, Hepzibah had been able to sustain them through her well-rooted confidence and her understanding and caring capacities. Now she is afflicted by grave anxiety about homelessness for herself and Mr Johnny, and is temporarily unavailable as a resource to help them with their worries. After putting a pie in the oven she says, 'You two make friends time that's cooked. Or you'll get the rough edge of my tongue. I'm short on patience this evening.' The children cannot bear the evidence of Hepzibah's distress, though later in the evening they are all soothed by the sound of her voice when she tells them a story about the Michaelmas fair of her childhood.

Thus the healing power of a story told to children by a loved adult (healing both for tellers and listeners) ends a chapter full of torment, and makes tolerable for the child reader the painfulness of identifying with all his or her heroes and heroines. So ends many a day of difficulty in a child's life.

Carrie's confusion persists, as she struggles to work out whether to believe in Mr Evans's honesty – would he steal and destroy a will? – and she feels her head 'spinning like a top'. Not being able to grasp what she herself is feeling, wishing, and fearing at this point intensifies her confusion. Her own motives are lost in a heap of speculations about his. A letter arrives from the children's mother to say they will be able to join her soon, and precipitates both children into further muddled feelings of not knowing where they want to be. Albert and Carrie are both taken up with schemes to rescue Hepzibah and Mr Johnny, whose potential homelessness makes them into symbolic containers for the children's own sense of displacement. Albert has to come close to his cowardice, and to bearing with the limits of being a child – the 'handicap' of being a child and the exposure to impotence this involves, just as Mr Johnny's handicap makes him so lacking in powers of self-determination. This brings him close to Carrie again who is feeling 'torn in two' by the impending separation. 'I wish there were two of me, really,' she says, 'one to stay in the village and one to go to mother.'

The emotional distance between Nick and Carrie becomes greater. Nick and Louisa are happy, while Carrie and Mr Evans are miserable. There is an apt rendering of the many 'last times' the children take note of, the last time they do each familiar thing, another instance of Bawden's splendid observation of children's ways. The children receive presents they really like from the Evanses, and Louisa is blossoming with the sense of life they have brought into the house for her. Mr Evans's burdensome and constricting depression has less hold on her now, but remains dominant for him, and he is aware that he will miss Carrie. For the very first time, Carrie finds herself speaking of her mother and anxiously imagining their reunion. The pressure of events and feelings is too much for her, and leads to her throwing out the skull in the belief that this act will magically destroy the house which Mr Evans should not be inheriting. She cannot put all her contradictory feelings and wishes together in a coherent way, and this impulse is unrestrained. In the really important matter of the farewells, things also go wrong. Neither she nor Albert can manage their goodbyes to each other gracefully (each wanting the other to make the first move and risk rejection, each constrained by the unease of early adolescent affection between the sexes) and it is even worse in the Evans household. For the basis of Nick's secret intimacy with Louisa is now out – Louisa has gone off to marry her American soldier, and Nick had known about it all along.

There is a pervasive anticipation of an ending – the children are to leave, Louisa also, and the household at Druid's Bottom is being dismantled. The external changes that are real enough for all of them mark very major life transitions, and it is Carrie's particular difficulty in coping with what this means to her which interests Bawden. Carrie cannnot bear the helplessness she is feeling – Hepzibah's future with Mr Johnny is solved by her own stoical practicality – Louisa's life is taking its own unexpected shape, and Mr Evans's faults turn out to be rather different from those Carrie had imputed to him. She stirs herself up into a state of righteous anger with him, only to feel moments later that it goes out of her like wind and leaves her 'becalmed' and confused. The goodbyes with mother she and Nick had been cheated of when they first came to Wales now bedevil her efforts to make the transition afresh. Louisa, Hepzibah and Mr Evans all make memorable farewell occasions for the children. Carrie's tragedy is that, feeling her heart breaking as the train passes by Druid's Bottom, breaking from the anguish of unspoken love and gratitude and unfulfilled wishes for magical reparative powers, she is appalled to glimpse a fire at the house. Mindful of the legend of the skull, she believes this to be her fault, and sees herself as the destroyer of what she has loved so much. Indeed, unconsciously she is drawn towards destruction in phantasy of what she cannot bear to leave behind; the lovely things she would no longer have access to become too much for her to leave intact.

This belief remains almost untouched at the core of herself into her adult life, because it involved the loss of an internal maternal figure to whom she could confide these fearful imaginings. Hepzibah had been the external representation of a receptive, listening, inner parent, sustaining her through her long separation from her actual parents. Once she was believed dead, Carrie had nowhere to turn. Nick is so paralysed by seeing Carrie's terror that he can never refer to all of this again, so that each child is terribly scared and unutterably lonely. There is probably a distortion in the consistency of Bawden's characterization of Nick here – he has shown himself to be more than the greedy and dependent baby brother that Carrie remembered him as, and that her children make him out to be later on when he is grown up. While we can see how Carrie would not be able to find a way to talk to her own mother or anyone else about what had happened, because of the intensity of her confusion between internal and external reality and her extreme anxiety about loyalty, there is no such convincing account of Nick's inhibition.

Bereaved in her later life, and thus opened afresh to the pain and anxiety of loss, Carrie is drawn back afresh to the place of these unresolved anxieties about herself. She is able to return to the Grove because her own eldest son perceives that she is terrified of the imagined powers of her thoughts, and he takes care both of her and of the younger children in a paternal fashion. When the children find Hepzibah and Mr Johnny still there, and learn the ordinary story which lies behind Carrie's nightmare beliefs, there is another chance for Carrie to recover from her life-long fear of loss of any happiness she may find. The true story being told, the question asked and answered, Bawden implies, gives new freedom to her character. Bawden has a writer's belief in the power of words (she even made the grown-up Albert provide Mr Johnny with a speech therapist to help him to talk!), allied with a sensitivity to the peculiar vulnerability of children to silences, to what cannot be said (in the Evans household as well as in Nick and Carrie's own family), and to the inner consequences of this in the psychological development of character. The healing quality of truth and knowledge is palpable in the final pages of the story and it is a pity that a fairy tale, too-good-to-be-true element is allowed to enter. An idealized bacon-and-egg breakfast cooked by Hepzibah seems to be the product of an excess of wish fulfilment, and does not allow either Carrie or Hepzibah the dignity of their many years of separate experience. The continuity between them would be unavoidably more fractured, in truth, than this event makes it seem.

As a document about wartime separations the story is, however, a very beautifully-conceived piece of work. There is conviction in Hepzibah's perception that 'Mr Head and Miss Heart', Albert and Carrie, could not get comfortably together, either in a friendship the children could sustain or in terms of an inner development of these different aspects of their own natures. We are, however, given enough of a glimpse of Carrie's husband to hear quite an echo of Albert. Albert's tragedy has been different from Carrie's. He has held on to a relationship with Hepzibah and Mr Johnny, but it seems that his adoption of them as a quasi-family is linked with both the entire loss of his own family and with an inability to form a new one. Mourning is evaded in various ways by the characters of the story, and the history of each is marked by these evasions.[2] There is a remarkable power and sympathy in the portrayal of these variations. Bawden's other novels for children deal with similar themes quite frequently (for example, *The Peppermint Pig* and *The Runaway Summer*), but there is a particular poignancy about the matching of the outer cultural context of mass evacuation and the inner experience of and response to multiple separations and losses which make this book outstandingly successful. It combines great psychological delicacy with a splendidly vivid evocation of a social world from a child's point of view.

11

Finding Oneself Among Strangers: Three Stories by Paula Fox

Paula Fox's books for children are written from the first person point of view, and the child's voice and viewpoint achieve access to the delicate interplay between inner preoccupations, the central themes of the child's mental and emotional life, and the readiness for particular experiences which are resonant with these internally powerful concerns. It is as if the children she writes about so beautifully have a not entirely conscious (pre-conscious, as Freud would say) idea of something they are looking for. The representation of a search for something not yet discovered in the internal or external world of the child, which yet has to be somewhere, is the thread which links the stories structurally. The psychoanalyst W.R. Bion has written of the 'preconceptions' of the infant, which need to meet up with lived experience, and it is this area of mental life which Fox explores compellingly, delineating the moments of developmental integration in which the child's dilemma comes to be resolved or restated through a poignant experience of him- or herself in-the-world in interaction with others. The moving quality of the stories, which are often quite simple in themselves, arises from this focus on the child's fresh grasping of him- or herself, and the extraordinary concomitant flowering of hopefulness, when the inner and outer worlds of experience are in dynamic connection. What is also very striking in Fox's works is the combination of such a depth of psychological understanding of her child characters and a rich and precise evocation of the social worlds they live in. The nature of the city child's world, whether twentieth-century Brooklyn or nineteenth-century New Orleans, is convincingly recreated, and the individual lives of her child heroes, located in a historical and social moment, allow the child's personal experience also to illuminate for the reader the nature of the place and time within which that child is finding a way to live.

We have chosen three of Paula Fox's stories for consideration in detail, and they illustrate the range of her intuitive grasp, and her capacity to find a tone for the younger reader say, aged between six and nine and the young adolescent. The first two stories belong to New York. *A Likely Place* concerns nine-year-old Lewis's struggle to find a place in which to be himself. He is a boy whom 'everyone wanted to help' and this anxious intrusive adult concern creates a fog of confusion in Lewis's mind; his initial solution to this is to run away. The problem is, where to? For the place he is looking for has no inner representation in his imagination as yet: one of his problems at school is not being able to distinguish 'there' and 'their'; the idea of a place (there) is confused with the idea of something personally located (their), and Lewis is stuck with his problem of not being able to find his personal sense of place and identity. When his mother inquires, 'Is there something on your mind, dear?' Lewis thinks about the literal surfaces of his head – his skin, his hair and a woollen hat that he has taken to wearing, even in bed. So uncertain is his sense of boundary between his mind and other minds and hence, so vulnerable and permeable, (he feels, for instance, that the doorman will read his mind), that he tries to hold himself more firmly together with an extra layer:[1] 'He didn't especially want to explain that wearing the hat made him feel everything inside his head was in the right place.' So at this point Lewis knows something about what he feels is wrong – *that* thought has crystallized and there is within the hat-protected head a small place where he can think personal thoughts. However, he suspects that any sharing of these private ideas will lead to their losing meaning for him. For example, if he lets his teacher or father know that he is interested in Pygmy bridges, they will become a 'School Project,' or evidence of his oddity. There is a pervasive expectation of being misunderstood by adults and great doubt about whether he can make sense of himself.

The story in fact portrays the less happy side of 'modern'

and 'progressive' methods of child-rearing and education that we normally tend to regard as an advance on the coercive and impersonal attitudes of the past. Basil Bernstein in several of his essays[2] has described 'progressive' methods of education and their characteristic focus on the individual child, their use of informal interaction to engage the child's own interests, and the attempt to relate schoolwork as much as possible to the child's everyday environment and interests. He also perceived, however, that these methods of education aimed to include more of the child's extra-curricular world in his or her schooling, and attempted a deeper penetration of the personality than older more conventionally structured forms. These methods, and parallel efforts to involve the parents and 'the community' as partners in the child's education, were sometimes developed specifically for work with children otherwise found inaccessible to schooling, where the gap between parental and school cultures was widest. They also reflected the concern of middle-class parents for the development of the child's talents and personality as his or her crucial resource in the competition for professional status and occupation. A high level of self-awareness and self-consciousness is characteristic of this 'new middle-class' world, and also of its educational practices, as also is a high level of parental anxiety about their children's progress and development. *A Likely Place* shows how this particular parental and educational style might be experienced by a child, especially one who for whatever reason feels somewhat vulnerable and marginal.

Everything in the child's environment in this culture seems to be there for a reason – to improve the child's mind is as ubiquitous a goal of parents of this kind as the improvement of his or her morals was for an earlier more religious generation. The child's father asks, for example, 'Lewis, do you have a plan for those batteries which are soaking in your spare fishbowl?' conveying the implicit message that there should be a plan for everything. Everything is done and provided for his own good, and always with a patient smile which makes it harder to refuse without feeling bad. Every activity and mood of Lewis's seems to be carefully monitored by his parents, sometimes in oppressive combination with each other:

That night he took a book from the shelf, and while he was lying

217

in bed looking at it, a hand turned it over to see the title. It was his mother's hand, but his father's voice said, 'Hmm . . . well . . . I see. Uh-huh . . . well, well!'

The educated middle-class milieu of the parents is deftly indicated by their tone of voice, their museum trips, and their mutual exchanges of the Sunday newspaper supplements.

The exercise of overt compulsion and the unselfconscious acceptance of conflicts of purpose between adult and child can merely set children in opposition to or withdrawal from the adult world, even in collective resistance to its demands. By requiring the child to develop 'interests', his own assent is sought to an adult-sponsored agenda of activities and thoughts. But this is painful for a child so unsure of himself that he doesn't know what his interests are, or whether he has any that are acceptable to his elders. *A Likely Place* pictures the dilemmas of a child who is reluctant to expose his tentative thoughts to adult scrutiny, lest they be rendered unspontaneous and inauthentic before he has got a proper hold of them. The adults to whom Lewis responds warmly are those who have a reality and preoccupations of their own, and who don't confuse or wrap up their own purposes in Lewis's. This way things can come Lewis's way without always making personal demands of him. He can take them or leave them, and maybe make something of them in his own time (like the damp booklet he finds on 'Mosquito Control in Southeastern Delaware').

A Likely Place doesn't disparage child-centred ways of bringing up children, and indeed it's our argument that books like this are an important part of this new child-oriented culture. In their own way, the adults who help Lewis are deeply interested in him, and in his own preoccupations. They also give him space to find things out for himself, and have respect for the spontaneous and impulsive aspects of development – 'the two babies crawling at high speed towards him' followed 'huffing and puffing' by a lady in a white uniform in the park. The story itself is an imaginative space in which this mode of experience of childhood can be thought about.

We become more sharply aware of the very small child aspect of Lewis, when his cousin comes to visit. It turns out that Lewis works out what day it is by reference to regular family events. Such is the natural first mode of defining time, which is how Lewis can perceive the passage of time as meaningful. This stands in painful juxtaposition with an experience of time organized *for* him – being 'taken to' places which should instruct or amuse him – in which he cannot even find enough space or time to know his own thoughts. The school corridor might serve as a much-needed in-between area, but the school principal comes up eager to help and hurries him into class: 'If he could have one wish it would be to make people stop asking him how he felt – or telling him how he felt.' His cousin hints that a litle patience goes a long way and his friend Henry, to whom he reads short stories on the service stairs, knows how to answer adult inquiries: 'Lewis wished he could get the hang of answering grown-ups. It seemed to him that everyone knew how to manage this problem except him.' But while reading to Henry and two other younger children, he feels happier; they represent the dependent younger part of himself and allow him to feel bigger and stronger in taking care of them, though this activity worries his parents because his friends are 'too young' for him. There is perhaps an evocation of Lewis's unconscious wish for a younger sibling which has not been gratified; the fish his parents bought 'to help him become responsible' only 'bore him to death'; they are a poor substitute, indeed.

So Lewis both feels himself as fundamentally unacceptable in some ways, always in the wrong, and yet hangs on to an image of being able to connect things up better and feel better:

> Pygmies did interest him. He had seen a picture of a Pygmy bridge in a magazine. It had been made from vines and then slung over a river somewhere in Africa. There were several Pygmies standing in the middle of the bridge with their arms around one another. They were all smiling.

This contrast develops as we read Lewis's ironic and wonderfully comic account of various babysitters he has had. They range from the stocky Mrs Carmichael, 'following him around all day,' to the neurotic Jake Elderberry and Miss Bender, whose anxieties drip out of them, calmly enumerated by Lewis. His capacity to notice things with interest begins to come to the fore despite the very unreceptive caretakers he seems burdened with. Observing the behaviour of city dogs heralds his efforts to follow his own nose. The city park, previously forbidden territory, becomes the very place he is looking for, the delimited but pleasantly undefined area in which he might find just the place he needs. A crucial ally appears to help him along in this direction: Miss Fitchlow, the babysitter who will take care of him while his parents go to Chicago. She is an unconventional character, keen on yoga, health food, and her own ideas. '"Something on your mind?"' she asks Lewis; '"So have I"'. She makes a hit with Lewis when she simultaneously notices the face he has drawn on his shoe to help him sort out left and right, and herself gets the two reversed. She also expresses confidence in his being able to 'figure out' how to dry up the dishes or make his own breakfast. As in several of the other stories we discuss in this book, the experience of his parents' absence is itself a push to Lewis's development. The story seems to tell us that it's useful to have to do things for yourself, but also good to have some limits set; Miss Fitchlow was 'starchy about matches'.

So he goes off to the park internally reinvigorated by this encounter with someone who thinks he can think. There is a lively and spontaneous quality to the scenes Fox describes. As might happen on a spring day in New York's Central Park, Lewis encounters all sorts of people, many of whom are quite willing to say what is on their minds, and pass on. Inside the park, he finds a snake, and meets a man who tells him its name – naming things is another huge help in emerging from his depression and muddle:

> 'What have you there?' he asked.
> 'A snake,' said Lewis.
> 'So I see,' the man said, 'but one must do better than that. It is known as DeKay's snake. Notice the chestnut color. Note the black dots along its sides.'
> The snake slid off Lewis's arm and disappeared beneath a bush.
> 'Easy come, easy go,' said the man. Lewis walked on. Everything in the world seemed to have a name.

The simplicity of language, aided by lovely Ardizzone pictures, leaves an absolutely clear image of all Lewis's adventures in the park.

The most important moment is still to come. Lewis makes friends with an old man, who is sitting talking to himself in 'a foreign language,' and who tries to start up a conversation with him. At first, Lewis is silent and a bit suspicious and he starts to leave. Then:

'Wait!' cried the old man. 'Don't you want to know where my home is? Have you no curiosity? . . . Barcelona!' shouted the old man. 'And I'll tell you something. If I could ride a bicycle in the first place, I could ride it across the Atlantic Ocean in the second place.'

Lewis asks if Barcelona is the capital of Honduras (a recent school poser):

'Barcelona in Honduras?' he repeated as if astonished. 'Why – it's in Spain, dear friend. Come over here and sit down. I must tell you a thing or two.' The old man tells his story, of living with his daughter and son-in-law, homesick for Barcelona, not allowed to work as a shoemaker, unable to spell English, which is a 'mad language'. He shows Lewis that he can spell Spanish words at once, banishing the boy's picture of himself as a hopeless dunce at spelling. The spelling problem is important because the old man wants to write a letter to his son-in-law. When Lewis asks why he can't talk to him directly, Mr Madruga replies 'Can you tell a rock?' The old man asks Lewis to help him with the letter and Lewis explains he wanted to find a cave, and they agree to help each other in both matters.

The symmetry of their predicaments makes these two natural allies, each infantilized (Mr Madruga has bought too many tooth brushes and is told off for dropping his spoon by his daughter and son-in-law), persecuted by English spelling, by intrusive attention from people who know better what is good for them, by an inauthentic relationship with their own family, who are experienced as impenetrable rocks. Lewis needs a cave in which to make a home, the old man wants a way to make his American home into a 'real' home. As he dictates in flowing phrases, Lewis writes a simplified version: 'Dear Charlie, I don't want to sit in a corner. I want to make some shoes.' Lewis recognizes the old man's *wanting* and discovers the name for it now that his wants have been heard by Miss Fitchlow and Mr Madruga, who perhaps together constitute a set of alternative parents by whom he feels understood. Their understanding is disparaged when Charlie appears to summon the old man home: '"Cut the cackle,"' he says, brutally. Speaking the same language and being heard is Fox's theme. When that process of dialogue collapses, inner thinking and identity are also disturbed. Now that Lewis has such splendid reasons for being interested in words, including how to spell them, his demeanour at school is quite different. Time in school goes quickly once he is feeling alive within time. Miss Fitchlow's comical equation of cleaning out the attic with meditation echoes Lewis's experience of gaining space to move and breathe in his own mind, no longer so cluttered: 'Miss Fitchlow reminded him of agreeable things even though he didn't understand what she was talking about.'

When he returns to the park to meet up with Mr Madruga, he is happy to find that his friend has remembered his wish for a cave; their happiness is the contentment of being kept personally in mind, the delight of recognition. They wander through the park, encountering all kinds of characters involved in their particular individual interests, and Lewis observes all this with wonder. Eventually an empty cave is discovered – Lewis's incipient discouragement when the earlier caves proved unsuitable is kept within bounds by Mr Madruga's hopefulness, which seems an especially important quality in him, to counterbalance Lewis's conviction that many people have given up hope in him, and a mutual exchange of despair is thus all that can be expected.

So they make themselves at home, and turn to the letter-writing, each enjoying the linguistic difference of the other. Together they write a letter in Lewis's simple English, completed by adding 'Adiós' and an enormously long Spanish signature. The successful interweaving of English and Spanish managed by a boy and an old man, seems to sum up the story's fascination with the problems of integration, stated at cultural, social, and linguistic levels, and in the context of the boy's inner development as a person whose difficulties arise from a poverty of understanding.

There is a story within the story, told to him by Miss Fitchlow, about an owl who chases a mouse all over the world. The mouse's efforts to escape are so energetic that 'by the time the owl had caught up with the mouse, the mouse had become a plump, smart, giant mouse, very strong in the legs because of all the running it had had to do to escape the owl.' This story recapitulates what is happening in Lewis's internal world – while confined within his identity as a dumb failure, Lewis the mouse lived in dread of being swallowed

222

up by the 'wise owl' grown-ups pursuing him at every turn; once he begins to feel his growing strength – in the mouse story it is physical strength, but in Lewis's story it is mental vigour which is at issue – the whole structure shifts.

At this point, Lewis can manage to wait and hold on to his own new capacity to enjoy himself in the wider world of park and mind: when Mr Madruga does not reappear for a few days, Lewis misses him but can go on making a place for himself to feel at home in the cave, and he practises the lotus position which Miss Fitchlow had shown him until he can do it alone. Within his cave home, he can keep in mind his two friends. There is a place for him to play, and an enlarged space in his mind which allows him to stretch and think. Fox is showing us the process of internalization[3] of good experience and the creative development which Lewis's identification with his friends' care of him make possible. When he feels too lonely, the sadness that is hard to bear (it becomes almost too much for him) takes its toll and he finds he can only remember half of Mr Madruga's name. Probably the 'Mad' part because he is feeling a bit maddened by waiting so long for news from his friend. (Somewhere buried in this is probably a link with feelings about his parents' absence, too.) He is afraid of being forgotten, and the image of a forgetful Mr Madruga is lived out in Lewis's impaired memory. Feeling hurt, neglected and angry, he quarrels with Henry, a neglected friend who is missing being read to – at this moment, Lewis cannot stand his own pained feelings and he tries to lodge them in Henry: '"I want to hear about the monkey," yelled Henry. Lewis leaned over the railing and looked down at Henry. "I'll haunt you myself," he said.' But he is helped both by Henry's giggling response (he is not too hurt) and by Miss Fitchlow, who knows something is wrong. The next day Mr Madruga reappears: 'Well, well, dear friend. I'm so glad you came . . . I was afraid you might have forgotten me or thought I had gone away.' So the two have shared the same painful anxieties and managed to go on hoping, and Mr Madruga's dilemma has been happily resolved by the letter.

The story chronicles the magical quality of their interchange: the boy knew there was something missing inside him but not what it was exactly, and Miss Fitchlow and Mr Madruga enable him to find it; the old man knew what he wanted and is helped by the boy to find a way to ask for it. It is, of course, the reciprocal gift which allows each to feel, like the mouse in Miss Fitchlow's tale, bigger and stronger at the end. Indeed, Miss Fitchlow even seems to reprove Lewis's homecoming parents for their oppressive anxiety about their son:

> 'Are you all right?' asked his mother.
> 'All right!' exclaimed Miss Fitchlow. 'Why he is extraordinarily well co-ordinated, having managed some very difficult Yoga exercises right off. He is also the best informed person on Delaware mosquitoes I have ever met.'

A related theme appears in *How Many Miles to Babylon?*, which also opens with a boy, ten-year-old James, thinking of running away. James is frightened and confused, and we learn only gradually how he comes to be in the care of three aunts living in a single room. Their anxious voices merge in a bombardment of demands from which he retreats. It is in tune with James's own befuddlement that the reader has to piece together the fragments of history which might make sense of his position, for that is James's own state of mind.[4] The memories which gradually cohere are of his father leaving one night, his mother later collapsing, his aunts explaining to him that mother was ill in hospital and was getting better. Unable to digest these catastrophes, James has another version: his mother is really in Africa, and he must go and find her.

With these underlying thoughts on his mind, James approaches a day at school. We are shown his aunts' kindly concern for him which does not penetrate his secret convictions. They know his aches and pains are an expression of not wanting to go to school; Aunt Paul, who calls him 'Little Bits' (perhaps seeing how little and how fragmented he feels), knows he 'likes to sleep in his underwear so he'll always be ready to *go*,' and tells him stories about their country childhood when he asks, hoping to regain thus a belief in some ordered continuity of existence. James wants to stay at home so as to lie in bed, eat 'soft' food and 'not think about anything' – he cannot swallow mentally his hard painful experiences, and part of him wants to empty his mind and shrink back to an infantile world in which everything would be processed for him, maybe even an image in phantasy of getting back inside mother's womb, where the pain of separation and loss can be obliterated. Walking through the tenement building, he hears fragments of conversation which he experiences as 'pieces of string he could tie together'. The image of an ill-assorted incoherent collection of oddments tied together is also descriptive of James's precarious sense of inner integration. Outside, he sees people moving 'like bits of paper in a high wind,' which demonstrates for us his fears for his own solidity.

The one focus which draws him together is a ring with a red stone he had found, which he feels was left for him as a sign by his mother, and which thus represents their ongoing link with each other. It is the one thing 'James was sure belonged to him.' On his walk to school, he encounters a dog – he doesn't like dogs – who tries to engage his attention: the dog's attraction to and interest in him disturbs James, who feels that any expression of attachment and dependence is best avoided. In school, disconnected memories of disturbed nights combine with his efforts to comprehend the school-children, who seem so numerous and bewildering, to exhaust him. He becomes wide awake only when he realizes he can walk out unnoticed.

Making his way to an empty house he has discovered in a nearby street, he constructs for himself a story of his mother 'across the ocean' in their 'real country' (James is a black child) preparing a place for him, the prince, who would then meet with all the other princes. His aunts' role is to take care of him until all is prepared. Fused in these images are James's memory of his mother's account of the enslavement of black Africans, pictures of American Indians from movies, James's transposition of a mother confined to bed in hospital to a queen who can reconstruct a black heritage and restore James to a family line of fathers and grandfathers. The child's shattered sense of family and personal worth is thus being restored in his imagination through belief in a more-than-humanly powerful mother, which allows him to distance himself from the recollection of the broken-down mother he last saw. Paula Fox has fictionally constructed here a configuration which is familiar in psychoanalytic work with distressed deprived children: images of despairing parental helplessness or violence are mixed with devotion to idealized omnipotent parental figures who are all the time working for the child's best interests.[5] In the house, James dresses up as a prince and dances to a giant cardboard representation of Father Christmas, believing that through these cardboard eyes he can reach his mother and reassure her that he has found the ring. The Christmas constellation of mother, father and child, magically housed and protected, has been ironically signalled in the title, which recalls the first line of a children's carol, 'How far is it to Bethlehem?' and the ring seems endowed with Star-of-Bethlehem significance by James. But to reach Bethlehem, the chaos of Babylon has to be endured.

James feels 'warmed and comforted' by the intensity of his longing – 'it seemed to him he was dancing before an immense fire' – and this moment of passionate hope is shattered by a cold intrusion, the mocking laughter of three boys who have also taken the empty house as their own. Stick, Blue and their mate Gino are street kids living by their wits. They have devised a scheme to make out, whereby they steal dogs and then hope to return them to frantic owners advertising in the newspaper offering a reward: 'Dog business incorporated'. None of this is remotely comprehensible to James at first. He is terrified and tries to escape, but the boys think he can help them: 'He look all sweet and cool' and people will trust him because he still looks cared-for if he offers to walk a dog. The atmosphere created by Fox conveys James's overwhelming terror; the boys are tough and threatening in gangster-style, and Stick knows intuitively how to drive James mad with fear:

> 'And if the people call the cops,' Stick was saying, 'so what? We be gone by that time and all they got is this little bitty kid. The cops going to think he's crazy. They'll lock him up!'
> James reached out behind him. It was like being on the edge of a cliff. If he didn't make it, he'd fall into a bottomless hole.

The most primitive infantile anxieties of falling[6] for ever are evoked for James, intensified by the rush of unconscious confusing thoughts concerning what has happened to his mother. '"Listen!" commanded Stick . . . How could he listen? They sounded like three radios going at once.' There is a nightmare echo here, in his incomprehending struggle to work out what is happening at this moment, to the voices of his three aunts which mingle confusingly in his mind in their night whisperings and their morning instructions to him.

'"Get your coat," Blue said to James. "I don't have a coat," James said instantly, almost grateful that one of them had said something he could understand.' James longs for the ring: 'If he could have the ring in his pocket, he wouldn't feel so terrible.' But the boys have thrown it in a dark corner, and without this one potent imaginary link with his mother he feels almost utterly lost. Just as they mention he'll be fed some 'dwarf food' if he's good, he notices Gino's thin wrists, and the idea of real hunger grips him. At the same time, he is made dizzy by their street-wise ways: Stick says '"Listen! Anyone ask you why you not in school, you say you go in the morning. You say your school get too many kids so some have to go in the morning and some have to go in the afternoon."'

The four of them set off on bikes. James's excited admiration of the boys (part of his dizziness) is alluded to when they pass Deacon, the teacher's favourite from his class at school, who is walking along the road and stares openmouthed at a vision of James rushing by on the back of a bike – for once, James is going to know something that Deacon does not know. However, the gang note James's laughter and terrorize him: 'He was turned upside down and all he could see were feet, and legs that shivered with cold, and bicycle wheels. Stick was holding him by his collar and swinging him back and forth. The sky was coming down on him.' James begins to understand something important for his self-preservation: while the gang can project their own fears (of hunger, of discovery, of falling right out of the human world) violently into him, he can guard his own thoughts by lying:

They hadn't known what he had been laughing about, James realized. They couldn't tell what he was really *thinking*. They could make him go when they wanted and they could scare him. But they couldn't get inside his head where his thoughts were. Maybe he'd have a great thought that would show him how he could get home.

In fact, James has already had a great thought, that home is where he wants to get; the invasion of his secret place in the house has been differentiated from the hidden interior of his mind where he can still have private thoughts. The idea of moving away has been replaced by the idea of getting back home; this is not simply a response to panic, but is to do with James's capacity to observe his captors, children lacking in

227

any credible human link beyond their gang's struggle to survive. He notices that Gino cannot bear to be touched, looks so old, his face like a stone, and can only laugh with a noise 'like a rusty sound'; that Stick's face is frozen, his voice 'low and awful,' his mouth a disappearing thin line. Blue is different; perhaps his name suggests some awareness in him of his depression and misery – he and Stick have taken names which deny their personal origin – and James keeps himself hidden behind his 'Prince' identity with which he had introduced himself. Blue talks to James, helping him to understand what is going on and trying to create a warmer spot between them. What James grasps is that he does have a place to go to, people noticing his absence, and that he longs for home and care, which is a framework the other three have left; but also that they have a capacity to struggle and think, to create a self-sustained existence, however pinched and uncertain, to show him the wider contours of the city, even the Atlantic Ocean, which helps him to realize the fantastic quality of his imaginings about his mother in Africa.

He acts the part of dog-walker successfully and acquires Gladys, a small white dog who attaches herself to him enthusiastically. Her owner gives him a cookie; 'James rested his hand in hers for a second. It was a warm hand. He wished he could crawl into it.' James likes Gladys, and is worried about kidnapping her. '"What are you going to do with this dog?" he asked. His voice rose at the end of his sentence as though he were going to cry. He was agry with himself.' His partially paralyzed feelings for himself, for the frightened little boy self that would like to be taken care of, are released though he were going to cry. He was angry with himself.' His partially paralysed feelings for himself, for the frightened Gladys even while 'his head was telling him: Go back! Go back!' James has not yet managed to bring together in his mind the desire for home, evoked by Gladys's trusting attachment to him, and the more canny scheming thoughtfulness which he can see in Stick. While feet and head are going in opposite directions, he is a prisoner, just as he had been a prisoner of his confused state of mind before his adventures began.

In the extremity of cold, hunger and exhaustion after the long bicycle ride to the Coney Island hideout, James's mind is filled with images of his aunts, the apartment building, and his mother imagined alone on the ocean in the dark. Mother and he are both lost, lost to each other, and away from home. His affectionate feelings for Gladys help him to survive the anxieties aroused by facing so much that is unknown and paradoxical to him; the Coney Island 'Fun House' seems a horribly frightening place, no fun at all:

> Gladys whimpered. 'Get it out of the box,' Stick said to James. He lifted the box lid. Gladys was all curled up on some rags. James lifted her out. She crept next to his feet and lay down. He bent down to scratch her head. Her ribbon had come untied and she didn't seem very lively . . . Inside it was pitch black. As they walked on the wooden floor, there were echoes. Gladys's nails clicked. It was a comforting sound . . . They went up a flight of stairs as long as the stairs in the home where James lived. Gladys was having a hard time. James bent down, picked her up and carried her the rest of the way.

Thus James cradles Gladys and learns to take care of his own pain and fear, to contain them within.

But his next effort at escape is foiled by Gladys's recognition of him hiding in the dark and her devotion to him. Courage and sensitivity to the moment of opportunity are not enough, though these awakening capabilities are crucial for James. However, he cannot leave without Gladys, for that departure would be based on a denial of his feelings for her, feelings of affection, concern, responsibility and guilt at his part in the kidnapping. So the story's concern with James's gathering together of his scattered self necessitates a further development before it can end. James learns in the moment of being discovered of his ambivalence towards Gladys: the pleasure of being individually valued by the little dog is offset by the burden of responsibility he then feels towards her.

> He ran towards the house. Gladys was tangled in his legs. How he hated her at that moment! . . . Gladys licked his hands. If only she'd be quick, or follow somebody else! . . . 'Oh, Gladys, you'll give me away,' whispered James. . . .He slid down, his back against the grille. Gladys crawled into his lap. He couldn't escape.

He cannot escape the gang nor can he escape the task of taking responsibility for restoring Gladys to her own house. Perhaps this is a particularly poignant moment because of the resonance with James's preoccupation with an image of a mother who could not cope with his need to be cared for by her. His hatred of Gladys may signify his recovery of an awareness of his having felt hated by mother; this time there has to be a solution which avoids idealization, collapse, and confusion.

James's private escape effort serves to provide knowledge of a way out when they are all locked in. The children are able to co-operate effectively to escape when they all experience the enemy as the hostile world outside, in the person of the policeman who has padlocked them in. For James's brains are now effectively mobilized when Stick proposes burning the place down (there are echoes for the reader here of the burning black ghetto areas of American cities of the 1960s):

> James's heart beat faster. Fire was the worst thing of all. He had seen fires, seen flaming mattresses hurled from windows, piles of charred sticks, baby carriages burned down to metal rims, heard people crying out, people wrapped in blankets, staggering, dazed, miserable.

Memories of past experience flood into his mind, together with a conviction that violent panic is profoundly destructive, and a hope that he might find a better way out, perhaps better than his alternately angry and despairing parents. Gino croaks and laughs when he sees James re-tie Gladys's ribbon. 'Blue said, "Now ain't that sweet? My! My! Wish I was a nice little old dog with a nice little prince for a mama!"' Thus the boys note James's gently maternal attention to Gladys, the little female dog that links him both with the softer vulnerable side of his own nature, and with his mother and aunts, whose care he recalls. As they ride off into the city, feeling better because of helping each other to escape,

> it all seemed to James like the beginning of a dream. The dream was without people, the only living thing in it was the smell of the ocean, sharp and sweet but especially new. It was a new smell that belonged entirely to him, not breathed by any other person alive.

Thus, brilliantly, Paula Fox sums up the newborn quality in James's enlarging personality. This new experience of himself takes him out of his Brooklyn despair into fresh possibilities, which have to begin with getting Gladys back home. 'He smiled, imagining how the lady would look when she saw the dog.' He begins to wonder more coherently about the three boys – do they have beds anywhere? – and to put together his own story and remember fully for the first time his mother's breakdown:

> That was the night his mother had gotten sick and had cried so much, sitting in a corner on the floor by herself and letting the tears run down her face without drying them . . . He hadn't remembered that night in a long time.

Instead of putting aspirin into the dog food to drug the dogs to sleep (this stratagem suggests the street boys' taking-for-granted of the drug use around them and which Blue reports of his elder brother), James slips the pills into his pocket. He needs the dogs to be wide awake to arrange their escape, and he himself is now ready to emerge from his dream-like adventure, no longer needing to be confused:

> 'I saw that big old cardboard Sandy Claus down there,' Blue whispered. 'Man, what were you *doing*, dancing round in front of that thing?' James didn't want to talk about that. He had known all along it was just a big cardboard cut-out.
> 'Where do you live?' James asked.
> 'All around,' said Blue.
> 'I live with my Aunts. There's junkies in my building. A man got killed in the alley back of my house.'

James and Blue talk at some length (the first conversation in the book that is more than a fragment) and, when James asks if Blue goes to school, Blue laughs: 'School? Now why would I want to do that for? I can read the street signs *now*.'

James tries to grasp the meaning of Blue's way of life and of his own running away, as Blue sleeps:

> It was funny about Blue wanting to be by himself . . . But how could you be by yourself? There was always someone breathing or snoring, talking or crying or humming. There was always someone fighting or moving furniture, or throwing it, or striking matches on the wall so that you could hear it all the way to the next room . . . The one place where James had ever been by himself was downstairs in the cellar of this old house. The only sound there had been his own breathing, his own footsteps. But he wasn't sure he really wanted to be by himself, the way Blue did.

Struggling on, he swallows his fear of Stick, his hunger, and puzzles over the emerging links of his history, coming to realize that he ran away from school because he could not think there; his aunts told him his mother would be proud of his learning, but his own inner conviction told him that his mother

> wasn't proud, just sick. He felt so bad, thinking about his mother being sick, not strong and well, that he forgot where he was. And no matter what he pretended, he knew she couldn't have gotten across the Atlantic Ocean. He had *seen* that water . . .

He is no longer lost in identification with a mother who can't listen ('Was there something wrong with his hearing?' his teacher, Miss Meadowsweet, had once yelled); he can now think about his mother, while remaining James. He is ready to make a move.

This time – the third try, rather like the three tries of many fairy stories – he makes it, with all three dogs. His last monumental effort is in getting Gladys home:

> He was stiff and sore . . . There was no use in thinking about all the walking he had to do . . . He wondered what was making him move. And no story could make the distance pass quicker. Too much had happened – it all got in the way of each story he tried to begin.

Once Gladys is safely home, he makes for home himself, realizing that he will have to tell his aunts 'what really happened'. His need to share his experience and conviction that he can find a way – that his aunts will somehow comprehend his story – is formed as he passes through the early morning city streets, observing a derelict man on a bench, an old woman talking to herself, bandaged men in loud conversation: he no longer defines himself as the loner with only himself to talk to, but is reaching home, returning from Babylon. His aunts and all the occupants of the building are there to greet him, but so is his mother, summoned out of her depression and withdrawal by his urgent need of her:

> He looked at his bed. A small woman was sitting on it. Her hair was cut close to her head [this is probably an allusion to mental hospital treatment] . . . She was hardly any bigger than Gino. James stood still: but where were her long white robes? Her long black hair?

232

Where were her servants and her crown? . . . Why, she was hardly any bigger than he was! How *could* she be his mother? . . . He thought, who am I? I'm not a prince.

'Hello, Jimmy,' she said.

James, Prince, the child burdened beyond his capacity, is reunited with Jimmy, the child who has a mother, with a place in her mind for him.

In an outstanding book for an older age group, *The Slave Dancer*, Paula Fox explores the links between damaged cultural identity and the personal maturation of an individual boy. The subtle interwining of the particular familial growth of persons and the delimiting conditions of the social and historical context, especially in relation to racial identities, is a most unusual aspect of her work. While these themes have been tackled by good writers of children's historical fiction (particularly successfully by Rosemary Sutcliffe), the contemporary setting is harder to deal with. In *The Slave Dancer*, Fox turns to the roots of black-white relations in slavery, as experienced by a New Orleans boy in 1840.

Thirteen-year-old Jessie lives with his widowed mother and sickly sister. They are poor, but his mother's long hours of needlework sustain their one-roomed existence, with occasional small additions earned by Jessie, playing his fife down in the town. The land and water world of New Orleans is Jessie's territory: despite the damp atmosphere of the house which makes his asthmatic sister ill, and the knowledge of his father's death by drowning at work cleaning the Mississippi riverbed, Jessie is drawn strongly to the sea. His mother's profound distrust of the 'drunken riverboat men,' the 'sinful' quarter of the town, are in opposition to the boy's fascination with his grandfather's sea-chest, the sewing-box decorated by a carved winged fish, the bright colours of her threads used for the clothes of the rich, illuminated by the window facing 'Pirate's Alley.' A boy alone with two females, he is excited by the wider world of city and sea, especially by forbidden glimpses of the Slave Market, of the houses and gardens of the white rich with their black slaves, of women's bodies. His delinquent explorations are linked both with dreams of his drowning father, whom he urges to swim, as if to draw him back into life, and with the pressure to understand the nasty seamy underbelly of the city. Caught watching the slave auction, he has been told to cut out his 'nasty peeking,' but just as he feels a 'prisoner' of the Mississippi fog and his mother's anxious moralism, so he feels imprisoned by ignorance of himself and his world which he must penetrate:

> I felt restless, and reluctant to return to the room full of brocade, so I took the longest way home, using alleys that kept me off the main streets where sailors and gentlemen and chandlers and cotton merchants and farmers went to make themselves drunk in taverns, and where women gotten up like parrots kept them company.

'Intoxicated' by a vision of himself as a rich chandler, he is unaware of danger, and is kidnapped. Finding himself on a raft, he realizes his captors are pirates, and looking down into the water thinks of his father. It is the unanswered questions about his father and his own blossoming manhood which have brought him into this terrifying position. An exhausting journey follows, prefiguring the terrible sea voyage to come. Jessie slowly learns that it is not death which awaits him, but enforced life aboard ship. He escapes the confines of childhood to be plunged into a fearful maturation, prepared for a confrontation with slavery through his own experience of being kidnapped, terror, incomprehension.

In the little boat which carries him to the ship, in which he finds it so hard to find a place to settle himself, 'the men spoke in undertones about nothing familiar to me.' He has been parted from the recognizable and familiar, and has to start from scratch. Every physical aspect of life at sea is profoundly distinct from life on land – the food, the beds, the lavatory arrangements, the male world replacing the female one. This is an adolescent *rite de passage* of terrifying proportions. The ship's name is *The Moonlight*. Jessie's personal preoccupation with the hidden areas of life, both the socially concealed and the not-yet-grasped inner relation to his own sexuality and aggression, are echoed in this name. It is in dreaming states that he has struggled with the image of his drowning father. Although writing with so light a touch, Fox has also given us the information that Jessie was four years old at the time of his father's death and that his mother was eight months pregnant; one can speculate on the confusion that may have been generated in Jessie's mind as he experienced intensified childish curiosity, awareness of parental sexuality, the violent death of a parent, and the arrival of a sickly sibling all in quick succession. His personal understanding of the impact of these events is continually open to reshaping in the light of his own experience, particularly so under the pressure of adolescence.

On board the big ship, he encounters a terrible stench 'so nauseating, that it stopped my breath'. He is filled with fear of death, as if it were palpable, in the air, like the awful smell, and despairingly imagines his mother thinking him dead, in this way shifting the worst fears out of his head and into his mother's, and gathering together some more self-preservative impulses. The sailors are gruff and crude, but one of them senses his panic and instructs his captors, Purvis and Sharkey, to explain to him where he is. He learns he is going on a long voyage, and has been kidnapped so that he can play his pipe on board.

'For the captain?' I asked.

Purvis opened his mouth so wide he looked like an alligator, and shouted with laughter. 'No, no. Not for the captain, but for kings and princes and other like trash. Why we'll have a ship full of royalty, won't we Ned?'

Jessie cannot understand this at all, but the readers are here introduced to the powerful mixture of feelings alive in the sailors who run the slave-ship. Bitterly ironic, Fox notes the revenge of the white 'trash' sailors for their own degradation (often press-ganged into sailing at sea in the first instance): the captured African negroes are mocked for their lost royal freedoms. In several of the sailors Jessie gets to know, there is a residual capacity to identify with the victims which is awoken by his arrival. Not one can see any human continuity between himself and a black slave, but Jessie's arrival serves to remind them of their younger selves, not yet hardened into life at sea, not yet moulded into permanent restlessness on land, not yet addicted to the primitive human relations of the ship. So Jessie draws forth a variety of kindnesses from the crew, which serve to modulate the shock of his encounter with the arbitrary terror of the captain's rule, and his realization that the ship is a slaver. His initial outrage recalls the decency of his mother's morality; she came from the North and has inculcated in him antipathy to the inhumanity of slave-owning. He is sustained in his long effort to grasp how the whole slave business works by memories of home; unlike the crew, who mostly lack any real place to be on land (drawn, as sailors so often have been, from the streets, from social *anomie*), Jessie feels his familial links as primary for his sense of himself. Captain Cawthorne, a man armoured in layers of prejudices, is after 'strong black youths' in his pursuit of the 'lucrative and God-granted' slave trade. His being comes alight with excited greed as he describes the trade to Jessie. 'Bollweevil' is the captain's belittling version of Jessie's family name, Bollier; summoned thus, Jessie is continually reminded of his now-distant family in a way that strips them of dignity.

Jessie has to find himself a place among the crew. His meeting with the captain has given him a sense of himself as one of the men, in contrast to the officers, and he now turns to the sailors who interest themselves in him. Ben Stout gives him clothes and explains the ship, attempting to make a friend of Jessie, and giving him good advice about the captain and mate. 'Saint Stout' is, however, not trusted by the others, and a link with him separates Jessie from the other sailors:

Unable to postpone any longer what Stout had called the needs of nature, I found my way back to that dreadful platform hanging above the water. I was so frightened, I held on to both ropes and shut my eyes tight as though by not actually *seeing* my circumstances, they would not exist. I heard a loud snort of laughter. Mortified I opened my eyes at once to see who was observing me . . .

Trying to distance himself from this humiliation, Jessie is challenged by Purvis to 'stop being so high and mighty' and hauled out of his superior isolation to be introduced to the rest of the crew and taken for a meal. The horrible food and loathsome cook (who 'was the thinnest man I'd ever seen. His skin was the color of suet except for uneven salmon-colored patches along the prominent ridges of his cheekbones') become bearable as Purvis teaches Jessie how to eat dried beef.

As I sat there on the narrow little bench, breathing in the close clay-like smell of lentils, and drinking tea from Purvis' bowl, I felt almost happy. When I remembered the wretchedness of my situation, I wondered if there was something about a ship that

236

makes men glide from one state of mind to another as effortlessly as the ship cuts through water.

This notion of effortless progress is modified by Jessie's gradual grasp of the work of sailors: 'I saw that day, and didn't forget, that a ship must be tended to day and night as though it was the very air one took into one's lungs . . .'[7] He observes the unceasing labour of the men, recalling his mother's long working hours, reminded of this particularly by Purvis's sewing of the sails. We recall too that his father had died in his work of making the river safe for ships. As Jessie, too, learns to work hard and uncomplainingly at given tasks – catching the rats, for instance – we can see his manly identification with the sailors take shape. The boy wandering the New Orleans streets with rather few real responsibilities is growing into a young man with a capacity for sustained effort.

There is already an implicit conflict between Stout and Purvis over the care of Jessie; each has been roused to parental concern for him. The intimacy and tenderness of such feelings, however much concealed by sailor style, are dangerous in the affection-starved climate aboard, probably also stirring latent homosexual jealousies. Jessie himself is struggling with his own sadistic excitement about the ship's foul smell, which he catches himself sniffing as if 'he was smelling a rose': the 'thrill of fear' he experiences when he gets an explanation for its origin is his introduction to the perverse sources of pleasure on this ship. Awareness of his own contradictory feelings is growing as he grasps the truth of the enterprise through his persistent questions: all the sailors have profit shares in slaving; both the American and British governments are against it; he is aboard an illegal ship out to beat the law, with a crew who admire their captain's skilful skullduggery. At the same time, he realizes his liking for Purvis, who shakes him violently out of a fit of breathless terror during a squall; he had been absorbed in an image of his mother and sister's life continuing as it had been and himself dead from their point of view, and Purvis forces him to hold on to life almost against his will: 'I thought I was choking to death . . . Purvis picked me up . . . If I didn't stop, he shouted, he'd have me up in the shrouds where I'd get more than air in my lungs.' Jessie is surprised to discover that for all Stout's kindnesses, he does not like him, though he does not yet understand why: 'But it was Purvis I was eager to see when I awoke in the morning, Purvis with his horrible coarse jokes, his brawling and cursing, Purvis whom I trusted.' He also comes to admire the strength, hard work, knowledge of the ship and the sea, and courage which is required for the ship to sail. Thus somewhat settled into the life aboard, he is disturbed afresh to note changes: a huge cauldron appears in the galley, a whip is being made which fascinates and horrifies him, gratings are placed over the hold. Purvis protects him from his own fears and the sadistic impulses of the sailors by dispatching him briskly to catch rats, a nasty task he has learned to reckon with. Later he also deals sharply with Jessie's incipient self-pity, and thus re-awakens Jessie's self-respect, for which Jessie is really grateful.

The ship is becalmed and the escalating tensions aboard explode: Stout's sea-chest is emptied out, one of the captain's eggs is stolen (by Stout), Stout and Purvis are quarrelling and the captain stages a demonstration of his absolute and irrational power: Purvis is accused (unjustly) of the stealing of the egg and flogged. Jessie is in turmoil, beside himself with rage at the injustice, at Stout's 'dreadful treachery' and unashamed contented snoring, at his own horrified perception of the mixture of dread, exhilaration, and misery within him. In the wake of this, Jessie rejects Stout and thus shifts the balance on board; this choice is also internally decisive because it is linked with his growing capacity to have a moral perception of his own about the slave trade, and to take up his own position. Though he is to fight about this with Purvis, his friend's stoicism and continued concern for the boy even in his own extreme pain (he reassures him that he will soon recover from the flogging) is important in providing a model of independent thought. Purvis knows he was beaten to protect the system of authority, and to invite the crew into identification with the master in relation to the slaves soon to be put in the ship's hold. Jessie refuses this abusive deal, and his nonconformity maddens Purvis, particularly as he knows that Purvis's sore back should remind him of the cruel lies by which the supposed morality of the system is upheld. The sight of land intensifies their quarrel:

Green and brown and white, trees and shore and waves. I

thought of home. At the same time I was overcome by a dreadful thirst. I thought I had grown accustomed to doing without everything that was familiar, accepting small rations of water and food without question. But the sight of the land, a longing to set foot on something that didn't rock and pitch and groan and creak, made the room on Pirate's Alley the only place in the world I wanted to be. To sit on a bench there in a private patch of sunlight and slowly peel and eat an orange! At that moment, I glimpsed Purvis dragging an enormous tarpaulin across the deck.

I hated him!

Jessie is overwhelmed with rage and shame at his recognition of having become part of the slaver's crew and of his mixed feelings for Purvis, who understands his mood quite accurately: 'Don't sulk so! It makes us all worried, to be near the shore like this and not able to walk on it. But think, the voyage is half over . . .' Jessie feels the affection in this in contrast with Stout's intrusive concern, which invites him into a hypocritical collusion: 'I softened a little in my feeling toward him (Purvis) partly because he'd spoken my very thoughts about the land teasing me then, so close, so out of reach.' The men start to drink as the captain's trade negotiations begin and Jessie comes to grasp a new dimension: '"Drink turns people round," commented Purvis somewhat importantly. "It's not drink," I protested. "It's the kidnapping of those Africans that turns everyone round!"' Jessie makes the link between Africans about to be sold into slavery and stories of slave uprisings in the South and a black woman he once watched in New Orleans. Purvis is roused to fury:

'Don't say such things!' he bellowed. 'You know nothing about it! Do you think it was easier for my own people who sailed to Boston sixty years ago from Ireland, locked up in a hold for the whole voyage where they might have died of sickness and suffocation? Do you know my father was haunted all his days by the memory of those who died before his eyes in that ship, and were flung into the sea? And you dare speak of my parents in the same breath with these niggers!'

Fox shows us here the impact of a horror that could not be dealt with by men's minds;[8] the memory is too painful and can only be lived with by a re-enactment in which new victims must bear the inherited unmetabolized pain, fear and guilt. Goaded and degraded for his Irishness by the captain (who calls him an 'Irish bucket'), Purvis can only find a way out by finding someone else to kick, as he now literally kicks Jessie.

All this prefigures the night-time arrival of the slaves, with the boat restructured around the task of the suppression of the blacks: shackles, whips, the sailors armed, forced feeding. Jessie watches the appalling happenings, from the sight of the first slave-child's face over the ship's rail; his breathing is strained and gasping, so immediate is his identification with the kidnapped captives, so close the memory of his own terrified arrival on board, so omnipresent the image of his drowning father, failing to reach the air. But he persists in asking questions when he cannot understand what he sees; since Purvis is on the watch, he wakes up Gardere from deep sleep to question him:

> 'Why was that man treated that way?' I asked, ignoring his complaints.
> 'What man?'
> 'The one who was forced to drink the rum?'
> 'Man?'
> 'That Purvis was flinging about so . . .'
> 'You mean the nigger!'
> 'Him,' I said.

Still able to feel for the sufferings of the blacks, he puts himself in danger by crying out as a dead black child is thrown overboard. Ned Grime both punishes and protects him from others by a huge swipe which fells him. As he staggers up, his eyes meet those of a black boy.

As they set sail, the sailors drown out the moans of the blacks by drinking and telling dreadful sea yarns. Stout is in charge of the slaves and his 'slowness of walk and gesture' is replaced by energy which Jessie finds 'repulsive'. Stout can speak a little of the natives' language and later Purvis tells Jessie that he has driven a black woman literally mad with torment through his special capacity to abuse through language. Though capable of physical cruelty, his real delight is in mental torture. One of Jessie's tasks is to empty the bucket latrines used by the blacks, and he now learns why his pipe-playing was wanted: a macabre performance is managed by Stout and Captain Cawthorne; the slaves are brought up on board, fed and then whipped into a fearful rhythmic parody of dance for which Jessie is to provide the music. Jessie's horror at this work makes him dread the daylight. He sees not only the extremes of mindless cruelty, but also the utter humiliation of the blacks, tormented by 'the bloody flux' which renders the buckets inadequate, and their nakedness before the sailors, who gaze at 'the unguarded difference between the bodies of the men and women'. These passages, written plainly, without any exploitative manipulation of the reader's emotions, bring to mind accounts of Nazi dealings with Jewish prisoners.

Jessie's relationship with Stout tortures him. Stout smilingly continues to make everything sound reasonable and Jessie perceives:

> He was not trying to excuse himself. No, it was only his usual trick. He knew I thought he was evil, but he liked to suggest that beneath that I held another opinion of him, that, in fact, I admired him. It was a complicated insult! . . . I found a dreadful thing in my mind. I hated the slaves! I hated their shuffling, their howling, their very suffering! . . . I would have snatched the rope from Spark's hand and beaten them myself! Oh, God! I wished them all dead! Not to hear them! Not to smell them! Not to know of their existence!

His hatred of the slaves at this moment for the pain they cause him to bear is so unbearable that momentarily the only solution he can find is to wish them dead, to kill his pain by killing the cause of the pain. Appalled by his own thoughts he defies ship's discipline, thus provoking punishment of himself, and is beaten by Stout at the captain's orders:

> I was not ashamed of my cries, for each time the rope fell, I thought of the slaves, of the violent hatred I had felt for them that had so frightened me that I had defied master and crew. My eyes flooded with tears . . . But as the blows fell I became myself again.

Jessie is now more alone, but clear-headed; although Ned and Purvis try to comfort him, they 'had become as remote from my understanding as were the lands that lay beneath the ocean. I became cautious. I observed the sailors with as little pity as they observed the blacks . . . I shuddered at the barbarousness of chance . . ' Later, he adds, 'I found a kind of freedom in my mind. I found out how to be in another place. You simply imagined it . . .'

He observes the sailors viewing the blacks as less than animals but as a source of gold, valuable objects. Only Stout, Spark and the captain take pleasure in cruelty, and Jessie gradually differentiates their motives, Stout's degraded perversity, Spark's mindlessness, the captain's greed. His questions continue to reveal both the natures of his companions and the way in which the inhumanity and irrationality of the slave trade is rationalized. The psychological and the historical and political are shown in intertwined discourse. It is an amazing achievement.

Drinking, fights and fever which spread to the crew begin to undermine the spurious unity of the master and men. The captain throws the mate overboard for wasting a black life, and elevates Stout. Jessie oscillates between the liberty of dreaming himself elsewhere, an enraged relation to the crew, and a developing preoccupation with the black boy who watches him, to whom he whispers his name. Stout, from his new position of power, offers an alliance to Jessie against the rest of the crew, but Jessie flees from him in terror and hatred. Purvis, still buoying him up with genuine affection (and talking of how he will never sail a slaver again, for Jessie's presence has affected him powerfully) helps him survive, promising that he and the others will protect him from Stout. Jessie is important to the crew because he represents the possibility that by saving him from the worst, they also feel in touch with the uncorrupted aspect of themselves, a part of the self that has not given up hope of some better future. However, it is the slaves themselves who help Jessie when Stout plans his revenge: Stout steals Jessie's pipe and hides it (stealing, like the egg-stealing, again serving as prelude to a vicious trick) then pushes Jessie down into the slave-hold to search for it. This is profoundly terrifying for him, as he realizes the hopelessness of finding his instrument in the mass of tightly packed bodies, and is horrified at having to walk over the slaves to search, and to experience their awful physical state, wounded from their shackles, ill, half-starved.

Suddenly I felt myself dropping, and I heard the wooden thunk of the two casks which I had, somehow, been straddling. Now I was wedged between them, my chin pressed against my chest. I could barely draw breath, and what breath I drew was horrible, like a solid substance, like suet that did not free my lungs but drowned them in the taste of rancid rot . . .. I began to choke.

Then arms took hold of me, lifting and pushing until I was sitting on a cask. I couldn't tell who'd helped me . . . my brain slept, my wits died. I could do nothing . . .. Then, through my wet eyes, I made out a figure rising from the throng . . .. In its hand, it held aloft my fife. In the steaming murk, I recognized the boy.

Jessie's recurrent claustrophobic anxiety about not being able to breathe, linked with his picture of his drowning father and feelings aroused by his sister's asthmatic attacks, almost overwhelms him. The slaves' assertion of their continuing humanity, through their recognition of his terror and their help, stands in massive contrast to the slavers' mode of being: the victims are still capable of identification with other victims; the persecutors, through the practice of cruelty and insensibility, can only live out their addiction to sadistic abuse. The slaves' arms, used to support his body and return the pipe to him, are an image of an unhoped-for gift, hauling him out of despair. Jessie learns in this moment that their appalling experiences have not made them mindless or feelingless; he sees himself being seen as a child tormented by Stout, and not as one of the slaving gang. Later, Purvis, too, recognizes the distraught little boy in Jessie, and draws him into a game of cat's cradle, trying to remind him that there is someone there to hold his emotional turmoil and distress in mind, and support him as a cradle holds an infant. '"I'm afraid of him (Stout),"' says Jessie, and Purvis, knowing that Stout 'sups on the fear he rouses up,' gently presses him into an effort to repair his self-respect through the work of the ship and the work of survival.

The ship is nearing Cuba, and Jessie's hopes of reaching home again come alive through Purvis's care. He sees flying fish, and recalls the one carved on his mother's sewing box. Purvis's affectionate concern has fathered Jessie through the crisis; Jessie's inner world is altered in an important way, for the preoccupation with a father who could not save himself has given way to an experience of a man who has survived and has helped him too. The strength Jessie can now find within himself through his experience of and appreciation of Purvis's love is the theme of the story's last part.

The dénouement of the story begins with disquieting 'festivities'; the slaves are 'dressed up' in fine clothes, shown how by the tongueless slave of the Spanish buyer, suppos-edly to enjoy a drunken and violent extravaganza before they are sold. (Fine clothes are repeatedly shown, both on shore and on board, as the false display of the 'aristocratic' slave-owning culture.) Sexual confusion and humiliation are enacted as elegant clothes are thrust on them, and captain and crew lose their heads in a rum-induced and sado-masochistic frenzy. The ship is surprised by an American government vessel; the slaves are thrown overboard alive (to the sharks) together with all the ghastly and torturing evidence (the shackles and chains) of their lives aboard. As the boarding party nears, a huge storm breaks. With his own scream, as he sees slave-children tossed into the water, Jessie wakes to knowledge of what he must do; finding the slave boy who returned his pipe, he takes him to hide in the hold. They lie there, terrified of the storm and even more so of discovery, talking to each other without understanding, but feeling some comfort:

> Neither of us knew what the other said, but the sound of our voices in the dark held back dread as the thunderous violence of the storm broke all around us. There were moments when I wanted only to give way, to become a noise, a thing, so as not to *know* the terror I was feeling.

This story is, indeed, an exploration of what it means to a child to come to know, to be able to bear, extreme feelings and of how such knowledge can be acquired through the sustenance of relationship.

As the ship begins to go down in sight of land, the boys grasp a bit of the boom in the hope of swimming ashore from the devastated vessel, awash with bodies. Jessie struggles to free himself from the long-feared death by drowning which claimed his father and now engulfs Captain Cawthorne before his eyes; he now has adequate internal resources for his task, and a companion to share the effort and danger: 'Even now I can feel the urgency of our struggle, the *hope* that delivered me from the depths and brought me up to air again and again . . .' (our italics).

They reach land and are found and cared for by an escaped slave, who first addresses Jessie as 'Master,' and then examines the black boy, wondering whether to trust Jessie and his white skin. Jessie struggles to explain how they came to be together. The man remarks '"He don't say nothing. Why is that?" "He speaks his own language," I replied. . . . "But he's not learned our language yet."' The issue is what is 'our' and who is to be seen as 'we'; Jessie gives his own name and then touches the black boy, who announces himself as 'Ras,' and acknowledges 'Jessie' aloud. Perceiving Ras's trust, the old man decides to take them both to his hut and feed them. Jessie, almost overwhelmed by a desire to bury himself in the mud, is gradually understanding his escape from the sea:

> How had I done it with my dog's pawing? Suddenly, I heard an inner voice crying out, 'Oh, swim!' as it had whenever I'd thought of my father sinking among the dead drowned trees in the Mississippi River.

Fed and clothed by the old man, Jessie's thoughts turn to his mother, as he experiences reciprocal involvement replacing terror as the basis of life together.

'At the end of the first week, the old man told me his name (Daniel).' This exchange of names signifies trust, as it had done when Jessie whispered his name to the slave boy, and in contrast to James, in *How Many Miles to Babylon?*, who never reveals his name to his kidnappers. Jessie is living with the two blacks in a temporary equality, and simultaneously coming to recognize his aloneness and difference as the old man makes preparations for Ras to escape to the North, plans from which he is excluded.

Both boys experience their parting after this interlude of peace, working and playing together, with pain but resignation, and Daniel helps Jessie through the 'hollowness' of Ras's departure by listening to the whole story of the voyage. For Jessie alone it is too much, but in sharing it he becomes able to bear what he now knows, of himself and of the world, and Daniel trusts him in return not to reveal his hidden home. As he sets out for home, he understands the complicated mixture of love and deeply rooted difference he confronts:

> I wanted him to touch my head as he had Ras's. But his arms remained unmoving at his sides. I looked into his face. He didn't smile. The distance between us lengthened even as I stood there,

245

listening to his breathing, aware of a powerful emotion, gratitude mixed with disappointment. I thought of Purvis.

'Go on now,' he said.

I stepped out of the hut. Daniel had saved my life. I couldn't expect more than that.

Fox conveys here how deeply wounded Daniel himself has been, and how much it means that he should care for even a kidnapped boy-member of a slaver's crew.

With the aid of Daniel's 'markers' he finds his way through the jungle, fearful of the snakes, echoes of the exotic horrors of the *Moonlight*, but comforted by his confidence that with Daniel's instructions he can get home. He re-enters the world of white power and black slavery, observing a white man in front of a grand house helped by three blacks to dismount from his horse and enter the house. For him, this sight is now inextricably linked to what he saw on board the slave-ship. In a rainstorm, he falters:

> To my dismay, I felt I could go no further. The water blinded me. It roared in my ears. I was filled with an apprehension that had no reasonable shape in my mind . . . . Suddenly, moved by an obscure impulse I held my breath. Somewhere, someone had once told me that there were people who could choke off their lives by an act of will . . . .. But . . . I couldn't not breathe.

This experience binds together his profound personal anxiety about survival, air defeating water, and a clear vision of the social relations of the South which drown human mutuality and capacity. Jessie's desire for life is established but he has to give up his wish for a life as a rich Southern gentleman, and promising himself that he 'would do nothing that was connected ever so faintly with the importing and sale and use of slaves,' he eventually realizes this means leaving Mississippi for the North.

His exceptional adventures have endowed him with exceptional capacities for emotional experience, for he cannot free himself from his memories though they are 'softened' by time, from homesick dreaming of the South, from an eternal search for Ras in every black face, from an incapacity to listen to music. The child's love of and talent for music-making has been transformed into a man's pained recollection of the humanly unbearable. The lost love of music represents the lost idealized hopes of childhood, for learning from experience is costly in mental pain.

Fox's achievement in this story is to write with magnificent restraint and precision about the interplay of personal and historical, inner growth and outer framework, the process of learning to think about self and world. Just as Jessie in the story learns to digest the acute painfulness of his direct experience of the most horrible aspects of slaving, yet has to bear this memory throughout his life, so Fox asks her readers to learn about the history and legacy of the slave trade through identification with her boy hero. A child reader, and indeed an adult one, may thus acquire a depth of understanding of the social and historical significance of slavery for a society still profoundly affected by the injuries of race.

Conclusion: Explorations of Loss

The stories we·have discussed in this book explore what must on the surface seem to be very dissimilar kinds of childhood experience. A journey made as a boy prisoner on a slave-ship (*The Slave Dancer*) is a much more terrible event than a short stay in quarantine with a well-meaning aunt and uncle (*Tom's Midnight Garden*). These narratives describe experiences of loss of different intensity, ranging from the minor separations from family involved in a holiday, (*Five Children and It*), to the larger anxieties evoked by evacuation, (*Carrie's War*), forcible eviction (*The Borrowers*), or a parent's mysterious absence through illness (*How Many Miles to Babylon?*). Holly, in *Holly and Ivy*, has no parents and lives in a children's home. Wilbur, the little pig, in *Charlotte's Web*, has to bear the death of his resourceful spider-guardian. The children in *The Lion, the Witch, and the Wardrobe* explore their response to their parents' absence through their entry into Narnia, where a state of war obtains between a seductive but heartless witch-mother, and the more vulnerable but protective Aslan. Sometimes loss is shown as an inescapable aspect of life which leads to personal development. There is something a little sad about Stuart Little saying goodbye to home and setting out on the open road in his quest for love, but he encourages the reader to face the pains of development by being so admirably adventurous and hopeful. The reader sees both Fern and Wilbur growing up, learning that there is more to life than being a baby or living by identification with babies. Omri, in *The Indian in the Cupboard*, begins to learn

248

something of a parent – indeed a mother's – feelings, at the stage of development when his mother is no longer completely available to him. We have tried to show that the pains evoked in children by loss of loved people and places and the loss of present security which all growth and change entails are the central theme of a number of the finest modern works of fiction that have been written for them.

States of loss have both external and internal meanings in these stories. Real social traumas are described in the narratives, sometimes in descriptively realist and frightening ways, as in *Carrie's War*, and *The Slave Dancer*. In other stories, writers have found metaphoric ways of constructing a situation quite recognizable as a representation of a moment in social history, while nevertheless writing within a chosen convention adapted to what child readers can imaginatively respond to. This is the case for the adventures of the Clock family in *The Borrowers*, for example, in which one can see clearly displayed a class society in transition. *The Mouse and His Child* depicts a social world with a frightening degree of turmoil and mobility, in which finding somewhere safe in which to make a life takes all the resources that a family has; in addition, and making another implicit reference to present times, it is a one-parent family. We have seen this as the representation of a specifically American experience, which makes use of some popular American cultural conventions, notably the genre of gangster fictions, to convey its frightening but also thrilling dangers. Other aspects of American character are displayed in the directness and warmth of contact that can occur between strangers, in Stuart Little's encounters, and in the meetings in the New York park of *A Likely Place*. We see also in the stories by E. B. White and Russell Hoban representations of a world in which success and fame are within the reach of everyone. Louis, Stuart, Charlotte and Wilbur all have their moment of public acclaim, and the mouse and his child's final home is a world-famous hotel for travellers (like their former selves) not just an ordinary domestic house.

The English stories, on the other hand, implicitly teach their readers that too much ambition can be dangerous, and that people do best if they don't stray too far from their place. The middle-class children of E. Nesbit's story have to learn that grand wishes can get them into trouble, and that it doesn't pay to lord it over the lower orders. The Clocks are nearly undone by Homily's greed for fine possessions; the Platters are sent off to Australia when they resort to stealing to keep their model village one step ahead of the village which Mr Pott and Miss Menzies have made. In *Carrie's War*, Mrs Gotobed's 'superior' marriage, and the jealousy it has (unintentionally) provoked in her family and in her Welsh Nonconformist village is the source of the bitterness between Mr Evans and his sister, whom Carrie then finds herself trying to reconcile. In a more indirect way, C. S. Lewis also evokes a particular moment of social experience in his Narnia stories. The starkness of the struggle between good and evil depicted in this series is not only a representation of a certain kind of Christian world-view, but also evokes the climate of world struggle against the forces of totalitarian darkness which belongs to the Second World War and Cold War periods. This is still more clearly the implicit theme of J. R. Tolkien's *The Hobbit* and *The Lord of the Rings*. In these and other ways, the writers we discuss offer their readers a way of imaginatively experiencing a particular social climate, and the ways in which people think and feel in these situations. Social situations are evoked and rendered through the ways in which individuals – recognizably typical of their kind – actually live and feel them.

Just as central to our argument, however, are the meanings in the inner or mental world of the events represented in the stories. Many of the children or child-like central characters in these stories are shown to experience relationships and states of loss not only in external fact, but in their imaginations, through symbolic representations of themselves or their loved objects. It is the relationship between the unconscious or phantasy representation of central figures in a child's life, and what is described of their actual real-life character, that gives many of these stories their distinctive depth and multi-dimensionality. For example, Carrie grieves for much of her life not for what she has in reality done, but under the sway of the phantasy that she has brought destruction to her temporary home, just as she felt unconsciously that she must have been responsible for the break-up of her old one! When her magical and omnipotent attempt to reconcile the estranged Mr Evans and his sister fails, her own sense of blamefulness becomes unbearable. In *The Battle of Bubble and Squeak*, the gerbils are unconsciously seen as new babies by everyone in this emotionally flat household. The children want them, seeking to find in caring for the gerbils some of the spontaneous warmth now missing from a mother worn down by her bereavement. Alice Sparrow, their mother, equally detests the little animals as reminders, in their simultaneous vulnerability and habit of turning the house upside down, of the young children she barely managed to care for when her first husband died, and of the new babies she has not been able to bear the thought of having with her new husband. The emotional crisis in this family, arising from the suppressed emotional needs of nearly every member, is powerfully rendered through the drama of the struggle over the animals, which stand as metaphors for internal babies. The story can thus engage readers both at an engaging and pleasurable surface level, and with these deeper emotional resonances. The point of the gerbils is that they have different internal significances for different family members, while not being an overwhelming presence in the story in themselves, as real babies might be. Philippa Pearce has found a fine symbolic container for this story of ordinary family life, which works so well because of the ways in which animals – real and imaginary – are used in many children's actual lives as projections of aspects of themselves and some of their central feelings, both tender and cruel.

Equally clearly, *A Dog So Small* explores the state of mind of a lonely child. While external reason enough is given in the story to indicate why Ben should feel the way he does, the main interest and power of the story lies in its depiction of his inner state, and his family's only intermittent and partial contact with it. This story is daring and path-breaking in the way that it moves between depicting a boy's relationship with a real dog, and a boy's states of daydream, phantasy, and even hallucination. This is also easily accessible to readers' experience because of the intensity of attachment which is so often felt towards animals.

Many of these stories depict in symbolic terms relationships between children (and some adults) and what psychoanalysts refer to as internal objects. Omri's Indian, Little Bear, and his friend's cowboy, Boone, are literally brought to life by the boys themselves, and live, we can readily see, in their minds. We can see the magic cupboard as a dramatic representation of the process of make-believe. The Indian and the cowboy 'stand for' aspects of the boys that the grown-up world – at school for example – cannot see. They allow the boys to be in touch with baby aspects of themselves, both the spirited, healthy, demanding infant like Little Bear, and the feeble cry-baby like Boone. The narrative shows Omri finding a way of being in touch with his mother, through feeling her preoccupations, noticing for the first time how she must feel, learning to feel more grown up by looking after someone else.

In *The Fairy Doll*, we see a youngest daughter a family doesn't have much time for, internalizing the image of a kindly grandmother, and keeping her as a resource in her mind to help her in her struggle to keep up with her competitive and crushing siblings. Great Grandmother understands Elizabeth better than anybody, but she is rather distant and strange for a little girl. Transformed into the fairy doll from the Christmas tree, Elizabeth can keep in *her* mind that *she* lives in the mind of someone strong, kind, and committed to her, and is given heart by this. Of course this is a version of the popular children's myth of the fairy godmother, and clearly sets out its emotional roots.

Several of the stories hint to us that the events they describe are to be taken as much as what can happen in a child's imagination than as literal truth. Mrs May hasn't actually seen the Borrowers herself, but has been told about them by her brother, who is now dead. The dolls talking with each other in *The Dolls' House*, or the toys in the shop discussing who will buy them at the beginning of *The Mouse And His Child* depict the ways children give a kind of life to their play-objects which can obviously only come from their own minds. It is because children's play is often an externalization of their inner preoccupations that it has become possible to use such play as a means of conversation with them in analytical psychotherapy with children.

Often the imaginary other in these stories is a representation of a part of the self or an aspect of parental figures. In other instances, the central figure is an imaginary brother or sister; in *Tom's Midnight Garden*, Tom encounters a little girl who brings to life his own feelings of abandonment by parents, his longing for his brother whom he had wanted to spend his holiday with, and a pre-pubertal dawning of interest in the opposite sex, which is also evoked by the anxious but generous affection of his aunt. In yet other cases, what is given a symbolic form is a rather impersonal kind of internal object, an inner parental voice rather than a whole

252

person. The Psammead in *Five Children and It* is something that grants wishes to the children, but while treated at first as an instrument of the pleasure principle, its own tacit inclinations seem more to be to uphold the reality principle. Most of the wishes turn out badly, and the children have to learn to listen and think before trying to indulge themselves.

Some of these stories succeed in representing specific internal figures and their role in the life of a child (for example, *The Fairy Doll* or *The Kitchen Madonna*, through a description of events in the life of a single family). Others, however, create a more complex and large-scale external representation of inner worlds, with many conflicting dimensions. This is certainly the case with *The Lion, the Witch and the Wardrobe*, where different kinds of response to anxiety are divided among the children in a fluid and dynamic way. *Charlotte's Web* is particularly subtle in the manner in which it sets one story of emotional development inside another. It is Fern's identifications with baby Wilbur which lead the reader into the barn; there, the child reader's identifications with the baby-self are transferred from Fern to Wilbur, and the identifications with a maternal object shift also from Fern, but in this case to Charlotte, who takes over Fern's mothering role as Fern loses interest and moves on, to her parents' astonishment, to Henry Fussy.

These stories represent and describe a process of symbolic and imaginary experience within their narratives, often in delicate detail. Characters like Tom, Omri, Carrie, the Mouse, Jessie, and Gregory are beings who are described as having complex mental lives, who experience feelings as well as being the subjects and objects of actions. Stories like these thus invite and encourage readers to develop space for mental reflection, through offering examples of what it is to hold feelings in the mind, and to experience them by thought and imagination. Writing which makes possible an identification with the practice of reflection on emotional experience is, we think, especially valuable to personal development. These stories at once represent and depict a process of symbolic representation in their own narratives, and also present themselves for readers as possible ways of thinking about their own states of mind or reflecting on inner and outer experiences which take place in their own lives.[1] Reading is one important way in which the meanings of such life-experiences, for children as well as adults, can be explored. Good writing for children both describes complex mental life, and invites its readers to share in it by identification, the narratives themselves providing material for reflection. Some of these stories make explicit reference to this crucial role of literacy and story-telling: Charlotte reads to Wilbur, as well as writing for him, and Arrietty's reading is a sign of her desire for growth and freedom.

The central characters have almost universally in common the capacity to hope. In Bion's terms, they carry in their minds a preconception of a good object,[2] and in their adventures they seek to find something which corresponds to it in experience. This is like the infant's innate preconception of the breast or maternal object, which is described both in the psychoanalytic and attachment theory literatures. The Mouse has an internal conception of the mother he hasn't got, and gives his father courage and persistence in looking for her. Several of the stories also describe the way in which these hopes are fulfilled, through a response in others to the hopefulness and trust seen in the child. It is shown that many adults have a mental preconception too, through which they can respond to a child's need. Thus Jessie evokes kind feelings and some remaining capacity for moral discrimination in members of the crew of the slave-ship – Purvis in particular – and it is this which enables him to survive. Charlotte responds to Wilbur's plight. Aunty Lou is brought to life by the children who come to her house in Wales. Mrs Sparrow is touched by the trust of her youngest daughter, which it is impossible for her to betray. In responding to the passionate hopefulness of children, many adults themselves are shown to change in their own lives. Aunty Lou manages to escape from her brother's house to marry an American officer. Alice Sparrow is able to laugh again with her husband. Mrs Bartholomew in *Tom's Midnight Garden* remembers her own children, and is able to become a friend to children who might be the grandchildren she never had.

The capacity to respond to children's needs – for the inner conceptions of adults and children to match each other – is represented as the crucial moral capacity in these stories. Not to have it is to be marked out as deficient or wicked as a person. It is even worse when this incapacity is hypocritically disguised and the subject of lies.[3] Ben Stout, in *The Slave Dancer*, is a monster, who for his own advantage seeks to befriend Jessie. Mrs Gotobed in *Carrie's War* never transcends her selfishness, even though she convinces Carrie that she means well by her brother. The claims of children on the adult world are shown to be so powerfully felt that even some wicked people make a pretence of responding to them, for external effect or for their own self-regard.

The stories we have discussed are fine examples drawn from a larger body of good modern writing for children in Britain and America. It is because these stories show that the pains of loss and development, both internal and external, can be surmounted in so many settings that they represent a positive moment in contemporary cultural life. We don't discuss many books written in the past decade, but the conclusion we draw from this mainly earlier period of post-war writing is that it was then felt widely possible to write in an authentically hopeful spirit about the world in which child readers would live. The existence of such writing itself contributes in no small way to the possibilities for life available to child and adult readers.

Notes

Introduction

1. On these two earlier periods of classic children's fiction, see Humphrey Carpenter's illuminating *Secret Gardens*, Allen and Unwin 1985. A study which provides a survey of the main genre of recent literature which we discuss is Ann Swinfen, *In Defence of Fantasy*, Routledge & Kegan Paul 1984.

2. Lawrence Stone, *The Family, Sex, and Marriage in England 1500–1800*, abridged edn, Penguin 1982.

3. Philippe Aries, *Centuries of Childhood*, Penguin 1972. See for a critique of this view of the modernity of affection towards children, Linda Pollock, *Forgotten Children: Parent-Child Relations from 1500 to 1800*, Cambridge University Press 1983.

4. Ian Watt, *The Rise of the Novel*, Chatto and Windus 1957.

5. On J.M. Barrie see Jacqueline Rose, *The Case of Peter Pan: The Impossibility of Children's Fiction*, Macmillan 1984, and a reply by M.J. Rustin, 'The Case of Peter Pan: A Defence of Children's Fiction', *Free Associations* 4, 1986.

6. For an account of Beatrix Potter's life which emphasizes the painfulness of her life with her parents, see Margaret Lane, *The Tale of Beatrix Potter*, Frederick Warne 1946. Humphrey Carpenter points out, however, in his *Secret Gardens* that Lane's account is not altogether supported by the more recently available evidence of Potter's own journal, published as *The Journal of Beatrix Potter from 1881 to 1897*, transcribed by L. Linder, Frederick Warne 1966.

7. On this genre of boys' adventure stories see Martin Green, *Deeds of Adventure, Dreams of Empire*, Routledge & Kegan Paul 1980. On the parallel genre of girls' stories see M. Cadogan and P. Craig, *The Girls' Story 1839–1985*, Gollancz 1976.

8. On *Scrutiny* see Francis Mulhern, *The Moment of Scrutiny*, New Left Books, London 1979.

9. On the history of this group, see Francis Mulhern, *The Moment of Scrutiny*, op. cit. Q.D. Leavis's critical writings have recently been collected and published in Q.D. Leavis, *Collected Essays* vol. 1: *Englishness and the English Novel*, Cambridge University Press 1983; vol. 2: *The American Novel and*

Reflections on the European Novel, Cambridge University Press 1985.

10. For one such connection, see Graham Greene's perceptive and amusing essay on Beatrix Potter in Sheila Egoff et al (eds) *Only Connect; Readings on Children's Literature*, Oxford University Press 1980.

11. For example, David Holbrook's books *English for Maturity*, Oxford University Press 1961; *English for the Rejected*, Oxford University Press 1964.

12. See the essays collected in Basil Bernstein, *Class, Codes, and Control*, vol. 3, Routledge and Kegan Paul 1977.

13. Susan Isaacs, *Intellectual Growth in Young Children*, Routledge 1930; *Social Development in Young Children*, Routledge 1932.

14. M.J. Rustin, 'A Socialist Consideration of Kleinian Psychoanalysis' *New Left Review* 131, Jan–Feb 1983.

15. D.W. Winnicott, *Playing and Reality*, Penguin, 1980.

16. For a useful introduction to such modern critical approaches see Catherine Belsey, *Critical Practice*, Methuen 1980. For the larger debate on realism see Terry Lovell, *Pictures of Reality*, British Film Institute, 1980.

17. The realist aesthetic of Georg Lukács depended on the idea of a transcendental reality which was illuminated in typified forms by representative literary works. Marx's theory of modes and relations of production is the deep structure of reality which underlies this view. We would argue in somewhat similar terms for the possibility of a psychoanalytic realism. On Lukács, see the essays collected in his *Writers and Critics*, Merlin Press 1970.

18. Umberto Eco, *Reflections on the Name of the Rose*, Secker and Warburg 1985.

19. See, for example, Malcolm Bradbury, *The Social Context of Modern English Literature*, Blackwell 1971; M. Bradbury and D. Palmer (eds), *The Contemporary English Novel*, Edward Arnold 1979; M. Bradbury, *The Novel Today: Contemporary Writers on Modern Fiction*, Manchester University Press 1977; Raymond Williams, 'Realism and the Contemporary Novel', in *The Long Revolution*, Chatto & Windus 1961; R. Williams, *The English Novel from Dickens to Lawrence*, Chatto & Windus 1970; David Lodge, *The Modes of Modern Writing*, Edward Arnold 1977.

20. On the authenticity or otherwise of children's experience of children's fiction, see the references given under note 5 above. Two useful collections besides Sheila Egoff's (see note 10) are G. Fox et al, *Writers, Critics and Children: Articles from 'Children's Literature in Education'*, Heinemann Education 1976; Margaret Meek et al (eds), *The Cool Web: The Pattern of Children's Reading*, The Bodley Head 1977. For a recent collection of articles on the subject from a psychoanalytic point of view, see J.H. Smith and W. Kerrigan (eds), *Opening Texts: Psychoanalysis and the Culture of the Child*, Yale University Press 1986; Ann Scott Macleod's article, 'An End to Innocence: the Transformation of Childhood in Twentieth-Century Children's Literature' makes the point that a sombre or even cynical tone seems to have become noticeable in the past two decades or so, e.g. in books by Robert Cormier and Paul Zindel.

21. Bruno Bettelheim, *The Uses of Enchantment: the Meaning and Importance of Fairy Tales*, Penguin 1978.

22. See the essay by Graham Greene on Beatrix Potter referred to in note 10 above.

23. Jack Zipes, *Breaking the Magic Spell: Radical Theories of Folk and Fairy Tales*, Heinemann Education/Gower Publishing Company 1979; see also Jack Zipes, *Fairy Tales and the Art of Subversion: the Classical Genre for Children and the Process of Civilisation*, Heinemann 1983.

24. Raymond Williams, *Culture and Society*, Chatto and Windus 1958.
25. See Martin Wiener, *English Culture and the Decline of the Industrial Spirit 1850–1980*, Cambridge University Press 1981.
26. For example, in his introduction to A. Alvarez (ed.), *The New Poetry*, Penguin 1966.
27. In E. Leach, 'Babar's Civilisation Analysed', in S. Egoff et al., op. cit.

Chapter 1

1. See Hanna Segal, *A Psychoanalytical Approach to Aesthetics* (1952) in *The Work of Hanna Segal*, Free Associations Books and Maresfield Library 1986.
2. Donald Winnicott, *Playing and Reality*, Penguin 1980.
3. For a psychoanalytic consideration of old age, see Lily Pincus, *The Challenge of a Long Life*, Faber 1981, and *Death in the Family: The Importance of Mourning*, Faber 1981; also Hanna Segal, *Fear of Death: Notes on the Analysis of an Old Man*, op. cit.
4. A contrast can be drawn between this concern to maintain an imaginative link with the past, and with a more escapist nostalgia for an idealized past world such as Humphrey Carpenter ascribes to a number of Edwardian children's writers (Grahame, Milne, et al.) in his *Secret Gardens*, Allen and Unwin 1985.
5. See D.W. Winnicott, *Playing and Reality* op. cit., and his 'Transitional Objects and Transitional Phenomena' in *Through Paediatrics to Psycho-Analysis*, Hogarth Press 1978.
6. See Hanna Segal's essay 'Delusion and Artistic Creativity' (in H. Segal, op. cit.) on William Golding's *The Spire* for a discussion of an adult novel exploring a similar theme.

Chapter 2

1. A similar idea inspires much science fiction writing for adults as well as children; for example, recent volumes by Doris Lessing and Ursula Leguin.
2. See Melanie Klein, 'A Contribution to the Psychogenesis of Manic-Depressive States' (1935), in Juliet Mitchell (ed.) *The Selected Melanie Klein*, Penguin 1986. Mitchell's introduction is also helpful on Klein's contribution.
3. See Donald Meltzer, 'Terror, Persecution and Dread' in *Sexual States of Mind*, Clunie Press 1978.
4. For a valuable discussion of the concept of aggression in psychoanalytic thought see Meira Likierman, 'The Function of Anger in Human Conflict', *International Review of Psychoanalysis*, vol. 14, part 2, 1987.
5. A similar use of language is found in J.R. Tolkien's writing for children.
6. There is a large autobiographical literature on this topic. See, for example, the early part of Robert Graves, *Goodbye to All That* (1929), Penguin 1969, and W.R. Bion, *The Long Weekend 1897–1917: Part of a Life* Fleetwood Press 1982.

Chapter 3

1. See M.J. Rustin, 'A Defence of Children's Fiction', *Free Associations* 2, 1985, p.135.

2. The popular *Galldora* books by Modwena Sedgwick and the *Mrs Pepperpot* stories by Alf Prøysen deal with these themes of social exploration for a younger age group.

3. On the emotions aroused by separation see John Bowlby, *Attachment, Separation, and Loss* (3 volumes), Penguin 1969–80; and films by James and Joyce Robertson such as *John Goes to Hospital*.

4. A much more critical reading of Nesbit's stories is given by Humphrey Carpenter (op. cit.).

Chapter 4

1. The increasing range of small figures available (together with Action Men perhaps) provides a resource for boys to play more comfortably with dolls.

2. W.R. Bion, *Learning from Experience* (1962), in the collection *Seven Servants*, Jason Aronson, 1977 ch. 12; see also for a clear exposition of many of Bion's idéas Donald Meltzer, *The Kleinian Development*, Clunie Press 1978, part 3.

3. Melanie Klein, 'The Psychogenesis of Manic-Depressive States' (1935) in J. Mitchell (ed.), op. cit.

4. Melanie Klein, 'Notes on sóme Schizoid Mechanisms' (1946), in J. Mitchell (ed.) op. cit.

5. This is a characteristic role of grandparents or others in the extended family in supporting parents in difficulties with their children.

6. On the topic of a transitional object which is able to be given up see Mattie Harris, *Thinking about Infants and Young Children*, Clunie Press 1975; and also D.W. Winnicott, *Transitional Objects and Transitional Phenomena*, op. cit.

7. See M. Boston and R. Szur, *Psychotherapy with Severely Disturbed Children*, Routledge & Kegan Paul, 1983.

8. W.R. Bion's ideas on preconceptions and their potential realization are developed in his *Elements of Psychoanalysis* (1963), in *Seven Servants*, op. cit.

9. See Hanna Segal, 'Notes on Symbol Formation', repr. in H. Segal, *The Work of Hanna Segal: a Kleinian Approach to Clinical Practice* (1981), Free Association Books and Maresfield Library 1986.

Chapter 5

1. Lynne Reid Banks's interest in sibling relationships is also evident in her book on the Brontë family, *Dark Quartet: the Story of the Brontës*, Penguin 1986.

2. David Lodge, *The Modes of Modern Writing*, Edward Arnold 1977.

3. A moving exposure of this myth is to be found in Dee Brown, *Bury My Heart At Wounded Knee*, Picador 1971.

4. Melanie Klein, 'A Contribution to the Psychogenesis of Manic-Depressive States', (1935); 'Mourning and its Relation to Manic-Depressive States' (1940); 'Notes on some Schizoid Mechanisms' (1946) all in J. Mitchell, op. cit.

Chapter 6

1. The reference to visible and invisible dogs in Russell Hoban's *The Mouse and His Child* may be an implicit tribute to this story, though the context does not make this entirely clear.

2. Examples of stories which feature love of horses are Mary O'Hara's *My Friend Flicka*, and J.D. and C. Pullein-Thompson, *Black Beauty's Clan*, Brockhampton Press 1975. The original of this genre is of course Anna Sewell's *Black Beauty*.

3. The distinction between metaphoric and metonymic symbolization in the novel is valuably explored in David Lodge's *The Modes of Modern Writing*, op. cit.

4. States of mourning and pathological mourning have been studied by Bowlby (op. cit., vol. 3), and Colin Murray Parkes, *Bereavement*, Penguin 1975.

Chapter 7

1. E.B. White, *The Essays of E.B. White*, Harper Row 1979; also *The Letters of E.B. White*, Harper Row 1986.

2. See W.R. Bion, *Second Thoughts*, Heinemann 1967, ch. 9; and D.W. Winnicott, *The Theory of the Parent-Infant Relationship* (1960) in *The Maturational Process and the Facilitating Environment*, Hogarth Press 1965.

Chapter 8

1. This celebration of the small has an obvious appeal to child readers and is a frequent theme in both traditional and modern literature for children. e.g., Tom Thumb, Alf Prøysen's *Mrs Pepperpot*, and E.B. White's *Stuart Little* discussed above in chapter 7.

2. Mary Douglas, *Purity and Danger* Routledge & Kegan Paul 1966; *Implicit Meanings*, Routledge & Kegan Paul 1976. See also the collection of anthropological articles, *Rules and Meanings* (ed.) Mary Douglas, Penguin 1973.

3. For the psychoanalytic concept of catastrophic change, first developed in the work of W.R. Bion, see Donald Meltzer, *The Kleinian Development*, part 3, chapter XIV, Clunie Press 1978.

4. Many providers of toys and entertainment have well understood the attractions of the miniature to both adults and children, from dolls' houses to Legoland.

5. For the idea of imprisoned internal objects see Melanie Klein's paper, 'A Contribution to the Psychogenesis of Manic-Depressive States' (1935), in J. Mitchell (ed.), *The Selected Melanie Klein*, Penguin 1986.

Chapter 9

1. Ursula Moray Williams, *The Little Wooden Horse*, (1938) Puffin Books 1959.

2. See for example John Dos Passos, *USA*, Houghton Mifflin 1963; E.L. Doctorow, *Ragtime*, Picador 1985.

3. See Raymond Williams, 'Social Darwinism' in his *Problems in Materialism and Culture*, Verso 1980.

4. There is now a large literature. Influential texts are Edward O. Wilson, *Sociobiology: The New Synthesis*, Harvard University Press 1980; and Richard Dawkins, *The Selfish Gene*, Paladin 1978.

5. Beatrix Potter's stories frequently deal with such risks to their animal characters.

6. This is also a common theme in American folk music, the blues, etc.

7. A. Joan Bowers has pointed out in 'The Fantasy World of Russell Hoban', *Children's Literature* 8, 1980, that three of Hoban's recent novels deal with the experience of a divorced man – *The Lion of Boaz Jachin and Jachin Boaz* (1973), Picador; *Kleinzeit* (1974), Picador; and *Turtle Diary* (1975), Picador. Her article mainly stresses Hoban's philosophical preoccupations. His tenderness towards young children is also shown in his Frances stories, *Bedtime for Frances*, etc.

8. For a substitute review of recent research on the development of the infant from birth see Daniel Stern, *The Interpersonal World of the Infant: a View from Psychoanalysis and Developmental Psychology*, Basic Books 1985.

9. Adele Geras's excellent novel *The Voyage Out*, Fontana Lions 1985, also explores the state of mind which makes emigration possible.

10. The dump is reminiscent at this point of a Nazi slave labour camp.

11. This may evoke for a child reader the need for courage in facing even the best-intended medical treatment.

Chapter 10

1. The subtlety of Bawden's understanding of Carrie's feelings about loyalty would make this story an excellent text for study by people involved in placing those children who come into statutory care in foster-homes.

2. On psychoanalytic approaches to mourning, see S. Freud, *Mourning and Melancholia* (1917), Standard Edition vol. 14, 1974 Hogarth Press; K. Abraham, 'A Short Study of the Development of the Libido Viewed in the Light of Mental Disorders' (1924), in *Selected Papers on Psychoanalysis*, Hogarth Press 1927. Melanie Klein, 'Mourning and its Relation to Manic-Depressive States' in J. Mitchell (ed.) op. cit.; John Bowlby, *Attachment, Separation and Loss* vol. 3., Penguin 1980.

Chapter 11

1. Esther Bick, 'The Experience of the Skin in Early Object Relations', (1968), in M. Harris and E. Bick, *Collected Papers*, Clunie Press 1987.

2. Basil Bernstein, *Class, Codes and Control* vol. 3, Routledge & Kegan Paul 1977.

3. Melanie Klein, *A Study of Envy and Gratitude* (1956) in J. Mitchell (ed.) op. cit.

4. There is a more despairing exploration of a similar theme for a more sophisticated and older child audience in R. Cormier's *I am the Cheese*, Pantheon 1977.

5. See M. Boston and R. Szur, op. cit., for clinical studies of children thinking in similar ways.

6. These are discussed in E. Bick, 'The Experience of the Skin in Early Object Relations', op. cit., and were noted in 'Alice in Wonderland' by William Empson in his *Some Versions of Pastoral*, Chatto and Windus 1935, ch. 7.

7. This view of the natural morality imposed by the sea is similar to that of Joseph Conrad in his sea stories.

8. On repetition compulsion, see S. Freud, *Instincts and their Vicissitudes* (1915), Standard Edition vol. 14, Hogarth 1974.

Conclusion

1. A recent book which explores the issue of how children relate reading to their own experience is Jeff Adams, *The Conspiracy of the Text: The Place of Narrative in the Development of Thought*, Routledge & Kegan Paul 1986. This book makes use of sophisticated procedures drawn from semiotic analysis of texts to demonstrate the way that a child interprets the fairy tale *Beauty and The Beast*. It is a useful supplement to Bruno Bettleheim's discussion of fairy tales in *The Uses of Enchantment: the Meaning and Importance of Fairy-Tales*, Penguin 1978.

2. On Bion's idea of the innate preconception of the good object, see D. Meltzer, *The Kleinian Development*, chapter 6, Clunie Press 1978.

3. On a psychoanalytic approach to the significance of lies for mental life, see W. R. Bion, *Attention and Interpretation* (1970) chapter 11, in *Seven Servants*, Jason Aronson, 1977; R. Money-Kyrle, 'Cognitive Development', *International Journal of Psychoanalysis* 48, 1968; and John Steiner, 'Turning a Blind Eye: the Cover-Up for Oedipus', *International Review of Psychoanalysis*, vol. 12, part 2, 1985.

List of Principal Works Discussed

Lynne Reid Banks *The Indian in the Cupboard*, Avon Books (USA) 1980, Dragon Books (UK) 1981.

Nina Bawden *Carrie's War*, Victor Gollancz 1973, Puffin Books 1974.

Paula Fox *A Likely Place* Macmillan (New York) 1967.

—— , *How Many Miles to Babylon*, Davis White & Co. (New York) 1967.

—— , *The Slave Dancer*, Dell Publishing Company (New York) 1973.

Rumer Godden *The Dolls' House*, Michael Joseph 1947.

—— , *The Fairy Doll*, Macmillan 1956.

—— , *The Story of Holly and Ivy*, Macmillan 1957.

—— , *The Kitchen Madonna*, Macmillan 1967.

Russell Hoban *The Mouse and His Child*, (USA) 1967, Faber and Faber 1969, Puffin Books 1976.

C.S. Lewis *The Lion, the Witch and the Wardrobe*, Geoffrey Bles 1950, Penguin Books 1959.

—— , *Prince Caspian*, Geoffrey Bles, 1951, Puffin Books 1962.

—— , *The Voyage of the Dawn Treader*, Geoffrey Bles 1952, Puffin Books 1965.

—— , *The Silver Chair*, Geoffrey Bles 1953, Puffin Books 1965.

—— , *The Horse and his Boy*, Geoffrey Bles 1954, Puffin Books 1965.

—— , *The Magician's Nephew*, The Bodley Head 1955, Puffin Books 1963.

—— , *The Last Battle*, The Bodley Head 1956, Puffin Books 1964.

E. Nesbit *Five Children and It*, first published 1902, Puffin Books 1984.

Mary Norton *The Borrowers*, Dent 1952.

—— , *The Borrowers Afield*, Dent 1955.

—— , *The Borrowers Afloat*, Dent 1959.

—— , *The Borrowers Aloft*, Dent 1961.

—— , *The Borrowers Avenged*, Kestrel Books 1982.

Philippa Pearce *Tom's Midnight Garden*, Oxford University Press 1958, Puffin 1976; (Carnegie Medal 1958).

—— , *A Dog So Small*, Constable 1962, Puffin 1964.

—— , *The Battle of Bubble and Squeak* André Deutsch 1978, Puffin 1980; (Whitbread Literary Award 1978).

E.B. White *Charlotte's Web*, Hamish Hamilton 1952, Puffin Books 1963.

—— , *The Trumpet of the Swan*, Harper and Row (USA) 1970.

—— , *Stuart Little*, Puffin Books 1969.

Index